AFTER WINNICOTT

AFTER WINNICOTT

Compilation of Works
Based on the Life,
Work and Ideas of
D.W. Winnicott

Harry Karnac

Routledge
Taylor & Francis Group

LONDON AND NEW YORK

First published 2007 by Karnac Books Ltd.

Published 2018 by Routledge
2 Park Square, Milton Park, Abingdon, Oxon OX14 4RN
52 Vanderbilt Avenue, New York, NY 10017

*Routledge is an imprint of the Taylor & Francis Group,
an informa business*

British Library Cataloguing in Publication Data

A C.I.P. for this book is available from the British Library

ISBN 13: 978-1-85575-506-2 (pbk)

Typeset by Vikatan Publishing Solutions, Chennai, India

CONTENTS

FOREWORD

I am delighted to welcome and introduce Harry Karnac's careful bibliography of works to date that have made use of the plethora of ideas introduced into the psychoanalytic lexicon by Donald Woods Winnicott. This is the core work. All serious Winnicott scholars will find it essential as a starting point for reference. Since Winnicott's ideas tangle with many other fields, this compilation of references is the touchstone for many others in whatever areas they are engaged.

Just as in his lifetime Winnicott regularly and frequently spoke to enormous numbers of different, not only professional audiences, so, after his death, his writings continue to engage all manner of people. Winnicott's work, no less than Freud's, has applications in, spans and influences 'Nothing Short of Everything' as he wanted to title his autobiography. Accordingly, his work has been discovered and influenced people in many fields of human endeavour.

With due acknowledgement of the limitations and gains, the interdisciplinary uses and cross-fertilization of psychoanalysis is part of that to which Winnicott aspired no less than Freud. This bibliography undoubtedly will require constant

updating as the relevance and originality of Winnicott's theories percolate through into the vast fields addressed in what
he referred to as 'the rich collective storehouse of mankind.'
Articles, doctoral theses and books will continue to appear in
exponentially increasing accretions to this work. Here is evi-
dence that Winnicott is as important in applied psychoanalysis
and the humanities as is Freud. Political scientists, politicians
and policy makers all too often neglect papers such as
"Thoughts on the meaning of the word 'democracy'" (1951), or
'The importance of the monarchy' (1970), or educationalists
'Sum: I AM' (1968). Winnicott explicitly wished "to be more
correlated", all too aware that this would have to be left to others. ('DWW on DWW', 1967, Winnicott 1989, p. 573). We find
here just how deeply his skeins of thought have stimulated
and become interwoven into many explorative excursions of
commentary in the realms of understanding.

Harry Karnac produced in 1966 the first bibliography of
Winnicott's own writings then available. It remains to date the
best we have until it will be superseded by one currently under
compilation by Dr Knud Hjulmand of Copenhagen University,
which will be included in the new edition of *The Language of
Winnicott* by Jan Abram. Everything is not yet available of the
work of a man who is undoubtedly amongst the most significant heirs to the mantle of Freud and already Harry Karnac has
listed more than 1200 articles, books and reviews of relevant
derivative scholarship interest. Until the unopened archives
become available no final evaluation of Winnicott's work will
be possible. Winnicott was a field scientist who noted down
and reflected on everything as he went along. The 'thirty thou-
sand' case studies [the number mentioned to me by Clare
Winnicott – perhaps a rhetorical number] in the Cornell
Medical School archives in New York contain important mate-
rial for additional Winnicott publications at a later date. He
constantly produced a spate of witty, pithy poems and doggerel,
composed songs, doodled, sketched and painted when not at

his piano. There are volumes of yet to be published correspondence.

Browsing one day in Harry Karnac's Gloucester Road bookshop, it was bibliophile Donald Winnicott who suggested that he specialize in psychoanalytic books which, he tells me, he agreed to do with considerable trepidation. Appropriately, Harry ends his engaging personal memoir on Psychoanalytic Bookselling (1991) with a pertinent anecdote about Winnicott's penchant for reading the beginnings of biographies. Only with Harry who was familiar with Winnicott's idiosyncratic reading habits can I find confirmation of my suspicion that had he lived to complete what was on his mind, he was planning and preparing for a 'Totem and Taboo' - "Moses and Monotheism" - like work in scope, looking at Female Goddesses.

Harry was never a bookseller unacquainted with the content of the works on his shelves, nor one disinterested in his customers. Some of us were privileged to become his friends, to enjoy his trenchant wit, and able to draw on his deep specialized knowledge in our field. Harry has always been as decent and tactful a human being as one might hope to know, a committed and thoughtful Socialist, a delightful raconteur. One can argue with Harry and hold different views, but the basic trust, affectionate bonding, banter and capacity for fun will only be strengthened. It will be a rare psychoanalyst or psychotherapist who will not be indebted to Harry for realizing the need for re-issues of certain classic psychoanalytic texts that led him to found the Karnac Books publishing house, initially re-issuing various volumes in the appropriately-named Maresfield imprint. On 'retiring' to pursue his transformed life as a hard-working bibliographer, Harry sold Karnac Books to Cesare Sacerdoti late in 1984, who opened the Finchley Road shop in the following year.

The company today is owned by Oliver Rathbone, who has effectively run the business for some years. Harry's personal touch, the hands-on know-how and ambience one encountered in the Gloucester Road bookshop is a matter of memory, now but of historical description. Karnac Books is currently concentrated in the Finchley Road and Tavistock Centre book-selling outlets. Oliver has brought the publishing house to a significant and respected force in its arena of influence and has vigorously built and expanded the publishing side into an important niche in the specialized psychoanalytic, psychotherapeutic and allied professional world. An informative Karnac newsletter arrives for customers. It is to Oliver's credit that this important bibliography is being published, will be updated and hopefully, eventually electronically available. It is appropriate, indeed seemly that Harry Karnac's work be published under the imprint of the Publishing House he founded.

This bibliography was the natural progression of Harry's career activities since 'retiring'. His bibliography of works relating to Bion's writing (2006) is of great value, and will shortly be updated and reformatted. When he had finished his first version I told him I had been working on and had given up on a bibliography of works relating to Winnicott's writing. In fact, what I had listed of works that mentioned Winnicott in their references or index and handed over to Harry was of little value. What is listed herein is worth reading.

The bibliography Harry Karnac has now compiled merits separate publication. There is no intention here to annotate or provide a critical bibliography, nor to reproduce summaries or abstracts of articles, nor to analyse the items in any depth. It is impossible for there not to be errors and omissions. In a different way, in my books that deal with Winnicott extensive bibliographies signpost the way to works which have affinities and parallels to his as well as to many listed here that I have managed to read. But the task is impossible because of the sheer volume and rate at which new writing appears.

This bibliography has been fascinating reading for me for whom it is essential, as I am confident it will be for many, many others now and in years to come.

How might Winnicott have reacted to this publication? To be a bibliographer today is much easier than it was even a decade back when one spent hours in libraries poring over abstracts in indexed references to publications in medicine, literary studies, theology, psychology, social work, education, paediatrics, sociology, public policy, political science, philosophy, anthropology, art history, child development, and more, always lighting on items that made reference to Winnicott's writing. Microfiche helped. But bibliographic research was a painstaking and tedious business. We live in revolutionary times. The frustration of Harry Karnac in his far-from-dotage computer-literate late eighties in the throes of a computer glitch or breakdown signals real distress. This kind of recurrent obstacle to this publication was no joking matter, although I am sure Harry will try to find an amusing anecdote to ease his annoyance.

How might Winnicott's writing have been altered in our computer-tools enriched world? Winnicott's reactions were too original to be predictable. There is little doubt about how very pleased he would have been with the bibliography itself, and how immensely grateful to Harry Karnac and all the authors listed. I suspect he might have tried to write a few personal words to each, and what a spate of ideas his comments might have set running.

From my mixed welter of feelings and memories I conjure him smiling, delighted. At the idea of the hours Harry has devoted so conscientiously and diligently, in solitude, how might Winnicott have reacted? In my mind D.W.W. shakes his head and grimaces; skips away with a blithe wave of his hand and will have none of it. He humps his shoulders, raises both hands to his head which sinks into himself curling up into some foetal yet wearily depressive and also amused slump. Then he wisely decides we must have a ceremonious and silent cup of tea and sips slowly, sometimes watchful, sometimes wandering off, keeping me waiting expectantly till his opinion is irrelevant.

This bibliography demonstrates amply how wide the range is of Winnicott scholarship. Harry Karnac has done a great and necessary job in facilitating post-Freudian Bion and Winnicott studies. We are immensely indebted to him for facilitating our writing and mapping out the terrain to date in the worlds of studies to which their writing has opened awareness and understanding. We need such selective and satisfying orderings in our ongoing human search for ways to deal with all our proclivities, including the wanton, witless and sublime.

Dr Judith Issroff is a child, family and social psychiatrist, psychoanalyst and child psychoanalyst who was supervised by Donald Woods Winnicott during her child psychoanalytic training. She organized the series of private seminars that Winnicott gave which resulted in the publication of *Therapeutic Consultations in Child Psychiatry* (1971). After D.W. Winnicott's death Clare Winnicott gave her the manuscript of what was eventually published as *Human Nature* (1988). Judith completed its initial editing by 1972. She edited and co-authored *Donald Winnicott and John Bowlby: Personal and Professional Perspectives* (2005). She is currently working on *Something Short of Everything about Donald Woods Winnicott (Free Association Books) and Mending Mischief: Masud Khan and Enough Winnicott Bashing* (Karnac), both due for publication soon.

ACKNOWLEDGEMENTS

I wish to express my thanks to those, without whose patient help and advice, I would have been obliged to spend many additional months of research for this work to reach its present state.

Firstly to Dr Issroff for her original research and continuing recommendations. To several librarians including Angela Douglas of the Tavistock Library and Saven Morris of the British Psychoanalytical Society I owe my thanks and in particular I would acknowledge the generosity of Richard Wakeford of the British Library for the valuable assistance in time and expertise provided during the months of research.

Finally, a word of thanks to Oliver Rathbone for providing an ever-ready source of materials vital for the compilations of this work.

Harry Karnac

PART I

Complete alphabetical listing

Aaltonen, J.,
Räkkökäinen V.
(1987)

The Paradox and the Dissolution of the
Œdipus Complex. *Scandinavian
Psychoanalytic Review, 10*: 117-132

Abadi, S. (2001)

Explorations: Losing and Finding
Oneself in the Potential Space
[in Bertolini, M. et al (2001) vol.1: 79-87]

Abend, S. (Ed.)
(1996)

*The Place of Reality in Psychoanalytic
Theory and Technique.* New York: Aronson

Ablon, S.L. (2001)

Continuities of Tongues: a
Developmental Perspective on the Role
of Play in Child and Adult
Psychoanalytic Process. *Journal of
Clinical Psychoanalysis, 10*: 445-459

Abram, J. (1994)

Dockar-Drysdale, B. (1990) review
Winnicott Studies, 9: 59-62

Abram, J. (1996)

The Language of Winnicott. London:
Karnac (reprint, New York: Aronson
2004)

Abram, J. (Ed.) (2000a)
André Green at the Squiggle Foundation. London: Karnac for the Squiggle Foundation

Abram, J. (2000b)
A Kind of French Winnicott [editor's foreword in Abram, A. (2000a): xi-xviii]

Abramowitz, S.A. (1995)
Killing the Needy Self: Women Professionals and Suicide (a Critique of Winnicott's False-self Theory). *Progress in Self Psychology, 11*: 177-188

Abrams, S., Neubauer, P. (1978)
Transitional Objects: Animate and Inanimate [in Grolnick, Barkin, Muensterberger (1978): 133-144]

Adams, W.W. (2006)
Love, Open Awareness and Authenticity: a Conversation with William Blake and D.W. Winnicott. *Journal of Humanistic Psychology, 46*: 9-35

Adler, G. (1989)
Transitional Phenomena, Projective Identification and the Essential Ambiguity of the Psychoanalytic Situation. *Psychoanalytic Quarterly, 58*: 61-104

Aguayo, J. (2002)
Reassessing the Clinical Affinity Between Melanie Klein and D.W. Winnicott, 1935-1951: Klein's Unpublished "Notes on Baby" in Historical Context. *International Journal of Psychoanalysis, 83*: 1135-1152

Aiken, S.C., Herman, T. (1997)
Gender, Power and Crib Geography: Transitional Spaces and Potential Places. *Gender, Place and Culture, 4*: 63-88

Aite, P. (2001)
Between C.G. Jung and D.W. Winnicott [in Bertolini, M. et al (2001) vol. 2: 242-244]

Akhtar, S. (1995)   Lewin, R.A., Schultz, G. (1992) review. *Psychoanalytic Quarterly, 64*: 583-588

Albiston, R.K. (1984)   The Advent of Object Representation: a Piagetian Critique of the British School Theorists Klein, Fairbairn, Winnicott and Guntrip. *Dissertation Abstracts (International), 44* (10-B): 3185

Alby, J-M. (1993)   Being English and a Psychoanalyst [in Goldman, D. (Ed.) (1993): 159-164]

Alford, C.F. (2000)   Levinas and Winnicott: Motherhood and Responsibility. *American Imago, 57*: 235-260

Alford, C.F. (2002a)   Levinas, Winnicott and the Ethics of Ruthlessness. *Journal for the Psychoanalysis of Culture and Society, 7*: 39-42

Alford, C.F. (2002b)   *Levinas, The Frankfurt School and Psychoanalysis.* New York: Wesleyan Univ. Press

Alford, C.F. (2006)   *Psychology and the Natural Law of Reparation.* Cambridge: Cambridge University Press

Aliprandi, M.T. (2001)   Antisocial Acting-out as a Substitute for the Spontaneous Gesture in Adolescence [in Bertolini, M. et al (2001) vol. 2: 133-138]

Alizade, A.M. (Ed.) (2006)   *Motherhood in the Twenty-first Century.* London: Karnac

Alphandary, I. (2002)   The Subject of Autonomy and Fellowship in Maupassant, Winnicott and Conrad. *Dissertation Abstracts (International), 62* (10A): 3376

Altman, N. (1994)	A Perspective on Child Analysis. *Psychoanalytic Psychology, 11*: 383-395
Altman, N. (et al) (2002)	*Relational Child Psychotherapy.* New York: Other Press
Altman, N. (2005)	Relational Perspectives on the Therapeutic Action of Psychoanalysis [in Ryan, J. (2005): 15-50]
Alvarez, A. (1992)	*Live Company: Psychoanalytic Therapy with Autistic, Abused and Borderline Psychotic Children.* London: Routledge
Alvarez, A. (1996)	The Clinician's Debt to Winnicott. *Journal of Child Psychotherapy, 22*: 377-382
Amado, G., Vansina, L. (Eds.) (2005)	*The Transitional Approach in Action.* London: Karnac.
Anderson, J.W. (2003)	Recent Psychoanalytic Theorists and their Relevance to Psychobiography: Winnicott, Kernberg and Kohut. *Annual of Psychoanalysis, 31*: 79-96
Anderson, J.W. (2004)	The Most Influential Psychoanalyst since Freud. *PsycCRITIQUES, 49*
André, J. (2002)	Separation [in Widlöcher, D. (Ed.) (2002) *Infantile Sexuality and Attachment.* London: Karnac: 123-131]
Andrews, J.C. (2001)	Manic Defence and its Place in Therapy [in Bertolini, M. et al (2001) vol. 1: 255-256] (see also Neri, F. (2001) for discussion)
Anshin, R.N. (1991)	Hughes, J.M. (1989) review. *Journal of the American Academy of Psychoanalysis, 19*: 497-499
Anshin, R.N. (1996)	*Thinking About Children* review. *The Lancet, 348 issue 9031*: 877-878

Anthony, E.J. (2002)   Memories of Donald Winnicott [in Kahr (2002a): 137-140]

Anzieu, D. (1989)   *The Skin Ego: A Psychoanalytic Approach to the Self*. New York & London: Yale University Press

Anzieu, D. (Ed.) (1990)   *Psychic Envelopes*. London: Karnac

Applegate, J.S. (1990)   Theory, Culture and Behavior: Object Relations in Context. *Child & Adolescent Social Work Journal, 7*: 85-100

Applegate, J.S. (1993)   Winnicott and Clinical Social Work: a Facilitating Partnership. *Child & Adolescent Social Work Journal, 10*: 3-19

Applegate, J.S., Bonovitz, J.M. (1995)   *The Facilitating Environment: a Winnicottian Approach for Social Workers and other Helping Professions*. Northvale, NJ: Aronson

Applegate, J.S. (1996)   The Good-enough Social Workers: Winnicott Applied [in Sanville, J.B. Ed. (1996) *Fostering, Healing and Growth: a Psychoanalytic Social Work Approach*: 77-96 Lanham, MD: Aronson]

Applegate, J.S. (1997a)   Kahr, B. (1996c) review. *Child and Adolescent Social Work Journal, 14*: 462-466

Applegate, J.S. (1997b)   The Holding Environment: an Organizing Metaphor for Social Work Theory and Practice. *Smith College Studies in Social Work, 68*: 7-29

Applegate, J.S. (1999)   Winnicott and the Paradoxes of Intersubjectivity. *Smith College Studies in Social Work, 69*: 203-220

Applegate, J.S. (2002)   Parallel Paths: a Personal Journey to Winnicott and Beyond. *Psychoanalytic Inquiry, 22*: 510-518

Apprey, M. (1992)   Little, M. (1990) review. *Psychoanalytic Books, 3*: 58-62

Armellini, M. (2001)   The Father as Function, Environment and Object [in Bertolini, M. et al (2001) vol. 2: 37-46

Aron, L. (1992)   Interpretation as Expression of the Analyst's Subjectivity. *Psychoanalytic Inquiry, 2*: 475-507

Arthern, J., Madill, A. (1999)   How do Transitional Objects Work?: The Therapist's View. *British Journal of Medical Psychology, 72*: 1-21

Athanassiou, C. (1991)   Construction of a Transitional Space in an Infant Twin Girl. *International Review of Psychoanalysis, 18*: 53-63

Atwood, G.E., Stolorow, R.D. (1984)   *Structures of Subjectivity: Explorations in Psychoanalytic Phenomenology.* Hillside, NJ and London: Analytic Press

Axelman, M. (2006)   *Playing and Reality* review. *PsycCRITIQUES, 51*

Azevedo, R. (2001)   Fetish-object, Transitional Object [in Bertolini, M. et al (2001) vol.1: 204-209]

Babits, M. (2001)   Using Therapeutic Metaphor to Provide a Holding Environment: the Inner Edge of Possibility. *Clinical Social Work Journal, 29*: 21-33

Bacal, H.A. (1987)   British Object Relations Theorists and Self-psychology: Some Clinical Reflections. *International Journal of Psychoanalysis, 68*: 81-98

Bacal, H.A. (1989)   Winnicott and Self Psychology: Remarkable Reflections [in Dettrick, D.W. & S.P.(1989): 259-271]

Bacal, H.A., Newman, K. (1990)
Theories of Object Relations: Bridges to Self Psychology. New York: Columbia University Press

Bacon, R.J.E. (2002)
Winnicott Revisited: a Point of View. *Free Associations, 50*: 250-170

Bacon-Greenberg, K. (1996)
Goldman, D. (1993a) review. *Contemporary Psychology, 41*: 383-386

Bacon-Greenberg, K. (2004)
Winnicott: the Man and his Theory. *PsyART, 8*

Balint, E. (2000)
The Broken Couch [in Rudnytsky (2000): 1-26]

Bank, R. (1999)
Mythic Perspectives and Perspectives on Truth: Approaching Winnicott by Way of Comparisons between Kohut and Freud. *Psychoanalytic Review, 86*: 109-136

Barak, Y., Rabinowitz, G. (1995)
Gestalt Elements in Winnicott's Psychoanalytic Technique. *Gestalt Journal, 18*: 87-91

Barkin, L. (1978)
The Concept of the Transitional Object [in Grolnick, Barkin, Muensterberger (1978): 511-536]

Barnett, B. (2001)
A Comparison of the Thought and Work of Donald Winnicott and Michael Balint [in Bertolini, M. et al (2001) vol. 2: 185-188] (see also Dreyfus, P. (2003) for discussion)

Barrat, B.B. (1984)
Psychic Reality and Psychoanalytic Knowing. Hillside, NJ: Analytic Press

Bartlett, A.B. (1999)
Slochower (1996a) review. *Bulletin of the Menninger Clinic, 63*: 260-262

Bass, A. (1992)
Little, M. (1990) review. *Psychoanalytic Dialogues, 2*: 117-131

Bassin, D.,
Honey, M.
Kaplan, M.M. (Eds.)
(1994)
Representations of Motherhood. New Haven, CT and London: Yale University Press

Belger, A.W. (2002)
Theory as Holding Environment: Using Winnicott to Explore the Beginning Psychoanalytic Psychotherpist's Relationship to Theory. *Dissertation Abstracts (International), 63(2-B)*: 1009

Benjamin, J. (1990)
An Outline of Subjectivity: The Development of Recognition. *Pychoanalytic Psychology, 7/Supp*: 33-46

Benjamin, J. (1993)
Reply to Burack (1993) on Donald Winnicott. *Psychoanalysis & Contemporary Thought, 16*: 447-454

Benjamin, J. (2000)
Reparative Projects [in Rudnytsky (2000): 233-275]

Berg, D.F. (1999)
Pluralism, Religious Bias and Pathologizing: the Interpretation and Use of Winnicott's Theories in the Psychoanalytic Study of Religion. *Dissertation Abstracts (International), 59 (10-A)*: 3849

Berger, B. (1999)
Deprivation and Abstinence in Psychoanalytic Psychotherapy. *Israel Journal of Psychiatry and Related Sciences, 3*: 164-173

Berger, L.R. (1980)
The Winnicott Squiggle Game: A Vehicle for Communicating with the School-aged Child. *Pediatrics, 66*: 921-924

Bergmann, M.S. (Ed.) (2004a)
Understanding Dissidence and Controversy in the History of Psychoanalysis. New York: Other Press

Bergmann, S. (2004b)	Rethinking Dissidence and Change in the History of Psychoanalysis [in Bergmann, M.S. (2004a): 1-110]
Berman, E. (1996a)	Goldman, D. (1993a) review. *Contemporary Psychoanalysis, 32*: 158
Berman, E. (1996b)	Goldman, D. (1993b) review. *Contemporary Psychoanalysis, 32*: 158-164
Berman, E. (1997)	Relational Psychoanalysis: a Historical Background. *American Journal of Psychotherapy, 51*: 185-203
Berman, E. (2003)	On Joseph Aguayo. "Reassessing the Clinical Affinity between Melanie Klein and D.W. Winnicott" (Aguayo 2002). *International Journal of Psychoanalysis, 84*: 445-446
Bertolini, M., Giannakoulas, A., Hernandez, M., Molino, A. (Eds.) (2001a)	*Squiggles and Spaces: Revisiting the Work of D.W. Winnicott* (2 volumes). London & Philadelphia: Whurr (Wiley)
Bertolini, M. (2001b)	Central Masturbatory Fantasy, Fetish and Transitional Phenomena [in Bertolini, M et al (2000) vol. 1: 210-217]
Bertolini, M., Neri, F. (2005)	Sex as a Defence against Sexuality [in Caldwell, L. (2005): 105-120]
Bethelard, F., Young-Bruehl, E. (1999)	The Wise Baby as the Voice of the True Self. *Psychoanalytic Quarterly, 68*: 585-610
Beyda, A. (2006)	Playing and Ultimate Reality: Dialectics of Experience in Jung and Winnicott. *Dissertation Abstracts (International), 66 (9-B)*: 5

Bingley, A. (2003)   In Here, Out There: Sensations between Self and Landscape. *Social and Cultural Geography*, 4: 329-345

Black, D.M. (Ed.) (2006a)   *Psychoanalysis and Religion in the 21st Century: Competitors or Collaborators?* Hove, Sussex: Routledge (in association with the Institute of Psychoanalysis, London)

Black, D.M. (2006b)   The Case for a Contemplative Position [in Black, D.M. (2006a): 63-80]

Blandy, E. (2003)   Kahr, B. (2002a) review. *Journal of Child Psychotherapy*, 29: 439-441

Blass, R. (2001)   On the Ethical and Evaluative Nature of Developmental Models in Psychoanalysis. *Psychoanalytic Study of the Child*, 56: 193-218

Blass, R.B. (2006)   Beyond Illusion: Psychoanalysis and the Question of Religious Truth [in Black, D.M. (2006a): 23-42]

Blatner, A. (2006)   Richards, V. (2005) review. *PsycCRITIQUES*, 51

Blum, H.P., Ross, J.M. (1993)   The Clinical Relevance of the Contribution of Winnicott. *Journal of the American Psychoanalytic Society*, 41: 219-235

Blum, H.P. (1997)   Clinical and Developmental dimensions of Hate. *Journal of the American Psychoanalytic Society*, 45: 358-375

Blumenson, S.R. (1986)   The Application of Modern Psychoanalytic Techniques of Winnicott's Concept of the Holding Environment: a Linear Study of Three

Emotionally Deprived Pre-œdipal Patients. *Dissertation Abstracts (International), 47(5-B)*: 2150

Bodin, G. (1994)
A comparison of Concepts in Self-Psychology and Winnicott's Theory of the Development of the Self. *Scandinavian Psychoanalytic Review, 17*: 40-58

Bollas, C. (1986)
The Transformational Object [in Kohon, (1986): 83-100]

Bollas, C. (1987)
The Shadow of the Object: Psychoanalysis of the Unthought Known. London: Free Association Books

Bollas, C. (1989)
Forces of Destiny: Psychoanalysis and Human Idiom. London: Free Association Books

Bollas, C. (1993a)
Being a Character, Psychoanalysis and Self-Experience. London: Routledge

Bollas, C. (1993b)
The Æsthetic Movement and the Search for Transformation [in Rudnytsky (1993): 40-49]

Bolognini, S. (2001)
The 'Kind-hearted' versus the Good Analyst: Empathy and Hatred in Countertransference [in Bertolini, M. et al (2001) vol. 2: 120-129]

Bomford, R. (2006)
A Simple Question? [in Black, D.M. (2006a): 252-269]

Bonamino, V. (1991)
D.W. Winnicott and the Position of the Analyst and the Analysand in the Psychoanalytic Situation. *Rivista di Psicoanalisi, 37*: 626-667

Bonamino, V., Di Renzo, M. (2000)
Creativity, Dreaming, Living: Overlapping Circles in the Work of Marion Milner and D.W. Winnicott [in Caldwell. L. (2000): 97-112]

Bonaminio, V. (2001)
Through Winnicott to Winnicott [in Bertolini, M. et al (2001) vol.1: 88-98]

Bonovitz, H. (1998)
Abram, J. (1996) review. *Psychoanalytic Books, 9*: 435-438

Borden, W. (1998)
The Place and Play of Theory and Practice: a Winnicottian Perspective. *Journal of Analytical Social Work, 5*: 25-40

Bowie, M. (2000)
Psychoanalysis and Art: the Winnicott Legacy [in Caldwell, L. (2000): 11-29]

Bowlby, R. (2004)
Fifty Years of Attachment Theory (with contributions from Kahr, B. and King, P.) London: Karnac on behalf of the Winnicott Clinic of Psychotherapy

Boyer, L.B. (1979)
Barkin, Grolnick, Muensterberger (1978) review. *Psychoanalytic Quarterly, 48*: 646-652

Boyer, L.B. (1990a)
Regression in Treatment: On Early Object Relations [in Giovacchini (1990a): 200-225]

Boyer, L.B., Giovacchini, P.(Eds.) (1990b)
Master Technicians on Treating the Regressed Patient. Northvale, NJ: Aronson

Boyer, L.B. (1990c)
Psychoanalytic Intervention in Treating the Regressed Patient [introduction to Boyer and Giovacchini (1990b): 1-33

Boyer, L.B. (1995)
Gaddini, E. (1992) review. *Psychoanalytic Quarterly, 64*: 603-606

Boyer, L.B. (1997) The Verbal Squiggle Game in Treating the Seriously Disturbed Patient. *Psychoanalytic Quarterly, 64*: 603-606]

Boynton, R. (2002) The Return of the Repressed: the Strange Case of Masud Khan. *Boston Review, 27(6)*: 23-29

Boz, S. et al (1994) Articulations between Antisocial Tendency and Depression. *Encounters (Argentina), 1*: 87-93

Brafman, A.H. (1997) Winnicott's *Therapeutic Consultations* Revisited. *International Journal of Psychoanalysis, 78*: 773-787

Brafman, A.H. (2000) The Child is Still Ill – How are the Parents? *Psychoanalytic Psychotherapy, 14*: 123-162

Brafman, A.H. (2001a) *Untying the Knot: Working with Children and Parents* London: Karnac

Brafman, A.H. (2001b) What About the Parents? [in Bertolini, M. et al (2001) vol. 2: 30-36

Brandchaft, B. (1986) 19 British Object Relations Theory and Self-Psychology. *Progress in Self Psychology, 2*: 245-272

Bratherton, W.J. (1997) *Thinking about Children* review. *Journal of Analytic Psychology, 42*: 535-536

Brazelton, T.B., Cramer, B.G. (1990) *The Earliest Relationship: Parents, Infants and the Drama of Early Attachment* Reading, MA: Addison-Wesley reprinted London: Karnac 1991

Brinich, P.M. (1998) *Thinking about Children* review. *Psychoanalytic Quarterly, 67*: 727-730

Brodie, K. (1993) *Talking to Parents* review. *Library Journal, 118 issue 3*: 104

Brody, H.S. (2001)   Paul Klee: Art, Potential Space and the
                      Transitional Process. *Psychoanalytic
                      Review, 82*: 369-392

Brody, S. (1980)   Transitional Objects: Idealization of a
                      Phenomenon. *Psychoanalytic Quarterly,
                      49*: 561-605

Bronstein, A.A.   The Fetish, Transitional Objects and
(1992)   Illusion. *Psychoanalytic Review,
                      79*: 239-260

Brusset, B. (2003)   The Intersubjective Relation and
                      Psychoanalytic Work. *Psychoanalysis in
                      Europe Bulletin, 57*: 62-69

Buckley, P. (1994)   Self Psychology, Object-Relation Theory
                      and Supportive Psychotherapy. *American
                      Journal of Psychotherapy, 48*: 519-524

Burack, C. (1993)   Love, Rage and Destruction: Donald
                      Winnicott and Social Theory.
                      *Psychoanalysis and Contemporary Thought,
                      16*: 429-446

Bürgin, D. (2004)   Winnicott's Squiggle Game in Practice.
                      *International Journal of Psychoanalysis,
                      85*: 1297-1303

Burgin, V. (2004)   *The Remembered Film.* London: Reaktion
                      Books

Burland, J.A. (1989) *Home is Where You Start From* review.
                      Psychoanalytic Quarterly, 58: 283-285

Burland, J.A. (1998) Kahr, B. (1996) review. *Psychoanalytic
                      Quarterly, 67*: 726-727

Burns-Smith, J.   Theology and Winnicott's Object
(1999)   Relations Theory. *Journal of Psychology
                      and Theology, 27*: 3-19

Busch, F. (1974)   Dimensions of the First Transitional
                           Object. *Psychoanalytic Study of the Child,*
                           29: 215-230

Busch, F.,   Theme and Variations of First
McKnight, J. (1977)   Transitional Object. *International Journal*
                           of Psychoanalysis, 58: 479-486

Busch, F. (1990)   Fromm, Smith (1989) review. *International*
                           Journal of Psychoanalysis, 71: 553-556

Caldwell, L. (Ed.)   *Art, Creativity, Living.* London: Karnac
(2000)   for the Squiggle Foundation

Caldwell, L. (Ed.)   *The Elusive Child.* London: Karnac for the
(2002a)   Squiggle Foundation

Caldwell, L. (2002b)   Introduction [Caldwell, L. (2002a): 1-13]

Caldwell, L. (2003)   The Outrageous Prince: Winnicott's
                           Uncure of Masud Khan [intro. to
                           Goldman, D. (2003) and in *British Journal*
                           of Psychotherapy, 19: 483-485]

Caldwell, L. (Ed.)   *Sex and Sexuality: Winnicottian*
(2005)   *Perspectives.* London: Karnac for the
                           Squiggle Foundation

Cameron, K. (1996)   Winnicott and Lacan: Selfhood and
                           Subjecthood [in Richards with Wilce
                           (1996): 37-45]

Campbell, D. (2001)   On Pseudo-normality: a Contribution to
                           the Psychopathology of Adolescence
                           [in Kahr, B. (2001a): 61-72]

Canter, H.M. (1995)   The Imagination of Peace: A
                           Winnicottian Relations Understanding
                           Dissertation. *Abstracts International,*
                           55(11-B): 5060

24

Caradoc-Davies, G. (1995) A Return Journey to the Concept of Top-Dog/Under-Dog Travelling with Winnicott and Others. *British Gestalt Journal*, 4: 129-133

Carr, A., Downs, A. (2004) Transitional and Quasi-objects in Organization Studies: Viewing Enron from the Object Relations World of Winnicott and Serres. *Journal of Organisational Change Management*, 17: 352-364

Carratelli, T.I. (2001) On De Goldstein, R.Z. (2001) [in Bertolini, M. et al (2001) vol. 1: 241-246

Carter, L. (2000) The Analyst and his Personality: Winnicott analyzing Guntrip as a Case in Point. *Journal of the American Psychoanalytic Association*, 45: 487-488

Casas de Pereda, M. (2001) Adolescent Resignification [in Bertolini, M. et al (2001) vol. 1: 218-227]

Casement, P.J. (1982) Samuel Beckett's Relationship to his Mother-tongue. *International Review of Psychoanalysis*, 9: 35-44 [also in Rudnytsky (1993): 229-246]

Casement, P.J. (1985) *On Learning from the Patient*. London: Routledge

Casement, P.J. (1989) *Human Nature* review. *International Journal of Psychoanalysis, 70*: 360-362

Casement, P.J. (1990) *Further Learning from the Patient* London: Routledge

Casement, P.J. (1995) Goldman, D. (1993a) review. *Journal of the American Psychoanalytic Association*, 43: 223-227

Casement, P.J. (2000)   The Issue of Touch: a Retrospective Overview. *Psychoanalytic Inquiry,* 20: 160-184

Casement, P.J. (2002a)   *On Learning from our Mistakes.* London: Routledge

Casement, P.J. (2002b)   Learning from Life. *Psychoanalytic Inquiry,* 22: 519-533

Casement, P.J. (2002c)   Foreword to Kahr, B. (2002a): xxi-xxix

Cassidy, J. (1999)   *Handbook of Attachment: Theory, Research and Clinical Applications.* New York: Guilford Press

Castelloe, M. (2004)   The Good-enough Setting of Anna Deveare Smith: Restaging Crown Heights. *Psychoanalysis, Culture and Society, 9:* 207-218

Castro, C. (1996)   A First Approach to Clinical Work .... Taken by the Hand of Winnicott. *Winnicott Studies, 11:* 62-70

Cedillo, J.C.S. (2001)   A Story of Losses and the Creation of an Alternate World. *International Forum of Psychoanalysis, 10:* 64-71

Chagas-Bovet, A.M. (2001)   Exploring the Pathways of Illusion [in Bertolini, M. et al (2001) vol. 1: 126-133]

Charles, M. (1998)   On Wondering: Creating Openings into the Analytic Space. *Journal of Melanie Klein And Object Relations, 16:* 367-387

Charles, M. (1999)   *The Piggle*: Confrontations with Non-Existence in Childhood. *International Journal of Psychoanalysis, 80:* 783-795

Chazan, S.E. (1997)   Ending Child Psychotherapy: Continuing the Cycle of Life. *Psychoanalytic Psychology,14:* 221-238

26

Chescheir, M.W. (1985)

Some Implications for Winnicott's Concept for Clinical Work Practice. *Clinical Social Work Journal, 13*: 218-233

Chescheir, M.W., Schultz, K.H. (1989)

The Development of a Capacity for Concern in Anti-Social Children: Winnicott's Concept of Human Relatedness. *Clinical Social Work Journal, 17*: 24-39

Cheshire, J. (2006)

Caldwell, L. (2005) review. *British Journal of Psychotherapy, 22*: 520-524

Claman, L. (1980)

The Squiggle Drawing Game in Child Psychotherapy. *American Journal of Psychotherapy, 34*: 414-425

Clancier, A., Kalmanovitch, J. (1987)

Winnicott and Paradox: from Birth to Creation. London: Tavistock

Clancier, A., Kalmanovitch, J. (1990)

A Splash of Paint in his Style [in Giovacchini, P. (1990a): 41-59]

Coco, J.H. (1999)

Exploring the Frontier from the Inside Out: John Sloan's Nude Studies. *Journal of the American Psychoanalytic Association, 47*: 1335-1376

Cohn, H. (1986)

Deprivation and Delinquency review. *Group Analysis, 19*: 95

Coles, P. (Ed) (2006)

Sibling Relationships. London: Karnac

Cooper, J. (1993a)

Different Ways of Structuring the Frame: According to Winnicott, Khan and Langs. *Bulletin of the British Association of Psychotherapy,* 23-35

Cooper, J. (1993b)

Speak of Me as I am: The Life and Work of Masud Khan. London: Karnac

Cooper, S.H., Adler, G. (1990) Toward a Clarification of the Transitional Object and Self-objects in the treatment of the Borderline Patient. *Annual of Psychoanalysis, 18*: 133-152

Coppolillo, H.P. (1967) Maturational Aspects of the Transitional Phenomenon. *International Journal of Psychoanalysis, 48*: 237-246

Coppolillo, H.P. (1976) The Transitional Phenomenon Revisited. *Journal of the American Academy of Child Psychiatry, 15*: pp.36-47

Coppolillo, H.O. (1987) *Psychodynamic Psychotherapy of Children.* Madison, CO: International Universities Press

Cornell, W.F. (1997) If Reich had Met Winnicott. *Energy and Character, 28*: 50-60

Cornell, W.F. (2000) If Berne Met Winnicott: Transactional Analysis and Relational Analysis. *Transactional Analysis Journal, 30*: 270-275

Corrigan, E.G., Gordon, P-E. (Eds.) (1995a) *The Mind Object: Precocity and Pathology of Self-Sufficiency.* London: Karnac

Corrigan, E.G., Gordon, P-E. (Eds.) (1995b) The Mind as an Object [in Corrigan, E.G., Gordon, P-E. (1995a): 1-23]

Cowan-Jenssen, S. (1995) Primal Psychotherapy [in Ryan, J. (2005): 137-163]

Cox, M. (2001) On the Capacity for Being Inside Enough [in Kahr, B. (2001a): 111-120]

Coyote, A.L. (2000) Two Perspectives on Selfhood: Donald Woods Winnicott M.D. and Dvaita Yoga Philosophy. *Dissertation Abstracts (International), 61(3-B)*: 1663

Crastnopol, M. (1999)
The Analyst's Personality: Winnicott Analyzing Guntrip as a Case in Point. *Contemporary Psychoanalysis, 35*: 271-300

Crème, P. (1994)
The Playing Spectator: a Study on the Applicability of the Theories of D.W. Winnicott to Contemporary Concepts of the Viewer's Relationship to Film. *Ph.D. Thesis: Kent* 45-9182

Crewdson, F. (1996)
The False Self as Explored in a Long-term Psychoanalysis. *Journal of the American Academy of Psychoanalysis, 24*: 29-43

Cunningham, M. (2006)
Vedanta and Psychoanalysis [in Black, D.M. (2006a): 234-251]

Curtis, R.C. (Ed.) (1991)
The Relational Self: Theoretical Convergences in Psychoanalysis and Social Psychiatry. New York: Guilford

Daehnert, C. (1998)
The False Self as a Means of Disidentification: A Psychoanalytic Case Study. *Contemporary Psychoanalysis, 34*: 241-271

Dajani, K.G. (2003)
Psychological Resilience: a Theoretical Contribution - Georg Wilhelm, Friedrich Hegel, D.W. Winnicott. *Dissertation Abstracts (International), 63(10-B)*: 4080

Dalley, T. (1992)
Handbook of Art Therapy. London: Routledge

Daniel, P. (2001)
Masud Khan and Winnicott. *Bulletin of the British Psychoanalytic Society, 37*: 30-33

Dauber, A.B. (1993)
Thomas Traherne and the Poetics of Object Relations [in Rudnytsky (1993): 133-160]

Davar, E. (2001)   The Loss of the Transitional Object –
Some Thoughts about Transitional and
"pre-transitional" Phenomena.
Psychodynamic Counselling, 7: 5-26

Davids, M.F. (2006)   'Render unto Caesar what is Caesar's':
is there a Realm of God in the Mind?
[in Black, D.M. (2006a): 45-62]

Davis, J.A. (1993a)   *Clinical Notes on Disorders of Childhood*
review. *Winnicott Studies, 7(Spring):* 95-97

Davis, J.A. (1993b)   *The Child, The Family and the Outside World*
review. *Winnicott Studies, 8(Autumn):* 73-76

Davis, M.E.V.,   *Boundary and Space: An Introduction to*
Wallbridge, D.   *the Work of D.W.Winnicott.* London:
(1981)   Karnac & NY: Brunner-Mazel (rev. ed.
London: Karnac (1991))

Davis, M.E.V.   Some Thoughts on Winnicott and
(1985)   Freud. *Bulletin of the British Association of*
Psychotherapy, 16: 57-71

Davis, M.E.V.   The Writing of D.W. Winnicott.
(1987)   *International Review of Psychoanalysis,*
14: 491-501

Davis, M.E.V.   Play and Symbolism in Lowenfeld and
(1990)   Winnicott. *Free Associations,*
23 vol.2/3: 395-422

Davis, M.E.V.   Destruction as an Achievement in the
(1993a)   Work of Winnicott. *Winnicott Studies,*
7(Spring): 85-92

Davis, M.E.V.   Winnicott and the Spatula Game (edited
(1993b)   and abridged by Sievers, R.). *Winnicott*
Studies, 8(Autumn): 57-67

Davis, M.E.V.   Winnicott and Object Relations (edited
(1995)   and abridged by Sievers, R.). *Winnicott*
Studies, 10: 33-45

Davis, M.R., Irving, H. (1985)	The Holding Environment in the In-Patient Treatment of Adolescents. *Adolescent Psychiatry, 12*: 434-443
Davoin, F. (1989)	Potential Space and the Space between Two Deaths [in Fromm, Smith (1989a): 581-603]
Daws, D., Boston, M. (Eds.) (1977)	*The Child Psychotherapist and Problems of Young People.* London: Routledge (rev. edition. 1981. Reprinted 1988, London: Karnac)
Daws, D. (1996)	The Spatula, The Electric Socket and the Spoon. *Journal of Child Psychotherapy, 22*: 392-393
De Astis, G. (2001)	The Influence of Winnicott on Francis Tustin's Thinking [in Bertolini, M. et al (2001) vol. 2: 189-195]
De Canteros, N.L. (1994)	Winnicott and Clinical Practice in Psychosomatics, Narcissistic Hypersensitivity and its Vicissitudes. *Encounters (Argentina), 1*: 61-69
De Goldstein, R.Z. (1994)	The Child as Transitional Object of the Mother: Reverted Dependence Demand. *Encounters (Argentina), 1*: 11-23
De Goldstein, R.Z. (2001)	The Matrix of the Psyche-soma [in Bertolini, M. et al (2001) vol. 1: 172-183] (see also Carratelli (2001) for discussion)
De Greif, L.M.V. (1994)	Illusion, Paradox and Metaphor in Psychoanalytic Practice. *Encounters (Argentina), 1*: 1-59
De Groba, A.M.S. (1994)	Some Vicissitudes of Displaying: The Capacity to be One's Own. *Encounters (Argentina), 1*: 95-101

DeLaCour. E.P.
(1989)

Fear of Breakdown: A Case with
Multiple Psychotic Episodes [in Fromm,
Smith (1989a): 558-580]

DeMause, L. (2006)

Issroff, J. (2005) review. *Journal
of Psycho-history, 33*: 402

Dent, K. (1994)

Little, M. (1990) review. *Journal of the
American Academy of Psychoanalysis,
42*: 352-354

Denzler, B. (2001)

Empathy: Love or Skill? [in Bertolini, M.
et al (2003) vol. 2: 232-235

Deri, S. (1978)

Transitional Phenomena: Vicissitudes of
Symbolization and Creativity [in
Grolnick, Barkin, Muensterberger
(1978): 43-60]

Deri, S. (1984)

Symbolization and Creativity.
New York: International
Universities Press

De Schvartzman,
A.R. (1994)

Initial Interviews with Adolescents.
Encounters (Argentina), 1: 79-86

De Silvestris, P.
(2001)

Interminable Illusion [in Bertolini, M.
et al (2001) vol. 2: 59-64

Detrick, D.W. & S.P.
(Eds.) (1989)

*Self Psychology: Comparisons and
Contrasts.* Hillside, NJ: Analytic Press

De Wet, V. (1990)

"Holding" as Therapeutic Manœuvre in
Family Therapy. *Journal of Family
Therapy, 12*: 189-194

Diamond, N. (2005)

When Thought is not Enough [in Ryan, J.
(2005): 113-136]

Di Cintro, J. (2002)

"Ordered Anarchy": Writing as
Transitional Object in *Moise and the
World of Reason. The Tennessee Williams
Annual Review, 5*

Dickes, R. (1978)   Parents, Transitional Objects and Childhood Fetishes [in Grolnick, Barkin, Muensterberger (1978): 305-320]

Dinnage, R. (1978)   A Bit of Light [in Grolnick, Barkin, Muensterberger (1978): 363-378]

Doane, J., Hodges, D. (1993)   *From Klein to Kristeva: Psychoanalytic Feminism and the Search for the 'Good Enough Mother'.* Ann Arbor: Michigan University Press

Dockar-Drysdale, B. (1974)   My Debt to Donald Winnicott. *Journal of Association of Workers for Maladjusted Children, 2:* 2-5

Dockar-Drysdale, B. (1990)   *The Provision of Primary Experience: Winnicottian Work with Children and Adolescents.* London: Free Association Books

Dockar-Drysdale, B. (1993)   *Therapy and Consultation in Child Care.* London: Free Association Books

Doron, A., Mendlovic, S. (1999)   Hypnosis and Winnicott's Transitional Phase. *Contemporary Hypnosis, 16:* 36-39

Douglas, A., Philpot, T. (1998)   *Care and Coping: A Guide to Social Services.* London: Routledge

Downes, C. (2006)   Kanter, J. (2004b) review. *British Journal of Psychotherapy, 22:* 384-388

Downey, T.W. (1978)   Transitional Phenomena in the Analysis of Early Adolescent Males. *Psychoanalytic Study of the Child, 33:* 19-46

Drapeau, P. (2002)   From Freud to Winnicott: an Encounter between Mythical Children [in Caldwell, L. (2002): 15-44]

Drell, M.J. (1991)   Clancier, Kalmanovitch (1987) review. *Infant Mental Health Journal, 12*: 81-83

Dreyfus, P. (2001)   A Discussion of Barnett, B. (2001) [in Bertolini, M. et al (2001) vol. 2: 236-241]

Dunstan, F. (1997)   *Thinking about Children* review. *Therapeutic Communities, 18*: 317

Dwyer, S. (2006)   Some Thoughts on the Work of D.W. Winnicott for Present-day Social Work Practice with Adults. *Journal of Social Work Practice, 20*: 83-89

Eddowes, L. (1997)   Sidemarkers and Teddy Bears: an Application of Winnicott's Ideas in Pædiatric Radiography. *Psychodynamic Counselling, 3*: 195-207

Ehrenberg, D.B. (1976)   The "Intimate Edge" and the "Third Area". *Contemporary Psychoanalysis, 12*: 489-496

Ehrlich, R. (2004)   Winnicott's Response to Klein. *Psychoanalytic Quarterly, 73*: 453-484

Eigen, M. (1980a)   On the Significance of the Face. *Psychoanalytic Review, 67*: 426-444 [also in Eigen (1993): 49-60]

Eigen, M. (1980b)   Instinctual Fantasy and Ideal Images. *Contemporary Psychoanalysis, 16*: 119-137 [also in Eigen, (1993): 61-75]

Eigen, M., Robbins, A. (1980c)   Object Relations and Expressive Symbolism: Some Structures and Functions of Expressive Therapy [in Robbins, A. (Ed.) *Expressive Therapy: A Creative Arts Approach to Depth-Oriented Treatment.* New York: Human Sciences Press (1980): 73-94]

Eigen, M. (1981a)   The Area of Faith in Winnicott, Lacan
                       and Bion. *International Journal of
                       Psychoanalysis, 62*: 413-433 [also in Eigen
                       (1993)109-138]

Eigen, M. (1981b)   Guntrip's Analysis with Winnicott – A
                       Critique of Glatzer. Evans (1977)
                       Contemporary Psychoanalysis, 17: 103-111
                       [also in Eigen (1993): 139-146]

Eigen, M. (1985)   The Sword of Grace: Flannery
                       O'Connor, Wilfred R. Bion and D.W.
                       Winnicott. *Psychoanalytic Review,
                       72*: 337-346

Eigen, M. (1986a)   *The Psychotic Core.* New York: Aronson
                       (reprinted London: Karnac 2004)

Eigen, M. (1986b)   Aspects of Mindlessness-Selflessness: A
                       Common Madness [in Travers, J.A. (Ed.)
                       Psychotherapy and the Selfless Patient.
                       New York: Haworth Press (1986): 75-82]
                       (*Psychotherapy and the Selfless Patient* also
                       published in *The Psychotherapy Patient,
                       Vol.2 No.2*)

Eigen, M. (1989)   Aspects of Omniscience [in Fromm,
                       Smith (1989a): 604-628]

Eigen, M. (1991)   Winnicott's Area of Freedom [in
                       Schwartz-Salant, N., Stein, M. Eds.
                       (1991) *Liminality and Transitional
                       Phenomena.* Wilmette, IL: Chiron
                       Publications: 67-88]

Eigen, M. (1992)   The Fire that Never Goes Out.
                       Psychoanalytic Review, 79: 271-287

Eigen, M. (1993)   *The Electrified Tightrope.* New York:
                       Aronson (reprinted London: Karnac
                       2004)

Eigen, M. (1995)   Mystical Precocity and Psychic Short-Circuits [in Corrigan, E.G., Gordon, P-E. (1995a): 109-134]

Eigen, M. (1996)   *Psychic Deadness.* New York: Aronson (reprinted London: Karnac 2004)

Eigen, M. (1998a)   Soundproof Sanity and Fear of Madness. *Journal of Melanie Klein & Object Relations, 16*: 411-423 [also in Eigen (1999): 171-185]

Eigen, M. (1998b)   *The Psychoanalytic Mystic.* London: Free Association Books

Eigen, M. (1999)   *Toxic Nourishment.* London: Karnac

Eigen, M. (2001)   *Damaged Bonds.* London: Karnac

Eigen, M. (2004)   *The Sensitive Self.* Middletown, CT: Wesleyan University Press

Eisenstein-Naveh,   The Center for Children and Families at
A.R. (2003)   Risk: a Facilitating Environment. *Family Journal, 11*: 19

Eklund, M. (2000)   Applying Object Relations Theory to Psychosocial Occupational Therapy: Empirical and Theoretical Considerations. *Occupational Therapy and Mental Health, 15*: 1-26

Ekstrom, S.R. (1984)   Self-theory and Psychoanalysis: The Evolution of the Self-concept and its Use in the Clinical Theories of C.G. Jung, D.W. Winnicott and Heinz Kohut. *Dissertation Abstracts (International), 45(1-B)*: 347

Elkind, S.N. (1992)   *Resolving Impasses in Therapeutic Relationships.* New York: Guilford Press

Elmhirst, S.I. (1980)   Transitional Objects in Transition. *International Journal of Psychoanalysis, 61*: 367-373

Endoh, T. (1990)   An Examination into Transitional Object
                        Origins: Transitional Object and
                        Maternal Care. *Japanese Journal of
                        Developmental Psychology, 1*: 59-69

Endoh, T. (1991)   Stress within Mother Infant Interactions
                        as a Determinant of the Occurrence of
                        Infant's Attachment to a Transitional
                        Object. *Japanese Journal of Educational
                        Psychology, 39*: 243-252

Epstein, L.,   *Countertransference.* Northvale, NJ:
Feiner, A.H. (1979)   Aronson

Epstein, L. (2001)   Further Thoughts on the Winnicott-
                        Khan Analysis [in Petrucelli and Stuart
                        (2001): 375-384]

Epstein, M. (1998)   *Going to Pieces without Falling Apart.*
                        New York: Broadway Books

Epstein, M. (2002)   *Going on Being.* New York: Broadway
                        Books

Epstein, M. (2005a)   *Open to Desire: Embracing a Lust for Life
                        Instincts from Buddhism and
                        Psychotherapy.* New York:
                        Gotham Books

Epstein, M. (2005b)   A Strange Beauty: Emmanuel Ghent
                        and the Psychologies of East and West.
                        Psychoanalytic Dialogues, 15: 125-138

Epstein, M. (2006)   The Structure of No-structure:
                        Winnicott's Concept of Unintegration
                        and the Buddhist Notion of No-self [in
                        Black, D.M. (2006a): 223-233]

Erlicher, P.,   Reparation in Respect of Mother's
Quarantini, A.Z.   Organized Defence Against Depression
(2001)   [in Bertolini, M. et al (2001) vol. 2: 24-29]

Esman, A.H. (1990) Three Books by and about Winnicott [Phillips, A. *Winnicott* (1988); Rodman, R. (Ed.). *Spontaneous Gesture* (1987); Winnicott, C., Shepherd, R. & Davis, M. (Eds.). *Psychoanalytic Explorations* (1987)] review. *International Journal of Psychoanalysis, 71*: 695-699

Etzi, J. (2005) Rodman, F.R. (2003) review. *Journal of Phenomenological Psychology, 36*: 247-248

Faber, M.D. (1988) The Pleasure of Rhyme: a Psychoanalytic Note. *International Review of Psychoanalysis, 15*: 375-380

Farhi, N. (1993) D.W. Winnicott and Personal Tradition [in Spurling, L. Ed. (1993): 78-105]

Farhi, N. (1996) The Squiggle Foundation. *Journal of Child Psychotherapy, 22*: 404-406

Farhi, N. (2001) Psychotherapy and the Squiggle Game: a Sophisticated Game of Hide-and-Seek [in Bertolini, M. et al (2001) vol. 2: 65-75] (see also Giannini (2003)for discussion]

Farhi, N. (2003a) Introduction to the Gaddini-Winnicott Correspondence. *Psychoanalysis and History, 5*: -3-12

Farhi, N. (2003b) In Her Mother's Name. *Contemporary Analysis, 39*: 75-87

Farrell, E. (2001) Vomit as a Transitional Object [in Kahr, B. (2002a): 73-82]

Favero, M., Ross, D.R. (2003) Words and Transitional Phenomena in Psychotherapy. *American Journal of Psychotherapy, 57*: 287-299

Feinsilver, D.B. (1989) Transitional Play with Regressed Schizophrenic Patients [in Fromm, Smith (1989a): 205-237]

Field, N. (1991)　　　　Projective Identification: Mechanism of
　　　　　　　　　　　　Mystery? *Journal of Analytic Psychology*,
　　　　　　　　　　　　36: 93-109

Fielding, J. (1985)　　　'To be or not to be': Hamlet, Culture
　　　　　　　　　　　　and Winnicott. *Winnicott. Studies*,
　　　　　　　　　　　　1: 58-67

Fielding, J. (1987)　　　The Creature there Never has Been:
　　　　　　　　　　　　'Alice' and Winnicott. *Winnicott Studies*,
　　　　　　　　　　　　2: 87-100

Fielding, J. (1988)　　　'Prove True, Imagination': Keats,
　　　　　　　　　　　　Coleridge and Winnicott. *Winnicott
　　　　　　　　　　　　Studies*, *3*: 4-12

Fielding, J. (1991)　　　'Men Children Only': Adolescence,
　　　　　　　　　　　　Fighting and Self-Definition. *Winnicott
　　　　　　　　　　　　Studies*, *6*: 48-59

Fielding, J. (1997)　　　"So Rare a Wonder'd Father":
　　　　　　　　　　　　Winnicott's Negotiation of the Paternal
　　　　　　　　　　　　[in Richards with Wilce (1997): 59-72]

Fielding, J. (2000)　　　"I Thought so Then": *Othello* and the
　　　　　　　　　　　　Unknown Thought [in Caldwell, L.
　　　　　　　　　　　　(2000): 49-62]

Fintzy, R.T. (1971)　　　Vicissitudes of the Transitional Object in
　　　　　　　　　　　　a Borderline Child. *International Journal
　　　　　　　　　　　　of Psychoanalysis*, *52*: 107-114

Firman, J. (1997)　　　*The Primal Wound: a Transpersonal View
　　　　　　　　　　　　on Trauma, Addiction and Growth* Albany,
　　　　　　　　　　　　NY: State University of New York Press

Firman, J., Gilla, A.　　*Psychosynthesis: a Psychology of the Spirit:*
(2002)　　　　　　　　Albany, NY: State University of New
　　　　　　　　　　　　York Press

First, E. (1994)　　　　Mothering, Hate and Winnicott [in
　　　　　　　　　　　　Bassin, Honey, Kaplan (1994): 147-161]

Fishman, E.A. (2003)
An Integrative Approach to Parent-child Attachment through the Work of Bowlby, Ainsworth, Winnicott and Kohut. *Dissertation Abstracts (International), 64(6-B)*: 2914

Flanders, S. (1992)
Dockar-Drysdale, B. (1990) review. *International Review of Psychoanalysis, 19*: 391-394

Flax, J. (1990)
Thinking Fragments: Psychoanalysis, Feminism and Post-modernism in the Contemporary West. Berkeley: University of California Press

Flew, A. (1978)
Transitional Objects and Transitional Phenomena: Comments and Interpretation [in Grolnick, Barkin, Muensterberger (1978): 483-502]

Flournoy, O. (1992)
Little, M. (1990) review. *International Journal of Psychoanalysis, 73*: 593-594

Flynn, C., Stirtzinger, R. (2001)
Understanding a Regressed Adolescent Boy through Story Writing and Winnicott's Intermediate Area. *Arts in Psychotherapy, 28*: 299-309

Flynn, D. (1998)
Jacobs, M. (1995) & Abram, J. (1996) review. *Therapeutic Communities, 19*: 334-335

Fogel, G.I. (1992)
Winnicott's Antitheory and Winnicott's Art: his Significance for Adult Analysis. *Psychoanalytic Study of the Child, 42*: 205-222

Fonsera, V.R. (1999)
The Phenomenon of Object-Presenting and its Implications for Development *International Journal of Psychoanalysis, 80*: 885-897

Forcey, L.R. (1987)   *Mothers of Sons: Toward an Understanding of Responsibility* Westport, CT: Praeger

Ford, D.H., Urban, H.B (1998)   *Contemporary Models of Psychotherapy: a Contemporary Analysis* New York: Wiley

Fordham, M. (1972)   *Therapeutic Consultations in Child Psychiatry* review *International Journal of Psychoanalysis*, 53: 555-556

Fordham, M. (1985)   *Explorations into the Self* London: Academic Press (new edition London: Karnac 2002)

Formaini, H. (2004)   Peering into One of Winnicott's "Blank Spots". *American Imago, 61*: 527-538

Forrester, J. (1997)   On Holding as Metaphor: Winnicott and the Figure of St. Christopher [in Richards with Wilce (1997): 41-58]

Fowler, C., Hilsenroth, M.J. Handler, L. (1998)   Assessing Transitional Phenomena with the Transitional Object Memory Probe. *Bulletin of the Menninger Clinic, 62*: 455-474

Fowler, J.C. (2005)   Transitional Relating and the Capacity for Play in Treatment. *Journal of Personality Assessment, 72*: 218-223

Fox, R.P. (1977)   Transitional Phenomena in the Treatment of a Psychotic Adolescent *International Journal of Psychiatric Psychotherapy, 6*: 147-164

Frankel, R. Ed. (1998)   *The Adolescent Psyche: Jungian and Winnicottian Perspectives* London and New York: Routledge

Frankel, R. (2002a)   A Winnicottian View of an American Tragedy [in Caldwell (2002): 153-175]

Frankel, R. (2002b)   Fantasy and Imagination in Winnicott's
                        Work. *British Journal of Psychotherapy,
                        19*: 3-20

Fraser, M.L (1997)   The Use of Transitional Space in Pastoral
                        Counselling: Psychological and
                        Theological Meaning Making. *Dissertation
                        Abstracts (International), 57(11-B)*: 7263

Frazier, R.T. (1993)   Space and Holding: Beginning Pastoral
                        Counselling with Incest Victims. *Pastoral
                        Psychology, 42*: 81-94

Frederickson, J.   From Delusion to Play. *Clinical Social
(1991)   Work Journal, 19*: 349-362

French, R. (1999)   The Importance of Capacities in
                        Psychoanalysis and the Language of
                        Human Development *International
                        Journal of Psychoanalysis, 80*: 1215-1226

Fromm, M.G.,   *The Facilitating Environment: Clinical
Smith, B.L. (Eds.)   Applications of Winnicott's Theory*
(1989a)   Madison, CT: International Universities
                        Press

Fromm, M.G.   Winnicott's Work in Relation to
(1989b)   Classical Psychoanalysis and Ego
                        Psychology [in Fromm, Smith (1989a):
                        3-26]

Fromm, M.G.   Impasse and Transitional Relatedness
(1989c)   [in Fromm, Smith (1989a): 179-204]

Fromm, M.G.   Photography as Transitional
(1989d)   Functioning [in Fromm, Smith
                        (1989a): 279-316]

Fromm, M.G.   Dreams Represented in Dreams: a
(1989e)   Discussion of the True Self/False Self
                        Duality [in Fromm, Smith
                        (1989a): 459-488]

Fromm, M.G. (1989f)	Disturbances of the Self in the Psychoanalytic Setting [in Fromm, Smith (1989a): 489-515]
Fromm, M.G. (1995)	Rudnytsky, P.L. (1993) review. *Contemporary Psychology, 40*: 953 [also in *PsycCRITIQUES* 2004]
Fujii, K. (1985)	A Developmental Study on Transitional Objects. *Japanese Journal of Educational Psychology, 33*: 106-114
Fuller, P. (1987)	Mother and Child in Henry Moore and Winnicott. *Winnicott Studies, 2*: 49-70
Furman, E. (1979)	*The Piggle* review. *Psychoanalytic Quarterly, 48*: 324-326
Gaddini, E. (1992)	*A Psychoanalytic Theory of Infantile Experience* (edited Limentani. A.) London: Routledge/Institute of Psychoanalysis
Gaddini, R. with Gaddini, E. (1970)	Transitional Objects and the Process of Individuation: a Study in Three Different Social Groups. *Journal of the American Academy of Child Psychiatry, 9*: 347-365
Gaddini, R. (1978)	Transitional Object Origins and the Psychosomatic Symptom [in Grolnick, Barkin, Muensterberger (1978): 109-132]
Gaddini, R. (1981)	Bion's "Catastrophic Change" and Winnicott's "Breakdown". *Rivista di Psicoanalisi, 27*: 610-625
Gaddini, R. (1985)	The Precursors of Transitional Objects and Phenomena. *Winnicott Studies, 1*: 49-57 (also in *Psychoanalysis and History, 5* (2003): 53-62)

Gaddini, R. (1987)   Early Care and the Roots of
Internalization. *International Review of
Psychoanalysis, 14*: 321-332

Gaddini, R.,   Clancier, Kalmanovitch (1987) review.
Bovet, A.C. (1988)   *International Review of Psychoanalysis,
15*: 534-535

Gaddini, R. (1990)   Regression and its Uses in Treatment: an
Elaboration in the Thinking of
Winnicott [in Giovacchini, P.L. (1990a):
182-199] also in Boyer and Giovacchini
(1990b): 227-244] and in Goldman, D.
(1993): 257-272]

Gaddini, R. (1993)   On Autism. *Psychoanalytic Inquiry,
13*: 134-143

Gaddini, R. (1996)   Lullabies and Rhymes in the Emotional
Life of Children and No-Longer
Children. *Winnicott Studies, 11*: 28-40

Gaddini, R. (1998)   Kumin, I. (1997) review. *Journal of the
American Psychoanalytic Society,
46*: 306-316

Gaddini, R. (2001)   The Psyche-soma Matrix: *Through
Pædiatrics to Psychoanalysis* [in Bertolini, M.
et al (2001) vol. 1: 167-171]

Gaddini, R. (2003a)   Correspondence between Donald
Winnicott and Renata Gaddini.
Psychoanalysis & History, 5: 13-48

Gaddini, R. (2003b)   The Precursors of Transitional Objects
and Phenomena. *Psychoanalysis &
History, 5*: 53-61

Gaddini, R. (2003c)   Creativity and the 'Nebulous' in
Winnicott (2000). *Psychoanalysis &
History, 5*: 63-70

Gaddini, R. (2004)	Thinking about Winnicott and the Origins of the Self. *Psychoanalysis & History*, 6: 225-235

Galligan, A.C. (2000)	That Place where we Live: the Discovery of Self through the Creative Play Experience. *Journal of Child and Adolescent Psychiatric Nursing*, 13: 169-176

Gallo, P., Nacinovitch, R. (2001)	Primary Maternal Preoccupation: Pregnancy and Child-rearing [in Bertolini, M. et al (2001) vol. 2: 155-160]

Garanzini, M. (1988)	*The Attachment Circle: An Object Relations Approach to the Healing Ministries* New York: Paulist Press

Gardner, R.A. (1973)	*Playing and Reality* and *Therapeutic Consultations in Child Psychiatry* review. *Contemporary Psychoanalysis*, 9: 392-399

Gargiulo, G.J. (1992a)	Sublimation: Winnicottian Reflections. *Psychoanalytic Review*, 9: 327-340

Gargiulo, G.J. (1992b)	Grolnick, S. (1990) review. *Psychoanalytic Books*, 3: 49-50

Gargiulo. G.J. (1994)	Giovacchini, P.L. (1990a) review. *Psychoanalytic Books*, 5: 214-218

Gargiulo, G.J. (1996)	Newman, A. (1995) review. *Psychoanalytic Books*, 7: 403-405

Gargiulo, G.J. (1998)	Winnicott's Psychoanalytic Playground [in Marcus, P. and Rosenberg, A. Eds. *Philosophies of Life and their Impact* New York: New York University Press (1998):140-146]

Gargiulo, G.J. (2003)	Hidden Boundaries/Hidden Spaces. *Psychoanalytic Review*, 90: 381-392

Garland, C. (1982) Group Analysis: Taking the Non-Problem Seriously. *Group Analysis, 15*: 4-14

Gau, J.V. (1991) The Theological and Psychological Foundations of Adult Faith as seen in Hans Urs von Balthasar, Melanie Klein and D.W. Winnicott. *Dissertation Abstracts International, 51(7-A)*: 2422

Gee, H. (2002) My Experience of Winnicott [in Kahr (2002a): 141-145]

Geissmann, C., Geissmann, P. (1998) *A History of Child Analysis.* London and New York: Routledge

Geleerd, E.R. (1967) *Family and Individual Development* review. *International Journal of Psychoanalysis, 48*: 106-111

Gerity, J.A. (2001) Josie, Winnicott and the Hungry Ghosts. *Art Therapy, 18*: 35-40

Gerrard, J. (1990) Use and Abuse in Psychotherapy. *British Journal of Psychotherapy, 7*: 121-128

Gerson, G. (2004) Winnicott, Participation and Gender. *Feminism & Psychology, 14*: 561-582

Gerson, G. (2005) Individuality, Deliberation and Welfare in Donald Winnicott. *History of the Human Sciences, 18*: 107-126

Ghent, E. (1990) Masochism, Subjection, Surrender: Masochism as a Perversion of Surrender. *Contemporary Psychoanalysis, 26*: 108-136

Ghent, E. (1992) Paradox and Process. *Psychoanalytic Dialogues, 2*: 135-139

Giannakoulas, A. (2005) Childhood Sexual Theories and Childhood Sexuality: the Primal Scene and Parental Sexuality [in Caldwell, L. (2005): 55-68)]

Giannini, G. del C. (2001)	Reflections on Farhi, C. (2001) [in Bertolini, M. et al (2001) vol. 2: 223-227]
Giannotti, V. et al (2001)	From the Æsthetics of External Objects to the Quality of Internal Objects: On the Diagnosis of Alopecia in Childhood and Adolescence [in Bertolini, M. et al (2001) vol. 2: 161-168]
Gibeault, A. (2001)	Art in Prehistory: a Potential Space for Play [in Bertolini, M. et al (2001) vol. 1: 136-145]
Gibson, M. (2004)	Melancholy Objects. *Mortality*, 9: 285-299
Gillespie, W.H (1971)	Donald W. Winnicott. *International Journal of Psychoanalysis, 52*: 227-228
Ginot, E. (2001)	The Holding Environment and Intersubjectivity. *Psychoanalytic Quarterly, 70*: 414-445
Giovacchini, P.L. (1978)	The Impact of Delusion and the Delusion of Impact: Ego Defect and the Transitional Phenomenon [in Grolnick, Barkin, Muensterberger (1978): 321-344]
Giovacchini, P.L. (1984)	*Character Disorders and Adaptive Mechanisms.* New York: Aronson
Giovacchini, P.L. (1986)	*Developmental Disorders: the Transitional Space in Mental Breakdown and Creative Imagination.* Northvale, NJ: Aronson
Giovacchini, P.L. (1989)	*Countertransference Triumphs and Catastrophes.* Northvale, NJ: Aronson
Giovacchini, P.L. (Ed.) (1990a)	*Tactics and Techniques in Psychoanalytic Therapy III: The Implications of Winnicott's Contributions.* Northvale, NJ: Aronson

Giovacchini, P.L.
(1990b)

Interpretations, an Obscure Technical Area: Winnicott's 'Interpretation in Psychoanalysis' [in Giovacchini (1990a): 71-89]

Giovacchini, P.L.
(1990c)

Absolute and Not Quite Absolute Dependence [in Giovacchini (1990a): 142-159] [also in Goldman, D. (1993): 241-256]

Giovacchini, P.L.
(1990d)

Regression, Reconstruction and Resolution: Containment and Holding [in Giovacchini, (1990a): 226-264]

Giovacchini, P.L
(1990e)

Hughes, J.M. (1989) review. *American Journal of Psychiatry*, 147: 807

Giovacchini, P.L.
(2001a)

Transitional Objects in Treatment of Primitive Mental States [in Kahr (2001a): 83-94]

Giovacchini, P.L.
(2001b)

Dangerous Transitions and the Traumatized Adolescent. *American Journal of Psychoanalysis*, 61: 7-21

Giraldo, M. (1990)

Phillips, A. (1988) review. *Psychiatry*, 53: 202

Glatzer, H.T.,
Evans, W.N. (1977)

On Guntrip's Analysis with Fairbairn and Winnicott. *International Journal of Psychoanalytic Psychotherapy*, 6: 81-98

Glatzer, H.T. (1985)

Early Mother-Child Relationships: Notes on the pre-Œdipal Fantasy. *Dynamic Psychotherapy*, 3: 27-37

Glenn, L. (1987)

Attachment Theory and Group Analysis: The Group Matrix as a Secure Base. *Group Analysis*, 20: 109-117

Godley, W. (2001a)

Saving Masud Khan. *London Review of Books* (Feb. 22)

Godley, W. (2001b)   My Lost Hours on the Couch. *The (London)Times* (Feb. 23)

Godley, W. (2004)   Commentary on Sandler, A.M (2004). *International Journal of Psychoanalysis,* 85: 42-44

Goetzmann, L. (2004)   "Is it Me or isn't it?" – Transplanted Organs and their Donors as Transitional Objects. *American Journal of Psychoanalysis,* 64: 279-289

Goldberg, B. (1999)   Spatial Transitions: Contesting the Limits of Social and Psychic Space. *Psychoanalysis and Contemporary Thought,* 22: 315-341

Goldberg, P. (1990)   The Holding Environment: Conscious and Unconscious Elements in the Building of a Therapeutic Framework [in Boyer and Giovacchini (1990b): 271-301]

Golden, G.K. (1991)   A Token of Loving: from Melancholia to Mourning. *Clinical Social Work Journal,* 19: 23

Golden, G.K., Hill, M.A. (1994)   Only Sane: Autistic Barriers in "Boring" Patients. *Clinical Social Work Journal,* 22: 9-26

Goldman, D. (1993a)   In Search of the Real: The Origins and Originality of D.W. Winnicott. *Dissertation Abstracts (International),* 54(4-B): 2200

Goldman, D. (1993b)   *In Search of the Real: The Origins and Originality of D.W. Winnicott.* Northvale, NJ: Aronson

Goldman, D. (Ed.) (1993c)   *In One's Bones: The Clinical Genius of Winnicott.* Northvale, NJ: Aronson

Goldman, D. (1996)   An Exquisite Corpse: the Strain of Working in and out of Potential Space. *Contemporary Psychoanalysis, 32*: 339-358

Goldman, D. (1998a)   Surviving as Scientist and Dreamer: Winnicott and "The Use of an Object". *Contemporary Psychoanalysis, 34*: 359-368

Goldman, D. (1998b)   Slochower, J.A. (1996). *Contemporary Journal of Psychoanalysis, 34*: 645-658

Goldman, D. (2001)   The Outrageous Prince: Winnicott's Uncure of Masud Khan [in Petrucelli and Stuart (2001): 359-374. Also in *British Journal of Psychotherapy, 19*: 486-501]

Gomer, G.M. (1994)   Embodiment as a Central Theme in the Work of D.W. Winnicott. *Dissertation Abstracts (International), 55(3-A)*: 592

Goodwin, J.M. (1997)   Kahr, B. (1996) review. *Journal of Psychohistory, 24*: pp. 302-303

Gordon, R. (2001)   Psychosomatics in Jung and Winnicott [in Bertolini, M. et al (2001) vol. 2: 169-172]

Graham, P. (2005)   Kanter, J. (2004b) review. *Children and Society, 19*: 418-419

Green, A. (1975)   The Analyst, Symbolization and Absence in the Analytic Setting (on Change in Analytic Practice and Analytic Experience). In Memory of D.W. Winnicott). *International Journal of Psychoanalysis, 56*: 1-22

Green, A. (1978)   Potential Space in Psychoanalysis: the Object in the Setting [in Grolnick, Barkin, Muensterberger, (1978): 167-190]

Green, A. (1986)   *On Private Madness.* London: Hogarth Press

Green, A. (1993)   Analytic Play and its Relationship to the
                      Object [in Goldman, D. Ed. (1993):
                      213-222

Green, A. (1997)   The Intuition of the Negative in *Playing
                      and Reality. International Journal of
                      Psychoanalysis, 78*: 1071-1084 [also in
                      Abram, J.(2000a): 85-106, and in Kohon,
                      G. (1999): 205-221 and in Bertolini, M.
                      et al (2001) vol. 1: 43-58]

Green, A. (1999)   *The Fabric of Affect in the Psychoanalytic
                      Discourse.* London and New York:
                      Routledge

Green, A. (2000a)   *Andre Green at the Squiggle Foundation*
                      (Ed. Abram, J.). London: Karnac

Green, A. (2000b)   Experience and Thinking in Analytic
                      Practice [in Green, A. (2000a): 1-15]

Green, A. (2000c)   Object(s) and Subject [in Green, A.
                      (2000a): 17-37]

Green, A. (2000d)   On Thirdness [in Green, A. (2000a): 39-68]

Green, A. (2000e)   The Posthumous Winnicott: on *Human
                      Nature* [in Green, A. (2000a): 69-83]

Green, A. (2001)   The Intuition of the Negative in *Playing
                      and Reality* [in Bertolini, M. et al (2001)
                      vol. 1: 43-58]

Green, A. (2003)   The Dead Mother Complex [in Raphael-
                      Leff, J. (2003): 162-174]

Green, A. (2004)   Thirdness and Psychoanalytic Concepts.
                      Psychoanalytic Quarterly, 73: 99-135

Green, A. (2005a)   *Play and Reflection in Donald Winnicott's
                      Writings.* London: Karnac on behalf of
                      the Winnicott Clinic of Psychotherapy

Green, A. (2005b)	Conjectures about Winnicott's Unconscious Countertransference in the Case of Masud Khan, in the Light of the Wynne Godley Case. [in Green, A. (2005a): 29-38]
Green, A. (2005c)	Winnicott at the Start of the Millennium [in Caldwell, L. (2005): 11-31]
Green, A. (2005d)	*Jouer Avec Winnicott* [Playing with Winnicott] (Rabain, J-F.) Paris Presses Universitaires de France 2004 review. *International Journal of Psychoanalysis, 86*: 1748-1754
Green, A., Kohon, G. (2005e)	*Love and its Vicissitudes.* Hove, Sussex: Routledge
Green, A. (2005f)	To Love or not to Love: Eros and Eiris [in Green, A., Kohon, G. (2005e): 1-39
Green, L.B. (2006)	The Value of Hate in the Countertransference. *Clinical Social Work Journal, 34*: 187
Greenacre, P. (1962)	Theory of the Parent-Infant Relationship: Further Remarks. *International Journal of Psychoanalysis, 43*: 235-237
Greenacre, P. (1969)	The Fetish and the Transitional Object. *Psychoanalytic Study of the Child, 24*: 144-164
Greenacre, P. (1970)	The Transitional Object and the Fetish with Special Reference to the Role of Illusion. *International Journal of Psychoanalysis, 51*: 447-456
Greenbaum, T. (1978)	The 'Analyzing' and the 'Transitional Object' [in Grolnick, Barkin, Muensterberger, (1978): 191-202]

| Greenberg, J., Mitchell, S. (1983) | *Object Relations Theory in Psychoanalytic Theory*. Boston, Mass. And London: Harvard University Press. pp. 188-232 |

Greenhalgh, P. (1994)
Emotional Growth and Learning London: Routledge

Greenson, R.R. (1978)
On Traditional Objects and Transference [in Grolnick, Barkin, Muensterberger, (1978): 203-210]

Grier, F. (2006)
Reflections on the Phenomenon of Adoration in Relationships, both Human and Divine [in Black, D.M. (2006a): 154-172]

Grieve, P. (2001)
On Schacht, L. (2001) [in Bertolini, M. et al (2001) vol. 1: 238-240]

Grimaldi, S. (2001)
Winnicott in Italy [in Bertolini, M. et al (2001) vol. 2: xvii-xix]

Groarke, S. (2000)
Winnicott and the Government of the Environment. *Free Associations*, 46: 74-104

Groarke, S. (2003)
A Life's Work: on Rodman's *Winnicott*. *Free Associations, 50*: 472-497

Grolnick, S.A., Barkin, L., Muensterberger, W. (Eds.) (1978)
Between Reality and Fantasy: Transitional Objects and Phenomena. New York: Aronson

Grolnick, S.A. (1978a)
Dreams and Dreaming as Transitional Phenomena [in Grolnick, Barkin, Muensterberger (1978): 211-232]

Grolnick, S.A., Lengyel, A. (1978b)
Etruscan Burial Symbols and the Transitional Process [in Grolnick, Barkin, Muensterberger (1978): 379-410]

Grolnick, S.A. (1982)	Davis, Wallbridge (1981) review. *Psychoanalytic Quarterly, 51*: 649-652
Grolnick, S.A. (1989)	Rodman, F.R. (1987) review. *Psychoanalytic Quarterly, 58*: 279-282
Grolnick, S.A. (1990)	*The Work and Play of Winnicott* New York: Aronson
Grolnick, S. (1993)	How to Do Winnicottian Therapy [in Goldman, D. Ed. (1993): 185-212]
Grotstein, J.S. (1989)	Winnicott's Importance in Psychoanalysis [in Fromm, Smith (1989a): 130-158]
Grotstein, J.S. (1990)	Invariants in Primitive Emotional Disorders [in Boyer and Giovacchini (1990b); 139-164
Grotstein, J.S. (1991)	Hughes, J.M. (1989) review. *Psychoanalytic Quarterly, 60*: 136-140
Guntrip, H. (1961)	*Personality Structure and Human Interaction: the Developing Synthesis of Psychodynamic Theory.* London: Hogarth Press (reprinted London: Karnac 1995)
Guntrip, H. (1968)	*Schizoid Phenomena, Object Relations and the Self.* London: Hogarth Press (reprinted London: Karnac 1992)
Guntrip, H. (1971)	*Psychoanalytic Theory, Therapy and the Self.* London: Hogarth Press and New York: Basic Books (reprinted London: Karnac 1985)
Guntrip, H. (1975)	My Experience of Analysis with Fairbairn and Winnicott. *International Review of Psychoanalysis, 2*: 145-156 (reprinted with editorial Introduction (1996). *International Journal of Psychoanalysis, 77*: 739-754) [also in Goldman, D. (1993): 139-158]

Guntrip, H. (1994)   *Personal Relations Therapy: the Collected Papers* (edited Hazell, J.). Northvale, NJ: Aronson

Gustafson, J., Dichter, H. (1983)   Winnicott and Sullivan in the Brief Psychotherapy Clinic. Part I – Possible Activity Part III (joint author Kaye, D.) – The Organization of the Clinic and its Passivity. Part II – The Necessity for New Theory and Practice Unsolved Problems. *Contemporary Psychoanalysis,* *19*: 624-672

Gutierres-Green, L. (2001)   'Had I only been Born a Woman...': the Feminine Element in Men [in Bertolini, M. et al (2001) vol. 1: 184-197]

Hägglund, T-B. (1976)   On the Psychoanalytical Conception of D.W. Winnicott. *Psychiatria Fennica*: 105-111

Hägglund, T-B. (1997)   On the Creative Experience in Psychoanalysis. *Scandinavian Psychoanalytic Review, 20*: 58-74

Hagman, G. (2005)   *Æsthetic Beauty: Beauty, Creativity and the Search for the Ideal.* Amsterdam and New York: Rodopi

Hagman, G. (2006)   Kanter, J. (2004b) review. *Psychoanalytic Social Work, 13*: 85-90

Hagood, L. (2006)   Awakening to Dreams. *Journal of Religion and Health 45*: 160-170

Haldipur, C.V. (1990)   *Psychoanalytic Explorations* review. *American Journal of Psychotherapy, 44*: 453

Hamalainen, O. (1999)   Some Consideration on the Capacity to be Alone. *Scandinavian Psychoanalytic Review, 22*: 33-47

Hamilton, V. (1982)   *Narcissus and Œdipus: the Children of Psychoanalysis.* London: Routledge and Kegan Paul

Hamilton, V. (1987)   Rhythm and Interpretation in Maternal Care and Psychoanalysis. *Winnicott Studies*, 2: 32-47

Hamilton, V. (1996a)   On the Otherness of Being: Winnicott's Ideas on 'Object Usage' and 'the Experience of Externality'. *Journal of Child Psychotherapy*, 22: 383-391

Hamilton, V. (1996b)   *The Analyst's Pre-Conscious.* Hillside, NJ: Analytic Press

Hanchett, S., Casale, L. (1976)   The Theory of Transitional Phenomena and Cultural Symbols. *Contemporary Psychoanalysis*, 12: 496-507

Hand, N. (1995)   D.W. Winnicott: the Creative Vision. *Annual Conference Proceedings*, 24: 167-170 (International Association of School Librarianship)

Handler, L. (1999)   Assessment of Playfulness: Hermann Rorschach Meets D.W. Winnicott. *Journal of Personality Assessment*, 72: 208-217

Hanna, E. (1992)   False-Self Sensitivity to Countertransference: Anatomy of a Single Session. *Psychoanalytic Dialogues*, 2: 369-382

Hansen, D., Drowdahl, R. (2006)   The Holding Power of Love: John Wesley and D.W. Winnicott in Conversation. *Journal of Religion and Psychology*, 25: 54-63

Hardy, D.S. (2000)   Re-describing Relationships in Christian
                      Spiritual Direction using Winnicott's
                      Psychoanalytic Object Relations Theory.
                      Dissertation Abstracts (International),
                      60 (12-B): 6398

Hardy, D.S. (2003)   Finding Spaces: Winnicott, God and
                      Psychic Reality. *International Journal for*
                      the Psychology of Religion, 15: 287-289

Harris, A.L. (2005)   The Holding Environment:
                      Considerations for Healthy Birthing
                      Care. *Dissertation Abstracts (International),*
                      66 (1-B): 554

Hartmann, L.   Rodman, F.R. (2003) review. *American*
(2003)   *Journal of Psychiatry, 160*: 2255-2256

Harwood, I. (1986)   The Need for Optimal, Available
                      Caretakers: Moving Towards Extended
                      Self-Object Experience. *Group Analysis,*
                      19: 291-302

Harwood, I. (1987)   The Evolution of the Self: an Integration
                      of Winnicott's and Kohut's Concepts [in
                      Honess, T. and Yardley, K. (Eds.) (1987).
                      Self and Identity: Perspectives Across the
                      Lifespan: 55-76 New York and London:
                      Routledge]

Harwood, I. (2005)   Distinguishing Between the Facilitating
                      and the Self-serving Charismatic Group
                      Leader. *Group, 27*: 121-129.

Hauptman, B.   Reflections on Donald Winnicott and
(2005)   John Bowlby [in Issroff, J.,
                      (2005): 101-113]

Hausner, R. (1985)   Medication and Transitional
                      Phenomena. *International Journal of*
                      Psychoanalytic Psychotherapy, 11: 375-407

Hayman, A. (1997)   Winnicott on Infancy. *Psychoanalytic Psychotherapy in South Africa, 5*: 23-34

Hazell, J. (1991)   Reflections on my Analysis with Guntrip. *Contemporary Psychoanalysis, 27*: 148-166

Hazell, J. (1996)   *H.J.S. Guntrip: a Psychoanalytical Biography.* London: Free Association Books

Healy, K.C. (2004)   Looking at the one we have Pierced: Repentance, Resurrection and Winnicott's "Capacity for Concern". *Pastoral Psychology, 53*: 53-62

Heard, D.H. (1978)   From Object Relations to Attachment Theory: a Basis for Family Therapy. *British Journal of Medical Psychology, 51*: 67-76

Hearst, L. (1981)   Emergence of the Mother in the Group. *Group Analysis, 14*: 25-32

Hedges, L. (1992)   *Interpreting the Countertransference.* Northvale, NJ: Aronson

Henderson, J. (1973)   Community Transference: with Notes on the Counter Response. *Bulletin of the Menninger Clinic, 37*: 258-269

Henderson, J. (1974)   Community Transference Reviewed: with Notes on the Clinic Community Interface. *Journal of the American Academy of Psychoanalysis, 2*: 113-128

Henderson, J. (1984)   Play in the Psychotherapy of Self-object Relating. *Canadian Journal of Psychiatry, 29*: 417-424

Henriques, M. (1993)   'Sum, I Am'. *Winnicott Studies, 8 (Autumn)*: 47-49

58

Hernandez, M.
(1998)

Winnicott's "Fear of Breakdown": on and Beyond Trauma. *Diacritics, 28*: 134-143

Hernandez, M.,
Giannakoulos, A.
(2001)

On the Construction of Potential Space [in Bertolini, M. et al (2001) vol. 1: 146-159]

Hicklin, M. (1957)

The Child and the Family review. *New Era in Home and School, 38 (May)*: 104-105

Hills, M. (2002)

Fan Cultures. London and New York: Routledge

Hinshelwood, R.,
Winship, G. (2006)

Orestes and Democracy [in Coles, P. (2006): 75-96]

Hinton, W.L. (1997)

Kahr, B. (1996) review. *Journal of Analytic Psychology, 42*: 697

Hirsch, A.T. (1986)

Predicting Child Adjustment from Early Mothering Behavior: A Longitudinal Examination of Winnicott's Theory. *Dissertation Abstracts (International), 46 (8-B)*: 2816

Hobson, P. (1998)

On Relationships and Relatedness: Winnicott's Set Situation. *Infant Behaviour and Research, 21*: 135

Hobson, P. et al
(2005)

Personal Relatedness and Attachment in Infants and Mothers with Borderline Personality Disorder. *Development and Psychopathology, 17*: 329-347

Hoey, B. (1996)

Who Calls the Tune?: a Psycho-dramatic Approach to Child Therapy. London: Routledge

Hoffman, M. (2004)

From Enemy Combatant to Strange Bedfellow: The Role of Religious Narratives in the Work of W. R. D.

Fairbairn and D. W. Winnicott. *Psychoanalytic Dialogues, 14*: 769-784

Hoffmann, J.M. (2000)   There is Such a Thing as an Infant. *Infant Mental Health Journal, 21*: 42-51

Hogan, P.C. (1992)   The Politics of Otherness in Clinical Psychoanalysis: Racism as Pathogen in a Case of D.W. Winnicott. *Literature and Psychology, 38*: 36-43

Holbrook, D. (1972)   *Sex and Dehumanization*. London: Pitman Publishing (new ed. Brunswick, NJ: Transaction 1997)

Holbrook, D. (1993)   Lawrence's False Solution [in Rudnytsky (1993): 189-215]

Holbrook, D. (1994)   *Creativity and Popular Culture*. Cranbury, NJ: Associated University Press

Holbrook, D. (2002)   D.W. Winnicott [in Kahr, B. (2002a): 146-150]

Hollins, S. (2006)   Young People with Learning Disabilities and Challenging Behaviour: a Winnicottian Perspective [in Morgan and Hollins (2006): 21-35]

Holmes, J. (1993)   *Between Art and Science: Essays on Psychiatry and Psychotherapy*. London: Tavistock/Routledge

Holmes, J.(2001)   *The Search for the Secure Base: Attachment Theory and Psychoanalysis*. Hove, Sussex and New York: Brunner-Routledge

Hood, C. (1975)   *Child Care and Development*. London: Mills and Boon

Hopkins, B. (1984)   Keats' Negative Capability and Winnicott's Creative Play. *American Imago, 41*: 85-100

Hopkins, B. (1989)   Jesus and Object-use: a Winnicottian Account of the Resurrection Myth. *International Review of Psychoanalysis*, 16: 93-100 [also in Rudnytsky (1993): 249-260]

Hopkins, B. (1997)   Winnicott and the Capacity to Believe. *International Journal of Psychoanalysis*, 78: 485-498 [also in *PsyArt*, 7, 2006 (June-Sept)

Hopkins, B. (2004)   Wordsworth, Winnicott and the Claims of the "Real". *PsyArt, 8*

Hopkins, B. (2005)   Winnicott and Imprisonment. *American Imago, 62*: 269-284

Hopkins, J. (1996)   The Dangers and Deprivations of Too-Good Mothering: a Type of Spoiling Observed by Winnicott. *Journal of Child Psychotherapy, 22*: 407-422 (also in *Educational Therapy & Therapeutic Teaching, 9*, 2000: 6-17)

Hopkins, J. (2002)   From Baby Games to Let's Pretend: the Achievement of Playing [in Kahr, B. (2002): 91-99]

Hopkins, L.B. (1998)   D.W. Winnicott's Analysis of Masud Khan: a Preliminary Study of Failures of Object Usage. *Contemporary Psychoanalysis, 34*: 5-47

Hopkins, L.B. (2000)   Masud Khan's Application of Winnicott's "Play" Techniques to Analytic Consultation and Treatment of Adults. *Contemporary Psychoanalysis, 36*: 639-663

Hopkins, L.B. (2001)   Masud Khan's Descent into Alcoholism [in Petrucelli and Stuart (2001): 319-346]

Hopkins, L.B.
(2004a)

Red Shoes, Untapped Madness and
Winnicott on the Cross: an Interview
with Marion Milner. *Annual of
Psychoanalysis, 14*: 233-244

Hopkins, L.B (2004b)

How Masud Khan Fell into
Psychoanalysis. *American Imago,
61*: 483-494

Hopkins, L.B.
(2006a)

Kanter, J. (2004b) review. *Psychoanalytic
Review, 93*: 136-139

Hopkins, L.B.
(2006b)

False Self: The Life of Masud Khan.
New York: Other Press

Horn, A. (1999)

*Handbook of Child and Adolescent
Psychotherapy.* Hove, Sussex:
Routledge

Horton, P.C. (1981)

Solace. Chicago: University of Chicago
Press

Horton, P.C. (1993)

Wright, K. (1990) review. *Psychoanalytic
Psychology, 10*: 611-619

Hudak, G.M. (2001)

On what is Labelled 'Playing': Locating
the 'True' in Education [in Hudak, G.M.,
Kihn, P. (2001). *Labelling: Pedagogy and
Politics*: 9-26 London and New York:
Routledge-Falmer

Hughes, A. (2002)

Brafman, A.H. (2001) review.
*International Journal of Psychoanalysis,
83*: 1205-1207

Hughes, J.M. (1989)

*Reshaping the Psychoanalytic Domain: The
Work of Melanie Klein, W. R. D. Fairbairn
and D. W. Winnicott.* Berkeley: California
University Press

Hurry, A. (Ed.)
(1998a)

Psychoanalysis and Developmental Therapy.
London: Karnac

Hurry, A. (1988b)   Psychoanalysis and Developmental
                     Therapy [in Hurry (1998a): 32-73]

Hutter, A.D. (1982) Poetry in Psychoanalysis: Hopkins,
                     Rossetti, Winnicott. *International Review
                     of Psychoanalysis, 9*: 303-316 [also in
                     Rudnytsky (1993): 63-86]

Hyllienmark, G.   Smoking as a Transitional Object. *British
(1986)   Journal of Medical Psychology, 59*: 263-267

Ilahi, M.N. (2005)   Rodman, F.R. (2003) review. *Journal of
                     the American Psychoanalytic Association,
                     3*: 311-316

Innes-Smith, J.   Breakdown, Madness and Health in
(2001)   Bertolini, M. et al (2001) vol.1: 18-30]
                     (see also Tonnesmann, M. (2001) for
                     discussion)

Irvine, E. (1973)   The Role of Donald Winnicott: Healing,
                     Teaching, Nurture. *British Journal of
                     Social Work, 3*: 383-390

Issroff, J. (1975)   Adolescence and Creativity [in
                     Meyerson, S. Ed. *Adolescence: The Crisis
                     of Adjustment – a Study of Adolescence by
                     Members of the Tavistock Clinic and other
                     British Experts.* 143-164. London: George
                     Allen & Unwin]

Issroff, J. (1983)   A Reaction to reading *Boundary and
                     Space: an Introduction to the Work of D.W.
                     Winnicott* by Madeleine Davis and
                     David Wallbridge. *International Review of
                     Psychoanalysis, 10*: 231-235

Issroff, J. (1988)   Suicide Provoked by Pathological
                     Mourning in Families: the Dynamics
                     and Dangers of Feeling 'Not Being
                     Wanted Enough' or 'Not Being Good

Enough' [in Chigler, E. (Ed.). *Counselling and Therapy in Grief and Bereavement.*; 197-212 Tel Aviv, Freund]

Issroff, J. (1991) The Healthy Adolescent and his Creativity. *Psychiatriki, 2*: 118-130

Issroff, J. (1993) Kitchen Therapy: Remembering the 'Theory of Salivation' and Advocating Cooking as an Aid in Psychoanalytic Child Psychotherapy with Latency Age Children. *Winnicott Studies, 7 (Spring)*: 67-84

Issroff, J. (1995) D. W. Winnicott's Ability to Facilitate Turning Points. *Voices: Art and Science of Psychotherapy, 31*: 4-10

Issroff, J. (2001) Reflections on *Playing and Reality* [in Bertolini, M. et al (2001 vol. 1): 59-70]

Issroff, J. (2005) *Donald Winnicott and John Bowlby: Personal and Professional Perspectives.* London: Karnac

Jackson, J. (1996) An Experimental Investigation of Winnicott's Set Situation: a Study of South African White, Black and Institutionalized Infants aged 7 to 9 moths old. *Journal of Child Psychotherapy, 27*: 343-361

Jacobs, M. (1995) *D.W. Winnicott* London & New Delhi: Sage

Jacobs, T.J. (1991) *The Use of the Self: Countertransference and Communication in the Analytic Situation.* Madison, CT: International Universities Press

Jacoby, M. (1990) *Individuation and Narcissism: the Psychology of Self in Jung and Kohut.* London: Routledge

Jallinsky, S. (1994)   Donald Winnicott, the Illusionist of Psychoanalysis. *Encounters (Argentina),* 1: 41-49

James, D.C. (1984)   Bion's 'Containing' and Winnicott's "Holding" in the Context of the Group Matrix. *International Journal of Group Psychotherapy, 34:* 201-213

James, M. (1962)   Infantile Narcissistic Trauma – Observations on Winnicott's Work in Infant Care and Child Development. *International Journal of Psychoanalysis, 43:* 69-80

James, M. (1979)   *The Piggle* review. *International Journal of Psychoanalysis, 60:* 137-139

James, M. (1982)   Davis, Wallbridge (1981) review. *International Journal of Psychoanalysis, 63:* 493-497

James, M. (1985)   The Essential Contribution of D.W. Winnicott. *Winnicott Studies, 1:* 26-35

Jarmon, H. (1990)   The Supervisory Experience: An Object Relations Perspective. *Psychotherapy, 27:* 195-201

Jemstedt, A. (1993)   A Comment on Teurnell's "The Piggle – a Sexually Abused Girl". *International Forum of Psychoanalysis, 2:* 145-148

Jemstedt, A. (2000)   Potential Space: The Place of Encounter between Inner and Outer Reality. *International Forum of Psychoanalysis, 9:* 124-131

Jenkyn, S.M. (1997)   *The Play's the Thing.* London: Routledge

Jerry, P.A. (1994)   Winnicott's Therapeutic Consultation and the Adolescent Patient. *Crisis*

Intervention and Time-limited Treatment,
1: 61-72

Johns, J. (1996) The Capacity to be Alone. *Journal of Child Psychotherapy, 22:* 373-376

Johns, J. (2001a) Winnicott: a Beginning [in Kahr, B. (2001a): 11-18]

Johns, J. (2001b) Personalisation [in Bertolini, M. et al (2001) vol. 1: 99-102]

Johns, J. (2002) Caldwell, L. (2000) review. *International Journal of Psychoanalysis, 83:* 195-120

Johnson, S., Ruszczynski, S. (Eds.)(1999) *Psychoanalytic Psychotherapy in the Independent Tradition.* London: Karnac

Johnson, S. (1999a) Who and Whose I am: the Emergence of the True Self [in Johnson, S., Ruszczynski, S. (1999): 9-26]

Johnson, S. (1999b) The Move from Object-relating to Object-usage: a Clinical Example [in Johnson, S., Ruszczynski, S. (1999): 111-132]

Johnson, S. (2005) D.W. Winnicott: "The Aims of Psychoanalytical Treatment". *Journal of the British Association of Psychotherapists, 43:* 124-128

Jones, J.W. (1992) Knowledge in Transition: Toward a Winnicottian Epistomology. *Psychoanalytic Review, 79:* 223-237

Jones, J.W. (1997) Playing and Believing: the Uses of D.W. Winnicott in the Psychology of Religion [in Capps, D. Ed. (1997). *Religion, Society and Psychoanalysis:* 106-126] Boulder, CO: Westview Press

Jones, J.W. (2002)   *Terror and Transformation: the Ambiguity of Religion in Psychoanalytic Perspective.* London and New York: Routledge

Jones, K. (2005)   The Role of Father in Psychoanalytic Theory: Historical and Contemporary Trends. *Smith College Studies in Social Work, 75*: 7-28

Jordan, M.J. (1998)   Winnicott's Contribution to the Concept of Patient Care in Medicine. *Dissertation Abstracts (International), 59 (5-B)*: 2104

Josselson, R. (1992)   *The Space Between Us: Exploring Dimensions of Human Relationships.* San Francisco: Jossey Bass

Kafka, J.S. (1969)   The Body as Transitional Object: a Psychoanalytic Study of A Self-mutilating Patient. *British Journal of Medicine, 43*: 207-212

Kahane, C. (1993)   Gender and Voice in Transitional Phenomena [in Rudnytsky (1993): 278-291]

Kahn, E.M. (1986)   The Discovery of the True Self. *Clinical Social Work Journal, 14*: 310-320

Kahn, W.A. (2004)   *Holding Fast: the Struggle to Create Resilient, Care-giving Organizations.* London & New York: Brunner/ Routledge

Kahne, M.J. (1967)   On the Persistence of Transitional Phenomena into Adult Life. *International Journal of Psychoanalysis, 48*: 247-258

Kahr, B. (1996a)   Donald Winnicott and the Foundations of Child Psychotherapy. *Journal of Child Psychotherapy, 22*: 327-42

Kahr, B. (1996b)   Newman, A. (1995) review. *Journal of Child Psychotherapy, 22*: 456-458

Kahr, B. (1996c)   *D.W. Winnicott: A Biographical Portrait* London: Karnac

Kahr, B. (1999a)   Winnicott's Boundaries. *International Journal of Communicative Psychoanalysis and Psychotherapy, 12*: 66-70

Kahr, B. (1999b)   *Talking to Parents* review. *Psychotherapy Review, 1*: 76-78

Kahr, B. (2000a)   Ethical Dilemmas of the Psycho-analytical Biographer: the Case of Donald Winnicott. *Free Associations, 8*: 105-120

Kahr, B. (2000b)   Abram, J. (1996) review. *Psychoanalytic Studies, 2*: 91

Kahr, B. (Ed.) (2001a)   *Forensic Psychotherapy and Psychopathology: Winnicottian Perspectives.* London: Karnac

Kahr. B. (2001b)   Winnicott's Contribution to the Study of Dangerousness [intro. Kahr, B. (2001a): ix-xxiv also in Morgan and Hollins (2006): 39-47]

Kahr, B. (Ed.) (2002a)   *The Legacy of Winnicott: Essays on Infant and Child Mental Health* London: Karnac

Kahr, B. (2002b)   Donald Woods Winnicott: the Cartographer of Innocence [in Kahr, B. (2002a): 1-12]

Kahr, B. (2002c)   Winnicottiana: Some Hitherto Unpublished Documents [in Kahr (2002a): 151-160]

Kahr, B. (2003a)   On the Memorialisation of Donald Winnicott [in McDougall (2003) (foreword): 9-14]

Kahr, B. (2003b)	Masud Khan's Analysis with Donald Winnicott: on the Hazards of Befriending a Patient *Free Associations,* *10*: 190-222
Kahr, B. (2004)	Rodman, R. 1934 – 2004. *American Imago, 61*: 539-542
Kahr, B. (2005)	The Fiftten Key Ingredients of Good Psychotherapy [in Ryan, J. (2005): 1-14]
Kahr, B. (2006)	Winnicott's Comtribution to the Study of Dangerousness [Appendix to Morgan and Hollins (2006): 39-47]
Kalsched, D. (1996)	*The Inner World of Trauma: Archetypal Defenses of the Personal Spirit* London: Routledge
Kaminer, H. (1978)	Transitional Object Components in Self and Other Relationships [in Grolnick, Barkin, Muensterberger (1978): 233-244]
Kanter, J. (1990)	Community-based Management of Psychotic Clients: the Contributions of D.W. and Clare Winnicott. *Clinical Social Work Journal, 18*: 23-41
Kanter, J. (2000)	The Untold Story of Clare and Donald Winnicott: How Social Work Influenced Modern Psychoanalysis. *Clinical Social Work Journal, 28*: 245-262
Kanter, J. (2004a)	"Let's Never Ask him what to Do": Clare Britton's Transformative Impact on Donald Winnicott. *American Imago, 61*: 457-482
Kanter, J. (Ed.) (2004b)	*Face to Face with Children: the Life and Work of Claire Winnicott* London: Karnac
Kaplinsky, C, (1996)	Goldman, D. (1993a) review. *Journal of Analytical Psychology, 41*: 150

Karnac, H. (1991)   On Psychoanalytic Bookselling
                    1950-1989 (paper presented at a meeting
                    of the Applied Section of the Brtish
                    Psychoanalytic Society 26th June 1991)

Kegerreis, D.   A Benevolently Dangerous Growth:
(1999)   Surviving the Trauma of Change with
                    Borderline Patients In Group
                    Psychotherapy. *Group Analysis*,
                    32: 427-438

Kegerreis, D. (2005)   Kanter, J. (2004) review. *Psychodynamic
                       Practice, 11*: 335-337

Keith, C. (1993)   Dockar-Drysdale (1990) review.
                    American Journal of Psychotherapy, 47: 151

Kennard, D. (1989) The Therapeutic Community Impulse:
                    What Makes it Grow *International
                    Journal of Therapeutic Communities*,
                    10: 155-163

Kermode, F. (2004) Clutching at Insanity: review of
                    Rodman, F.R. (2003). *London Review of
                    Books* (Apr. 3)

Kernberg, O. (1980) *Internal World and External Reality: Object
                     Relations Theory Applied* New York:
                     Aronson

Kerr, A. (1991)   The Unmet-Need: Can Severely
                    Disturbed Children Become Good-
                    Enough Parents? *Winnicott Studies*,
                    6: 21-38

Kestemberg, E.   A Yeast for Thought [in Goldman, D.
(1993)   Ed. (1993): 1165-170]

Kestenberg, J.S.   Transsensus-outgoingness and
(1978)   Winnicott's Intermediate Zone [in
                    Grolnick, Barkin, Muensterberger
                    (1978): 61-74]

Kestenberg, J.S., Weinstein, J. (1978)   Transitional Object and Body Image Formation [in Grolnick, Barkin, Muensterberger (1978): 75-96]

Khan, M.M.R. (1971a)   Obituary: D.W. Winnicott. *British Journal of Medical Psychology, 44*: 387-388

Khan, M.M.R. (1971b)   Donald Winnicott. *International Journal of Psychoanalysis, 52*: 225-226 [also in Goldman, D. (1993) with Tizard, J.P.M. (1971): 111-116]

Khan, M.M.R., Davis, J.A. Davis, M.E.V. (1974)   The Beginning and Fruition of the Self: an Essay on D.W. Winnicott [in Davis, J.A., Dutting, J. *The Scientific Foundations of Pædiatrics*: 274-289 London: Heinemann] Medical Books (1974)

Khan, M.M.R. (1975)   *The Privacy of the Self: Papers on Psychoanalytic Theory and Technique*. London: Hogarth Press (reprinted London: Karnac 1996)

Khan, M.M.R. (1979)   *Alienation in Perversions*. London: Hogarth Press (reprinted London: Karnac 1989)

Khan, M.M.R. (1983)   *Hidden Selves: Between Theory and Practice in Psychoanalysis*. London: Hogarth Press (reprinted London: Karnac 1989)

Khan, M.M.R. (1988)   *When Spring Comes: Awakenings in Clinical Psychoanalysis*. London: Chatto and Windus (published as *The Long Wait* New York: Summit Books 1989)

Killick, K., Schaverein, J. (1997)   *Art, Psychotherapy and Psychosis*. London: Routledge

King, L. (1994)   'There is No Such Thing as a Mother'. *Winnicott Studies, 9*: 18-24

King, P. (2001)   Remembering Winnicott [in Bertolini, M. et al (2001) vol. 1: 268]

King, P. (2005)   *Time Present and Times Past: Selected Papers*. London: Karnac

Kingsbury, P. (2003)   Psychoanalysis, a Gay Spatial Science? *Social & Cultural Geography*, 4: 347-367

Kinst, J.M. (2003)   Trust, Emptiness and the Self in the Practice of Soto Zen Buddhism: an Exploration including the Insights of Self-psychology – Erik Erikson and D.W. Winnicott. *Dissertation Abstracts (International), 64 (6-A)*: 2122

Kirschner, S.R. (1996)   *The Religious and Romantic Origins of Psychoanalysis, Individuation and Integration in Post-Freudian Theory*. Cambridge: Cambridge University Press

Kirshner, L.A. (1991)   The Concept of the Self in Psychoanalytic Theory and its Philosophical Foundations. *Journal of the American Psychoanalytic Association, 39*: 157-182

Klein, J. (1987)   *Our Need for Others and its Roots in Infancy*. London: Routledge

Klein, J. (1995)   *Doubts and Certainties in the Practice of Psychotherapy*. London: Karnac

Klein, R.S. (1990)   *Object Relations and the Family Process*. Westport, CT: Praeger

Kluzer, A.U. (1992)   The Significance of Illusion in the Work of Freud and Winnicott: a Controversial Issue. *International Review of Psychoanalysis, 19*: 179-187

Kluzer, A.U. (2001)　Illusion and Reality in the Work of D.W. Winnicott [in Bertolini, M. et al (2001) vol. 2: 49-58]

Knauss, W. (1999)　The Creativity of Destructive Fantasies. *Group Analysis, 32*: 397-411

Kobrick, J.B. (1998)　Kahr, B. (1996) review. *Canadian Journal of Psychoanalysis, 6*: 336-337

Koepele, K.C., Tebeira, M.A. (2000)　Annihilation Anxiety: a Metapsychological Exploration of D.W. Winnicott's *The Piggle. Psychoanalysis and Psychotherapy, 17*: 229-256

Kohon, G.(Ed.) (1986)　*The British School of Psychoanalysis: the Independent Tradition.* New Haven, CT. Yale and London: Free Association Books

Kohon, G.(Ed.) (1999)　*The Dead Mother: The Work of André Green.* Hove, London and New York: Routledge

Kohon, G. (2005)　Love in a Time of Madness [in Green, A., Kohon, G. (2005e): 41-100]

Konigsberg, I. (1996)　Transitional Phenomena, Transitional Space, Creativity and Spectatorship in Film. *Psychoanalytic Review, 83*: 865-889

Kotowicz, A. (1993)　Tradition, Violence and Psychotherapy [in Spurling, L. (Ed.) (1993): 132-157]

Kramer, R. (1994)　Rudnytsky, P. (1991) review. *Bulletin of the History of Medicine, 68*: 540

Kramer, S. (1974a)　*Therapeutic Consultations in Child Psychiatry* review. *Psychoanalytic Quarterly, 43*: 315-318

Kramer, S. (1974b)　*Playing and Reality* review. *Psychoanalytic Quarterly, 43*: 318-319

Kristovich, D. (2002)   Late Adolescents' Use of Music as Transitional Space. *Dissertation Abstracts (International), 62 (8-A)*: 2883

Kuhns, R. (1992)   Loss and Creativity: Notes on Winnicott and Nineteenth Century American Poets. *Psychoanalytic Review, 79*: 197-208

Kulka, R. (1995)   Revolutionary Evolution in Psychoanalysis. *Israel Journal of Psychotherapy, 9*: 100-110

Kumin, I. (1997)   *Pre-Object Relatedness: Early Attachment and the Psychoanalytic Situation.* New York, Guilford Press

Kumin, I.M. (1979)   *The Piggle* review. *Journal of the American Academy of Psychoanalysis, 7*: 453-455

Kupersmidt, J. (1997a)   Rudnytsky (1991) review. *Psychoanalytic Review, 84*: 469

Kupersmidt, J. (1997b)   Rudnytsky (1993) review. *Psychoanalytic Review, 84*: 469-474

Kuriloff, E. (1998)   Winnicott and Sullivan: Playing with the Interpersonal Model in a Transitional Space. *Contemporary Psychoanalysis, 34*: 379-388

Kwawer, J.S. (1981)   Object Relations and Interpersonal Theories. *Contemporary Psychoanalysis, 17*: 276-288

Kwawer, J.S. (1998)   On Using Winnicott. *Contemporary Psychoanalysis, 34*: 389-396

Lally, E. (2002)   *At Home with Computers.* Oxford and New York: Berg

Lambert, K. (1981)   *Analysis, Repair and Individuation.* London: Academic Press (new edition London, Karnac 1994)

Lambert, K. (1987)   Some Religious Implications of the
                     Work of Freud, Jung and Winnicott.
                     Winnicott Studies, 2: 49-70

Lamothe, R. (1995)   Messengers of Hate: a Psychoanalytic
                     and Theological Analysis of
                     Intransigence in Religion. *Dissertation
                     Abstracts (International), 56 (1-B)*: 0557

Lamothe, R. (2000)   The Birth of Reality: Psychoanalytic
                     Developmental Considerations.
                     *American Journal of Psychotherapy,
                     54*: 355-371

Lamothe, R. (2005a) Creating Space: the Fourfold Dynamics
                     of Potential Space. *Psychoanalytic
                     Psychology*, 22: 207-233

Lamothe, R. (2005b) *Becoming Alive: Psychoanalysis and
                     Vitality*. Hove, Sussex and New York:
                     Routledge

Langs, R. (2002)   D.W. Winnicott: the Traditional Thinker
                     [in Kahr (2002a): 13-22]

Lanyado, M. (1996)   Winnicott's Children: the Holding
                     Environment and Thepautic
                     Communication in Brief and
                     Non-intensive Work. *Journal of Child
                     Psychotherapy*, 22: 423-443

Lanyado, M. (1999)   Abram, J. (1996) review. *Journal of Child
                     Psychotherapy*, 25: 143-145

Lanyado, M. (2003)   The Emotional Tasks of Moving from
                     Fostering to Adoption: Transitions,
                     Attachment, Separation and Loss.
                     Clinical Child Psychology and Psychiatry,
                     8: 337-349

Lanza, A.M.,   Self-States and the Maternal Integration
Bucci, S.P.,   Function [in Bertolini, M. et al (2001)

Chagas-Bovet, A.M. (2001) vol. 2: 13-23]

Larkin, J. (1987) The Judicious Use of 'Good Enough' Therapy in the Treatment of Borderline and Narcissistic Disorders. *International Journal of Partial Hospitalization*, 4: 227-234

Larson, L.R. (1995) Goldman, D. (1993a) and (1993b) review. *Clinical Social Work Journal*, 23: 232

Larson, R., Lee, M. (1996) The Capacity to be Alone as a Stress Buffer. *Journal of Social Psychology*, 136: 5-16

Last, J.M. (1988) Transitional Relatedness and Psychotherapeutic Growth. *Psychotherapy, 25*: 185-190

Laufer, M. (2001) Reflection on Central Masturbation Fantasy, the Fetish and Transitional Objects [in Bertolini, M. et al (2001) vol. 1: 201-203]

Lavender, J. (1992) Winnicott's Mind Psyche and its Treatment American. *Journal of Dance Therapy, 14*: 31-39

Lawler, S. (2000) *Mothering the Self: Mothers, Daughters, Subjects* London and New York: Routledge

Layland, M. (1996) Kahr, B. (1996) review. *International Journal of Psychoanalysis, 77*: 1269-1271

Lebovici, S. (1993) An Inimitable Genius [in Goldman, D. (Ed.) (1993): 1171-176]

Lee, C. (1985) The Good-Enough Family. *Journal of Psychology and Theology, 13*: 182-189

Lee, G. (1997) Alone Among Three: The Father and the Œdipus Complex [in Richards with Wilce (1997): 73-87]

Leiman, M. (1992) The Concept of Sign in the Work of Vygotsky, Winnicott and Bakhtin: Further Integration of Object Relation Theory and Activity Theory. *British Journal of Medical Psychology, 65*: 209-221

Lemma, A. (2003) *Introduction to Practice of Psychoanalytic Psychotherapy* Chichester: Wiley

Lemma, A. (2005) The Many Faces of Lying. *International Journal of Psychoanalysis, 86*: 737-753

Lerner, P.M. (1985) The False Self Concept and its Measurement. *Ontario Psychologist, 17*: 3-6

Lerner, P.M. (2005) On Developing a Clinical Sense of Self. *Journal of Personality Assessment, 84*: 21

Le Roux, E.E. (2001) Loneliness in the Therapeutic Dialogue: the Concepts of Winnicott and Heidegger *Dissertation Abstracts (International), 61 (9-B)*: 4991

Lester, E. (1992) Hughes, J.M. (1989) review. *Journal of the American Psychoanalytic Association, 40*: 936-941

Lett, M.K. (1997) *Thinking About Children* review. *American Journal of Psychiatry, 154*: 1032-1033

Levine, H. (2006) Rodman, F.R. (2003) review. *Psychoanalytic Quarterly, 75*: 585-591

Levinge, A. (1999) Music Therapy and the Theories of Donald Winnicott *Ph.D. Thesis*, Birmingham 51-10071

Levy. E., Campbell, K.J. (2000)   D.W. Winnicott in the Literature Classroom. *Teaching English in the Two-Year College*, 27: 320-328

Lewin, R.A., Schultz, G. (1992)   *Losing and Fusing: Borderline Transitional Object and Self Relations*. Northvale, NJ: Aronson

Litt, C.J. (1986)   Theories of Transitional Object Attachment: an Overview. *International Journal of Behavioral Development*, 9: 383-399

Little, M.I. (1981)   *Transference Neurosis and Transference Psychosis*. Northvale, NJ: Aronson & London: Free Association Books

Little, M.I. (1985)   Winnicott Working in Areas where Psychotic Anxieties Predominate: a Personal Record. *Free Associations*, 3: 9-42

Little, M.I. (1987)   On the Value of Regression to Dependence. *Free Associations*, 10: 7-22

Little, M.I. (1990)   *Psychotic Anxieties and Containment: a Personal Record of an Analysis with Winnicott*. Hillside, NJ: Aronson

Little, M.I. (1993)   Psychotherapy with D.W.W. [in Goldman, D. (Ed.) (1993): 123-138]

Lomas, P. (1973)   *True and False Experience*. London: Allen Lane

Lomas, P. (1981)   *The Case for a Personal Psychotherapy*. Oxford: Oxford University Press

Lomas, P. (1987)   *The Limits of Psychoanalysis: What's Wrong with Psychoanalysis?* Harmondsworth: Penguin Books

Lomas, P. (1998)   *Personal Disorder and Family Life*. New Brunswick, NJ: Transaction Publications

Lomas, P. (2000)   An Independent Streak [in Rudnytsky (2000): 51-62]

Lomas, P. (2001)   Godley, W. (2001a) review. *Outwrite, 3*: 42-44 (*Journal of Cambridge Society for Psychotherapy*)

Lomax-Simpson, J. (1989)   *Babies and their Mothers* review. *Group Analysis, 22*: 347-348

Lomax-Simpson, J. (1990)   Phillips, A. (1988) review. *Group Analysis, 24*: 85-86

Lombardie, K.L. (2006)   When a Body Meets a Body: a Neo-Kleinian View of Language and Bodily Experience. *Psychoanalytic Review, 93*: 379-390

Lonie, I. (1985)   From Humpty Dumpty to Rapunzel: Theoretical Formulations Concerning Borderline Personality Disorders. *Australian and New Zealand Journal of Psychiatry, 19*: 372-381

Lonie, I. (1992)   The Winnicott Baby. *Australian Journal of Psychotherapy, 11*: 11-18

Lopez-Corvo, R.E. (2006)   The Forgotten Self: with the Case of Bion's Theory of Negative Links. *Psychoanalytic Review, 93*:363-377

Lorenzer, A., Orban, P. (1987)   Transitional Objects and Phenomena: Socialization and Symbolization [in Grolnick, Barkin, Muensterberger (1987): 469-482]

Lubbe, T. (2000)   *The Borderline Psychotic Child: a Selected Integration.* London: Routledge

Luborsky, E.B. (2001)   "No Talking": the Possibility of Play. *Journal of Clinical Psychoanalysis, 10*: 445-459

79

Lucas, T.,
Hughes, P.M.
(1988)
Holding and Holding-on: Using
Winnicott's Ideas in Group
Psychotherapy with twelve- to thirteen-
year olds. *Group Analysis, 21*: 135-151

Luepnitz, D.
(2005)
Orwell, Winnicott and Lacan: Notes of a
Psychoanalyst from Project H.O.M.E.
Psychoanalysis, Culture and Society,
10: 328-334

MacAskill, N.D.
(1982)
The Theory of Transitional Phenomena
and its Application to the
Psychotherapy of the Borderline Patient.
British Journal of Medical Psychology,
55: 349-360

McCarthy, J.B.
(1995)
Adolescent Character Formation and
Psychoanalytic Theory. *American Journal*
of Psychoanalysis, 55: 245-267

McCarthy, J.B.
(2003)
Disillusionments and Devaluation in
Winnicott's Analysis of Masud Khan.
American Journal of Psychoanalysis,
63: 81-92

McDonald, M.
(1970)
Traditional Tunes and Musical
Development. *Psychoanalytic Study of the*
Child, 25: 503-520

McDougall, J. (1986) *Theatres of the Mind: Illusion and Truth in*
the Psychoanalytic Stage New York:
Norton and London: Free Association
Books

McDougall, J. (1987) *Theatres of the Body* New York, Norton.
London: Free Association Books

McDougall, J.
(1993)
Of Sleep and Dream. *International Forum*
of Psychoanalysis, 2: 204-218

McDougall, J.
(1999)
Violence and Creativity. *Scandinavian*
Psychoanalytic Review, 22: 207-217

McDougall, J. (2003)
Donald Winnicott the Man: Reflections and Recollections. The Donald Winnicott Memorial Lecture. London: Karnac (on behalf of the Winnicott Clinic of Psychotherapy)

Machado, L.M. (2001)
Transitional Phenomena, Potential Space and Creativity [in Bertolini, M. et al (2001) vol. 1: 71-75]

MacIntyre, A. (2004)
The Unconscious: A Conceptual Analysis. London: Routledge

McMahon, L. (1992)
The Handbook of Play Therapy. Hove, Sussex: Routledge

McWilliam, N. (2004)
Psychoanalytic Psychotherapy: a Practitioner's Guide. London and New York: Guilford

Madden, K. (1997)
The Dark Interval: Inner Transformation through Mourning and Memory. *Journal of Religion and Health, 36*: 29-52

Maffei, G. (2001)
C.G. Jung's *Memories, Dreams, Reflections*: Notes on the Review by D.W. Winnicott [in Bertolini, M. et al (2001) vol. 2: 196-203]

Magherini, G. (2001)
The Parent-Child Relationship in Italian Renaissance Painting: External and Internal Realities in Giovanni Bellini's 'Families' [in Bertolini, M. et al (2991) vol. 2: 76-88] (see also Trinci, M. (2003) for further notes)

Magid, B. (2005)
Rodman, F.R. (2003) review. *Journal of the American Academy of Psychoanalysis, 33*: 408-411

Magro, E.P. (2001)
The Role of Imagination in Catechesis in Light of D.W. Winnicott's Theory of

	Emotional Development. *Dissertation Abstracts (International), 61(11-A)*: 4422
Mahon, P. (2004)	Kanter, J. (2004) review. *Child Care in Practice, 10*: 405-406
Marcus, E.R. (1994a)	*Psychoanalytic Explorations* review. *Journal of the American Psychoanalytic Association, 42*: 268-271
Marcus, E.R. (1994b)	Little, M. (1990) review. *Journal of the American Psychoanalytic Association*, 42: 937-940
Mariotti, P. (1997)	*Thinking About Children* review. *International Journal of Psychoanalysis, 78*: 166-168
Mariotti, P. (2001)	Cumulative Trauma: When All Does Not Go Well in the Everyday life of the Infant (in Bertolini, M. et al (2001) vol. 2: 93-102]
Marlkillie, R. (1996)	Guntrip's Analysis with Fairbairn and Winnicott. *International Journal of Psychoanalysis, 77*: 763-771
Martellock, A.K. (2003)	She who is Not: a Psychobiography of Catherine of Siena Using the Theories of D.W. Winnicott. *Dissertation Abstracts (International), 64 (1-B)*: 1910
Martin-Cabrè, L.J. (2001)	Winnicott and Ferenczi: Trauma and the Maternal Analyst [in Bertolini, M. et al (2001) vol. 2: 179-184
Maw, M. (1957)	*The Child and the Outside World* review. *New Era in Home and School, 38 (July/August)*: 147-149
Meares, R. (1986)	On the Ownership of Thought: an Approach to the Origins of Separation Anxiety. *Psychiatry, 49*: 80-91

Meares, R. (1992)   *The Metaphor of Play: The Self, The Secret and the Borderline Experience.* Melbourne: Hill of Content

Meares, R. (1993)   *The Metaphor of Play: Disruption and Restoration in the Borderline Experience.* Northvale, NJ: Aronson. 3rd edition (1995). Hove, Sussex and New York: Routledge

Meares, R. (2005)   *The Metaphor of Play: Origin and Breakdown of Personal Being.* Hove, Sussex: Routledge (Updated edition of Meares, R. (1992) and Meares, R. (1993))

Mednick, R.A. (1982)   Guntrip's "Diary": Resistance or Mirroring? *Hillside Journal of Clinical Psychiatry, 4*: 235-249

Meisel, P., Kendrick, W. (Eds.) (1986)   *Bloomsbury/Freud: The Letters and Times of James and Alix Strachey 1925-1925.* London: Chatto and Windus

Meissner, W.W. (1984a)   *Psychoanalysis and Religious Experience.* New Haven: Yale University Press

Meissner, W.W. (1984b)   *The Borderline Spectrum and Developmental Issues.* Hillside, NJ: Aronson

Meissner, W.W. (1988)   *Treatment of Patients in the Borderline Spectrum.* Hillside, NJ: Aronson

Meissner, W.W. (1992)   Religious Thinking as Transitional Conceptualization. *Psychoanalytic Review, 79*: 175-196

Meline, C.W. (2004)   The Creative Dimension of Subjectivity in Lacan, Freud and Winnicott. *Dissertation Abstracts (International), 65 (4-A)*: 1398...

Mendelsohn, E. (2002)   The Analyst's Bad-Enough Participation. *Psychoanalytic Dialogues,* 12: 331-358

Mesas, B.C. (1991)   The Brief Psychoanalytic Psychotherapy technique of D.W. Winnicott. *Dissertation Abstracts (International), 52 (4-B):* 2307-2308

Mezan, P. (1985)   Beyond the Reality Principle: An Enquiry into the Ego Psychology of D.W. Winnicott. *Dissertation Abstracts (International), 46 (8-B):* 1693-1694

Mikardo, J. (1996)   Hate in the Countertransference. *Journal of Child Psychotherapy,* 22: 398-401

Mikics, D. (2006)   Psychoanalytic Criticism of Shakespeare. *Literature Compass,* 3: 529-546

Milivojevic, L., Strakali, I.S. (2004)   Importance of Object Relations for Development of Capacity for Normal Love. *Croatian Medical Journal,* 45: 18-24

Miller, J.C. (2004)   *The Transcendent Function: Jung's Model of Psychological Growth.* Albany, NY: State University of New York Press

Miller, M.C. (1992)   Winnicott Unbound: The Fiction of Philip Roth and the Sharing of Potential Space. *International Review of Psychoanalysis,* 19: 445-456

Miller, R. (1978)   Poetry as a Traditional Object [in Grolnick, Barkin, Muensterberger (1987): 447-468]

Milligan, J. (2001)   Deprivation and Delinquency in the Treatment of the Adolescent Forensic Patient [in Kahr, B.(2001a): 44-50]

Mills, J. (Ed.) (2002)   *A Pedagogy of Becoming*. Amsterdam and New York: Rodopi

Milner, M. (1969)   *The Hands of the Living God: an Account of a Psychoanalytic Treatment*. London: Hogarth Press

Milner, M. (1977)   Winnicott and Overlapping Circles [in Milner, M. (1987): pp.287-298]

Milner, M. (1978)   D.W. Winnicott and the Two-way Journey [in Grolnick, Barkin, Muensterberger (1978): 35-42 also in Goldman, D. (1993): 117-122]

Milner, M. (1987)   *The Suppressed Madness of Sane Men*. London: Tavistock

Milner, M. (2001)   On Winnicott [in Bertolini, M. et al (2001) vol. 1: 265-267]

Minsky, R. (1995)   Reaching Beyond Denial – sight and insight – a Way Forward? (drawing on the theory of Freud, Klein, Winnicott, Lacan and Kristeva). *Free Associations*, 5: 326-351

Mirella-Back, J. (2000)   The Relationship between Maternal History of Victimization, Arrests, Social Supports and Abusive Parenting Behavior: a Winnicottian Perspective. *Dissertation Abstracts (International)*, 60 (9-A): 3528

Mitchell, G. (2002)   An Introduction to the Work of D.W. Winnicott. *Representing Children*, 14: 251-273

Mitchell, J. (2001)   Femininity from the Margins [in Bertolini, M. et al (2001) vol. 1: 247-254]

Mitchell, J. (2006)   Sibling Trauma: a Theoretical
                       Consideration [in Coles, P. (2006):
                       155-174]

Mitchell, L. (2000)   Attachment to the Missing Object:
                       Infidelity and the Missing Love. *Journal
                       of Applied Psychoanalytic Studies,*
                       2: 383-395

Mitchell, S.A.   Between Philosophy and Politics [in
(2000)   Rudnytsky (2000): 101-136]

Modell, A.H. (1970)   The Transitional Object and the Creative
                      Act. *Psychoanalytic Quarterly, 39:* 240-250

Modell, A.H. (1975)   A Narcissistic Defence against Affects
                      and the Illusion of Self-sufficiency.
                      International Journal of Psychoanalysis,
                      56: 275-282

Modell, A.H. (1983)   Davis, Wallbridge (1981) review.
                      International Journal of Psychoanalysis,
                      64: 111-112

Modell, A.H. (1985)   The Works of Winnicott and the
                      Evolution of his Thought. *Journal of the
                      American Psychoanalytic Association,*
                      33(S): 1133-137

Modell, A.H.   The Roots of Creativity and the Use of
(1990a)   an Object [in Giovacchini (1990a):
                      113-127]

Modell, A.H.   *Other Times, Other Realities: Toward a
(1990b)   Theory of Psychoanalytic Treatment*
                      Cambridge, MA and London: Harvard
                      University Press

Modell, A.H. (1993)   "The Holding Environment" and the
                      Therapeutic Action of Psychoanalysis
                      [in Goldman, D. Ed. (1993): 273-290]

Mody, Z.R., Bucchold, E.S. (1988)
Milieu for Change: the Therapeutic Education of a Mother-Child Relationship. *Journal of Child Psychotherapy, 14*: 81-97

Momigliano, L.N. (1992)
Continuity and Change in Psychoanalysis (especially chapter 2). London: Karnac

Montgomery, J.D. (1989)
Chronic Patienthood as an Iatrogenic False Self [in Fromm, Smith (1989a): 345-364]

Montreal Winnicott Study Group (2003)
A Note on What Winnicott Might have Said about the Terrorist Attack on the World Centre, in New York 11 September 2001. *Free Associations, 54*: 190-202

Morey, J.R. (2005)
Winnicott's Splitting Headache: Considering the Gap between Jungian and Object Relations Concepts. *Journal of Applied Psychology, 50*: 330-350

Morgan, R., Hollins, C. [contributors] (2006)
Young People and Crime – Improvising Provision for Children who Offend The Donald Winnicott Lecture. London: Karnac on behalf of The Winnicott Clinic of Psychotherapy

Morris, M. (1994)
Little, M. (1990) review. *Psychoanalytic Quarterly, 63*: 562-567

Morse, S.J. (1972)
Structure and Reconstruction: a Critical Comparison of Michael Balint and D.W. Winnicott. *International Journal of Psychoanalysis, 53*: 487-50

Moyer, D.M. (1995)
Goldman, D. (1993a & b) review. *Psychoanalytic Books, 6*: 456-463

Mulder, F. (1994)
Sanville, J. (1991) review. *Winnicott Studies, 9*: 72-75

Muensterberger, W. (1978) Between Reality and Fantasy [in Grolnick, Barkin, Muensterberger (1978): 3-14]

Murray, L. (1989) Winnicott and the Developmental Psychology of Infancy. *British Journal of Psychotherapy, 5*: 333-348

Murray, L. (1996) Winnicott: a Research Perspective. *Journal of Child Psychotherapy,* 22: 362-372

Natterson, J. (1991) *Beyond Countertransference: the Therapist's Subjectivity in the Therapeutic Process.* New York: Aronson

Nayowith, S.A. (2000) The Development of a "Good-enough Shelter" and a "Secure Base". *Dissertation Abstracts (International), 61 (2-A)*: 770

Nelson, C.R. (1996) *Thinking About Children* review. *Library Journal, 121 issue 13*: 95

Neri, F. (2001) Discussion of Andrews, J.C. (2001) [in Bertolini, M. et al (2001) vol. 1: 257-261]

Neri, C. (2005) What is the Function of Faith and Trust in Psychoanalysis? *International Journal of Psychoanalysis, 86*: 79-98

Neu, J. (2000) *A Tear is an Intellectual Thing: the Meanings of Emotion.* Oxford: Oxford University Press

Neubauer, P.B. (1966) *The Family and Individual Development* review. *Psychoanalytic Quarterly,* 35: 610-611

Newirth, J. (2003) *Between Emotion and Cognition: the Generative Unconscious.* New York: Other Press

Newman, A. (1985)   D.W. Winnicott and Friendship or
                     Where is Playing? *Winnicott Studies,*
                     1: 68-76

Newman, A. (1988)   The Breakdown that Was: Winnicott and
                     the Fear of Breakdown. *Winnicott*
                     Studies, 3: 36-47

Newman, A. (1991)   The Breakdown That Was, part two:
                     'There is No Such Thing as a Baby'.
                     Winnicott Studies, 6: 39-47

Newman, A. (1995)   *Non-Compliance in Winnicott's Words: A*
                     Companion to the Work of D.W. Winnicott.
                     London: Free Association Books

Newman, G.M.   *Locating the Romantic Subject: Novalis*
(1997)   *with Winnicott.* Detroit: Wayne State
                     University Press

Newman, K. (1999)   The Usable Analyst: the Role of the
                     Affective Engagement of the Analyst in
                     Reaching Usability. *Annual of*
                     Psychoanalysis, 26: 175-194

Newman, K.M.   Winnicott Goes to the Movies: the False
(1996)   Self in Ordinary People. *Psychoanalytic*
                     Quarterly, 65: 787-807

Nickman, S.L.   The Holding Environment in Adoption.
(2004)   *Journal of Infant, Child and Adolescent*
                     Psychotherapy, 3: 329-341

Nicolò, A.M. (2001) Antisocial Acting-out as a Defence
                     Against Breakdown [in Bertolini, M.
                     et al (2001) vol. 2: 139-144]

Nolasco, R.R. (2002) Interpreting the Transforming Function
                     of Eucharist using Winnicott's Object
                     Relations Theory and Neville's Theory
                     of Religious Symbols. *Dissertations*
                     Abstracts (International), 63 (3-A): 1007

Noonan, E. (1993)   Tradition in Training [in Spurling, L. (Ed.) (1993): 18-39]

Nussbaum, M.C. (2001)   *Upheavals of Thought: the Intelligence of Emotions* Cambridge: Cambridge University Press

Nussbaum, M.C. (2003)   Rodman, R. (2003) review. *New Republic, 4632*: 34-38

Nussbaum, M.C. (2004)   *Hiding from Humanity: Disgust, Shame and the Law* Princeton, NJ: Princeton University Press

Nutkevitch, I.V. (1987)   The Transitional Object and Transitional Phenomena: Winnicott Revisited. *Dissertation Abstracts (International), 47 (9-B)*: 3966...

Ochsner, J.K. (2000)   Behind the Mask: A Psychoanalytic Perspective on Interaction in the Design Studio. *Journal of Architectural Education, 53*: 194-206

O'Connor, P.A. (2000)   *Facing the Fifties: from Denial to Reflection* London: Allen & Unwin

Ogden, T.H. (1979)   On Projective Identification. *International Journal of Psychoanalysis, 60*: 357-373

Ogden, T.H. (1983)   The Concept of Internal Object Relations *International Journal of Psychoanalysis, 64*: 227-241

Ogden, T.H. (1985a)   On Potential Space. *International Journal of Psychoanalysis, 66*: 129-141 [also in Giovacchini, P. (1990a): 90-112 and in Goldman, D. (1993): 223-240]

Ogden, T.H. (1985b)   The Mother, The Infant and the Matrix: Interpretations of Aspects of the Work of Donald Winnicott. *Contemporary Psychoanalysis, 21*: 346-371

Ogden, T.H. (1986)   *The Matrix of the Mind: Object Relations and the Psychoanalytic Dialogue*. New York: Aronson (reprinted London: Karnac 1992)

Ogden, T.H. (1987)   The Transitional Œdipal Relationship in Female Development. *International Journal of Psychoanalysis, 68*: 485-498 [also in Ogden, T.H. (1989a): 109-140]

Ogden, T.H. (1988)   Misrecognitions and the Fear of Not Knowing. *Psychoanalytic Quarterly, 57*: 643-666

Ogden, T.H. (1989a) *The Primitive Edge of Experience*. New York: Aronson (reprinted London: Karnac 1992)

Ogden, T.H. (1989b) Playing, Dreaming and Interpreting Experience: Comments on Potential Space [in Fromm, Smith (1989a): 255-278]

Ogden, T.H. (1989c) On the Concept of an Autistic-Contiguous Position. *International Journal of Psychoanalysis, 70*: 127-140 [also in Ogden, T.H. (1989a): 47-81]

Ogden, T.H. (1990)   On Potential Space [in Giovacchini, P. (1990a): 90-112

Ogden, T.H. (1991)   Some Theoretical Concepts on Personal Isolation. *Psychoanalytic Dialogues, 1*: 377-390 [also in Ogden, T.H. (1994): 167-181]

Ogden, T.H. (1992)   The Dialectically Constituted/ Decentred Subject of Psychoanalysis, II: the Contributions of Klein and Winnicott. *International Journal of Psychoanalysis, 73*: 613-626 [also in Ogden, T.H. (1994): 33-60]

Ogden, T.H. (1993)   *The Electrified Tightrope* Northvale, NJ: Aronson (reprinted London: Karnac 2004)

Ogden, T.H. (1994)   *Subjects of Analysis*. London: Karnac

Ogden, T.H. (1995)   Analyzing Forms of Aliveness and Deadness of the Transference Countertransference. *International Journal of Psychoanalysis, 76*: 695-709 [also in Ogden, T.H. (1997a): 23-63]

Ogden, T.H. (1996)   *Psychic Deadness* Northvale, NJ: Aronson (reprinted London: Karnac 2004)

Ogden, T.H. (1997)   *Reverie and Interpretation* Northvale, NJ: Aronson (reprinted London: Karnac 1999)

Ogden, T.H. (1999)   *Toxic Nourishment*. London: Karnac

Ogden, T.H. (2001a)   *Conversations at the Frontiers of Dreaming* London: Karnac

Ogden, T.H. (2001b)   Reading Winnicott. *Psychoanalytic Quarterly, 70*: 299-324 [also in Ogden, T.H. (2001a): 205-235]

Ogden, T.H. (2004)   On Holding and Containing, Being and Dreaming. *International Journal of Psychoanalysis, 86*: 737-753

Olvin, M.,   The Pre-Conscious and Potential Space.
Lombardi, K.L.   *Psychoanalytic Review, 77*: 573-587
(1990)

Orbach, S. (1995)   Countertransference and the False Body. *Winnicott Studies, 10*: 3-13

Orbach, S. (2002)   The False Self and the False Body [in Kahr (2002a): 124-134]

Ornstein, A. (1984)   The Function of Play in the Process of Psychotherapy. *Annual of Psychoanalysis, 12*: 349-366

92

Ornston, D. (1978)   Projective Identification and Maternal Impingement. *International Journal of Psychoanalytic Psychotherapy, 7*: 508-532

Padel, J. (1988)   An Appreciation of John Turner's Paper "Wordsworth and Winnicott in the Play Area". *International Review of Psychoanalysis, 15*: 497-498

Padel, J. (1990)   Hughes, J.M. (1989) review. *International Journal of Psychoanalysis, 71*: 715-717

Padel, J. (1991)   The Psychoanalytic Theories of Melanie Klein and Donald Winnicott and their Interaction in the British Society of Psychoanalysis. *Psychoanalytic Review, 78*: 324-345

Padel, J. (1996)   The Case of Harry Guntrip. *International Journal of Psychoanalysis, 77*: 755-761

Padel, J. (2001a)   Nothing so Practical as a Good Theory [in Bertolini, M. et al (2001) vol. 1: 3-17]

Padel, J. (2001b)   Winnicott's Thinking [in Bertolini, M. et al 2001 vol.1: 269]

Painceira, A.J. (2001)   The Capacity to Be Alone [in Bertolini, M. et al (2001) vol. 1: 107-111]

Pang, L.B. (1997)   The Psychological Meaning of Playing: a Phenomenological Exploration of the Subjective Experience of Adults. *Dissertation Abstracts (International), 58 (5-B)*: 2722

Parker, R. (1994)   Maternal Ambivalence. *Winnicott Studies, 9*: 3-17

Parrish, D. (1978)   Transitional Objects and Phenomena in a Case of Twinship [in Grolnick, Barkin, Muensterberger (1978): 271-288]

Parsons, Marianne (1999) The Logic of Play in Psychoanalysis. *International Journal of Psychoanalysis, 80*: 871-884

Parsons, Michael (2000) *The Dove that Returns, the Dove that Vanishes: Paradox and Creativity in Psychoanalysis.* London: Routledge

Parsons, Michael (2006) Ways of Transformation [in Black, D.M. (2006a): 117-131]

Pasquale, G. (2001) A Clinical Approach to Empathy [in Bertolini, M. et al (2001) vol. 2: 115-119]

Pass, S.F. (1997) The Relationship between Mother's Response to Children's Developing Autonomy and Children's Utilization of Symbolic Play Dissertation. *Abstracts (International), 57 (7-B)*: 4749

Pearson, J. (Ed.) (2004) *Analyst of the Imagination: The Life and Work of Charles Rycroft.* London: Karnac

Pedder, J.R. (1977) The Role of Space and Location in Psychotherapy, Play and Theatre. *International Review of Psychoananlysis, 4*: 215-223

Pedder, J.R. (1982) Failure to Mourn, and Melancholia. *British Journal of Psychiatry, 141*: 329-337

Peltz, R. (2005) The Manic Society. *Psychoanalytic Dialogues, 15*: 347-366

Peña, S. (2001) The Presence of Winnicott in Me [in Bertolini, M. et al (2001) vol. 1: 31-37]

Petrucelli, J., Stuart, C. (Eds.) (2001) *Hungers and Compulsions.* Northvale, NJ: Aronson

Phillips, A. (1988)   *Winnicott* [Fontana Modern Masters
                        Series] London: Collins (reprinted
                        Cambridge, MA: Harvard University
                        Press 1988)

Phillips, A. (1989)   Winnicott: an Introduction. *British
                        Journal of Psychiatry, 155*: 612-618

Phillips, A. (1995)   The Story of the Mind [in Corrigan,
                        E.G., Gordon, P-E. (1995a): 229-240]

Phillips, A. (1998)   *The Beast in the Nursery.* London: Faber

Phillips, A. (2000)   Winnicott's Hamlet [in Caldwell, L.
                        (2000): 31-47]

Phillips, A. (2005)   Talking Nonsense, and Knowing When
                        to Stop [in Caldwell, L. (2005):
                        145-161]

Pinkney, T.A. (1982)   An Interpretation of some Aspects of
                        the Work of T.S. Eliot in the Light of the
                        Psychoanalysis of Melanie Klein and
                        D.W. Winnicott. *M.Litt. thesis*, Oxford
                        32-363

Piontelli, A. (1992)   *From Fœtus to Child: an Observational and
                        Psychoanalytic Study.* London and New
                        York: Tavistock/Routledge

Pizer, S.A. (1992)   The Negotiation of Paradox in the
                        Analytic Process. *Psychoanalytic
                        Dialogues, 2*: 215-240

Poirier, R. (1993)   Frost, Winnicott, Burke [in Rudnytsky
                        (1993): 216-228]

Pontalis, J.-B. (1981) *Frontiers in Psychoanalysis: Between the
                        Dream and Psychic Pain.* London:
                        Hogarth Press

Pontalis, J.-B. (2006) Noble Encounters. *American Imago,
                        63*: 145-157

Posner, B.M. et al (2001) In Search of Winnicott's Aggression. *Psychoanalytic Study of the Child*, 56: 171-192

Pound, K.S. (2002) The Challenges for Self-disclosure for Student Therapists and the Development of the Provisional Clinical Self. *Dissertation Abstracts (International)*, 63 (4-B): 2069

Prendeville, B. (1997) Jacobs, M. (1995) review. *Psychodynamic Counselling*, 3: 95-97

Price, A. (1994) Effects of Maternal Deprivation on the Capacity to Play: a Winnicottian Perspective on Work with Inner City Children. *Psychoanalytic Psychology*, 11: 341-355

Priel, B. (1999) Bakhtin and Winnicott: On Dialogue, Self and Cure. *Psychoanalytic Dialogues*, 9: 487-504

Prodgers, A. (1990) The Dual Nature of the Group as Mother: the Uroboric Container. *Group Analysis*, 23: 17-30

Propato, N.C. (1994) The Third Space: its Theoretical Fundamentation and its Application in Psychoanalytical Practice (the Thematic of the Psychic Spaces). *Encounters (Argentina)*, 1: 71-77

Pruyser, P.W. (1983) *The Play of Imagination: Toward a Psychoanalysis of Culture.* New York: International Universities Press

Pullen, N.C. (2002) Layers of Self: Extending Winnicott's Theory on the Self. *Dissertation Abstracts (International)*, 62 (11-B): 5387

Pulver, S. E. (1992)   *Psychoanalytic Explorations* review.
                           Psychoanalytic Books, 3: 53-57

Rafferty, M.A.   A Conceptual Model for Clinical
(2000)   Supervision in Nursing and Health
                          Visiting Based upon Winnicott's (1960)
                          Theory of Parent-infant Relationship.
                          *Journal of Psychiatric and Mental Health
                          Nursing, 7*: 153-161

Ransohoff, P.M.   Rudnytsky (1991) review. *International
(1994)   Journal of Psychoanalysis, 75*: 427-428

Raphael-Leff, J.   Primary Maternal Persecution [in Kahr,
(2001)   B. (2001a): 27-42]

Raphael-Leff, J.   *Parent-Infant Psychodynamics: Wild
(Ed.) (2003)   Things, Mirrors and Ghosts.* London: Whurr

Ratner, D.G. (2006)   A Buddhist Re-Interpretation of D.W.
                          Winnicott. *Dissertation Abstracts
                          International, 66 (9-B)*: 5072

Rayner, E. (1971)   *Human Development.* London: Allen and
                          Unwin (3rd ed. 1986)

Rayner, E. (1990)   *The Independent Mind in British
                          Psychoanalysis.* London: Free Association
                          Books

Reardon, D.B. (2002)   Erotic Play and Live Dreaming.
                          *Dissertation Abstracts (International),
                          63 (4-B)*: 2070

Redfearn, J. (1988)   *Myself, My Many Selves.* London:
                          Academic Press (new ed. London:
                          Karnac 1994)

Rees, C. (1995)   The Dialectic between Holding and
                          Interpreting in Winnicott's
                          Psychotherapy. *Psychoanalytic
                          Psychotherapy in South Africa, 3*: 13-30

Reeves, C. (1993)   The Role of Milieu Therapy in the
                      Treatment of Sexually Abused Children
                      Child & Youth Care Forum, 22: 111-124

Reeves, C. (1996a)   Interview with Barbara Docker-
                      Drysdale. *Journal of Child Psychotherapy*,
                      22: 402-403

Reeves, C. (1996b)   Transition and Transience: Winnicott on
                      Leaving and Dying. *Journal of Child
                      Psychotherapy*, 22: 444-455

Reeves, C. (2002)   A Necessary Conjunction: Docker-
                      Drysdale and Winnicott. *Journal of Child
                      Psychotherapy*, 28: 3-28

Reeves, C. (2003)   Creative Space: a Winnicottian
                      Perspective on Child Psychotherapy in
                      Britain-Past, Present and Future.
                      Insikten, 4 (Sweden): 22-29

Reeves, C. (2004a)   On Being "Intrinsical": a Winnicott
                      Enigma. *American Imago, 61*: 427-456

Reeves, C. (2004b)   Rodman, F.R. (2003) review. *Journal of
                      Child Psychotherapy*, 30: 120-123

Reeves, C. (2005a)   Singing the Same Tune?: Bowlby and
                      Winnicott on Deprivation and
                      Delinquency [in Issroff, J. (2005):
                      71-100]

Reeves, C. (2005b)   A Duty to Care: Reflections on the
                      Influence of Bowlby and Winnicott on
                      the 1948 Children Act [in Issroff, J.
                      (2005): 179-207]

Reeves, C. (2005c)   Postscript: From Past Impact to Present
                      Influence [in Issroff, J. (2005): 209-215]

Reeves, C. (2005d)   Kanter, J. (2004) review. *Journal of Child
                      Psychotherapy*, 31: 137-140

Reiland, P.H. (2004)   The Object beyond Objects and the
                        Sacred: Reflection on Freud's and
                        Winnicott's Contribution to the
                        Psychology of Religion. *Scandinavian
                        Psychoanalytic Review*, 27: 78-86

Reis, B.E. (2004)   You are Requested to Close your Eyes.
                        Psychoanalytic Dialogues, 14: 349-371

Resch, R.C. et al   The Later Creation of a Transitional
(1988)   Object. *Psychoanalytic Psychology*,
                        5: 369-387

Retallack, J. (2003)   *The Poetical Wager*. Berkeley: University
                        of California Press

Rich, W. (2001)   Grace and Imagination: from Fear to
                        Freedom. *Journal of Religion & Health*,
                        40: 213-230

Richards, B. (Ed.)   *Capitalism and Infancy: Essays on
(1984)   Psychoanalysis and Politics*. London: Free
                        Association Books

Richards, J. (1999)   The Concept of Internal Cohabitation
                        [in Johnson, S., Ruszczynski, S.
                        (1999): 27-52]

Richards, V. (1993)   Time-Sickness. *Winnicott Studies*,
                        8 (Autumn): 17-29

Richards, V. (1994)   Mothers, Mirrors and Masks. *Winnicott
                        Studies*, 9: 35-48

Richards, V.   *The Person Who is Me: Contemporary
with Wilce, G. (Eds.)   Perspectives on the True and False Self*.
(1996a)   London: Karnac for the Squiggle
                        Foundation

Richards, V. (1996b)   Hunt the Slipper [in Richards with
                        Wilce (1996a): 23-35]

Richards, V. (1997a)	*Fathers, Families and the Outside World.* London: Karnac for the Squiggle Foundation with Wilce, G. (Eds.)
Richards, V. (1997b)	Papa Versus Pooh [in Richards with Wilce (1997a): 1-8]
Richards, V. (1997c)	"If Father Could Be Home—" [in Richards with Wilce (1997a): 89-97]
Richards, V. (2005)	*The Who You Dream Yourself: Playing and Interpretation in Psychotherapy and Theatre.* London: Karnac
Ringel, S. (2003)	Play and Impersonation: Finding the Right Intersubjective Rhythm. *Clinical Social Work Journal, 31:* 371-381
Rizzutto, A.-M. (1979)	*The Birth of the Living God: Psychoanalytic Study* Chicago: Chicago University Press
Rizzuto, A.-M. (1990)	*Deprivation and Delinquency* review. *Journal of the American Psychoanalytic Association, 38:* 811-815
Roazen, P. (1997)	Kahr, B. (1996) review. *International Forum of Psychoanalysis, 6:* 207-208
Roazen, P. (2002)	A Meeting with Donald Winnicott in 1965 [in Kahr (2002a): 23-35]
Roazen, P. (2004)	Rodman, R. (2003) review. *Psychoanalysis and History, 6:* 117-122
Robinson, H.T. (1996)	Jacobs, M. (1995) review. *International Journal of Psychoanalysis, 77:* 837-838
Robinson, H.T. (2005)	Adult Eros in D.W. Winnicott [in Caldwell, L. (2005): 83-103]
Rodman, F.R.(Ed.) (1987)	*The Spontaneous Gesture: Selected Letters of Donald Winnicott.* Cambridge, MA: Harvard University Press and London: Karnac

Rodman, F.R. (1990)   Insistence on Being Himself [in Giovacchini (1990a): 21-40]

Rodman, F.R. (1992)   Grolnick, S.A. (1990) review. *International Journal of Psychoanalysis*, 73: 594-597

Rodman, F.R. (1993)   Fromm, Smith (1989) review. *Psychoanalytic Quarterly*, 62: 131-136

Rodman, F.R. (1999)   Winnicott's Laughter [in Barron, J.W. Ed. (1999). *Humor and Psyche: Psychoanalytic Perspectives*. Hillside, N.J: Analytic Press: 177-202]

Rodman, F.R. (2003)   *Winnicott: Life and Work*. Cambridge, MA: Perseus

Rogers, R. (1990)   Hughes, J.M. (1989) review. *Psychoanalytic Books*, 1: 459-463

Rogers, R. (1991)   *Self and Other: Object Relations in Psychoanalysis and Literature*. New York: New York University Press

Rogers, R. (1995)   Rudnytsky, P.L. (1993) review. *Psychoanalytic Books*, 6: 418-422

Rollin, L., West, M.I. (1999)   *Psychoanalytic References to Children's Literature*. Jefferson, NC: McFarland

Romano, E. (1994)   Time for Encounter, Regression and Creativity in Winnicott. *Encounters (Argentina)*, 1: 25-39

Rosegrant, J. (2002)   Rhymes and Animals: Aspects of the Development of Play. *Journal of the American Psychoanalytic Society*, 50 (4): 1321-1328

Rosen, M. (2001)   Winnicott's Complex Relationship to Hate and Hatefulness [in Petrucelli and Stuart (2001): 347-358]

Rosorea, B.P. (2004)   Abstinence and Neutrality Revisited: an
                         Examination of Two Child Therapy
                         Cases – Axline's *Dibs* and Winnicott's
                         Piggle. *Dissertation Abstracts
                         (International), 65 (6-B)*: 3181

Ross, M. (2000)   "Good-enough" isn't so Bad: Thinking
                         about Success and Failure in Ethnic
                         Conflict. *Management Journal of Peace
                         Psychology, 6*: 37-47

Rubin, J.B. (1998)   *A Psychoanalysis for Our Time: Exploring
                         the Blindness of the Seeing I*. New York
                         and London: New York University Press

Rubin, J.B. (2006)   Psychoanalysis and Spirituality [in
                         Black, D.M. (2006a): 132-153]

Rudnytsky, P.   Redefining the Revenant: Guilt and
(1988)   Sibling Loss in Guntrip and Freud.
                         *Psychoanalytic Study of the Child,
                         43*: 423-432

Rudnytsky, P.   Winnicott and Freud. *Psychoanalytic
(1989)   Study of the Child, 44*: 331-350

Rudnytsky, P.   *The Psychoanalytic Vocation: Rank,
(1991)   Winnicott and the Legacy of Freud*. New
                         Haven and London: Yale University
                         Press

Rudnytsky, P.(Ed.)   *Transitional Objects and Potential Spaces:
(1993)   Literary Uses of D.W. Winnicott.*
                         New York: Columbia University Press

Rudnytsky, P.   *Psychoanalytic Conversations: Interviews
(2000)   with Clinicians, Commentators and Critics.*
                         Hillside, NJ: Analytic Press

Rudnytsky, P.   Willoughby, R. (2005) review. *Journal of
(2005)   the American Psychoanalytic Society,
                         53*: 1365-1371

Russell, J. (2003)   Differance and Psychic Space. *American Imago, 60*: 501

Russo, L. (1991)   Some Notes on the Letters of D.W. Winnicott. *Rivista di Psicoanalisi,* 37: 668-693

Ryan, J.(Ed.) (2005)   *How Does Psychotherapy Work.* London: Karnac

Rycroft, C. (1970)   Symbolism and its Relation to Primary and Secondary Sources. *Rivista di Psicoanalisi, 27*: 365-392

Rycroft, C. (1985)   *Psychoanalysis and Beyond.* London: Chatto and Windus

Rycroft, C. (1991)   *Viewpoints.* London: Hogarth Press

Rycroft, C. (2000)   A Science of the Mind [in Rudnytsky (2000): 63-80]

Sabbadini, A. (2003)   Encounter with Renata Gaddini. *Psychoanalysis and History, 5*: 1-2

Sacksteder, J.L. (1989)   Personalization as an Aspect of the Process of Change in 'Anorexia Nervosa' [in Fromm, Smith (1989a): 392-423]

Safran, J.D., Muran, J.C. (2000)   *Negotiating the Therapeutic Alliance: a Relational Treatment Guide.* New York: Guilford Press

Samuels, L. (1996)   A Historical Analysis of Winnicott's "The Use of an Object". *Winnicott Studies, 11*: 41-50

Sandbank, T. (1993)   Psychoanalysis and Maternal Work – some Parallels. *International Journal of Psychoanalysis, 74*: 15-727

Sandler, A-M. (2004)   Institutional Responses to Boundary Violations: the Case of Masud Khan. *International Journal of Psychoanalysis, 85*: 38-41

Sanville, J. (1991)   *The Playground of Psychoanalytic Therapy.*
                          Hillside, NJ: Analytic Press

Sarno, L. (2001)   Winnicott and Bion: on some Uncanny
                          Affinities [in Bertolini, M. et al (2001)
                          vol. 2: 204-220

Sayers, J. (2002)   Marian Milner, Mysticism and
                          Psychoanalysis. *International Journal of
                          Psychoanalysis, 83*: 105-120

Sayers. J. (2004a)   Intersubjective Winnicott. *American
                          Imago, 61*: 519-526

Sayers, J. (2004b)   Kanter, J. (2004) review. *British Journal of
                          Social Work, 334*: 1203-1205

Sayers, J. (2004c)   Robert Rodman: a Memorial Tribute.
                          American Imago, 61: 519-523

Scarfone, D. (2005)   Laplanche And Winnicott Meet [in
                          Caldwell, L. (2005): 33-53]

Schaedel , M. (2005)   Working with Women in an NHS
                          Outpatient Clinic for Sexual Dysfunction
                          [in Caldwell, L.(2005): 126-143]

Schacht, L. (1972)   Psychoanalytic Facilitation into the
                          "Subject-Uses-Subject" Phase of
                          Maturation. *International Journal of Child
                          Psychotherapy, 1*: 71-88

Schacht, L. (1988)   Winnicott's Position in Regard to the
                          Self with Special Reference to
                          Childhood. *International Review of
                          Psychoanalysis, 15*: 515-529

Schacht, L. (2001)   Between the Capacity and the Necessity
                          of Being Alone [in Bertolini, M. et al
                          (2001) vol. 1: 112-125] (see also Grieve, P.
                          (2001) for further notes)

Schacht, L. (2003)   The Paradox of Creativity.
                          Psychoanalysis in Europe, 57: 54-62

Scharff, J.S. (2003)   The British Object Relation Theorists: Fairbairn, Winnicott, Balint, Guntrip, Sutherland and Bowlby. (Paper read at a symposium "Understanding Dissidence and Controversy in the History of Psychoanalysis" – published 2004 New York: Other Press: 175-200)

Schermer, V. (2003)   *Spirit and Psyche: a New Paradigm for Psychology, Psychoanalysis and Psychotherapy.* London: Jessica Kingsley

Schlachet, P.J. (1986)   The Concept of Group Space. *International Journal of Group Psychotherapy, 36*: 33-53

Schlauch, C.R. (1990)   Illustrating Two Complementary Enterprises at the Interface of Psychology and Religion through Reading Winnicott. *Pastoral Psychology, 39*: 47-63

Schlierf, C. (1983)   Transitional Objects and Object Relations in a Case of Anxiety Neurosis. *International Review of Psychoanalysis, 10*: 319-332

Schneider, E. (1996)   Holding and Caring: a Borderline Patient in a New Psychotherapy Group. *Group Analysis, 29*: 125-126

Schneiderman, L. (1999)   Willa Cather: transitional Object and Creativity. *Imagination, Cognition and Personality, 19*: 131-147

Schoenberg, P. (2001)   Winnicott and the Psyche-Soma [in Bertolini, M. et al (2001) vol. 2: 147-154]

Schoenwolf, G. (1990)   *Turning Points in Analytic Therapy: from Winnicott to Kernberg.* New York: Aronson

Schreuder, B.J.N.
(2001)

The Violation of Inner and Outer Boundaries in Political Persecution. *Journal of Applied Psychoanalytic Studies, 3*: 231-242

Schwartz, M.M.
(1978)

Critic, Define Thyself [in *Psychoanalysis and the Question of the Text* Ed. Hartmann, G. (Baltimore and London: Johns Hopkins University Press) pp. 1-17]

Schwartz. M.M.
(1992)

Introduction: D.W. Winnicott's Cultural Space. *Psychoanalytic Review, 79*: 169-174

Schwartz, M.M.
(1993)

Where is Literature? [in Rudnytsky (1993): 50-62]

Scurlock, A. (2005)

Early Disillusionment. *Dissertation Abstracts (International), 65 (11-B)*: 6058

Searles, H.F. (1979)

Countertransference and Related Subjects: Selected Papers. New York: International Universities Press

Segal, H. (1951)

The Ordinary Devoted Mother and her Baby review. *International Journal of Psychoanalysis, 32*: 327-328

Selvin, J. (2003)

Winnicottian Reading of Gwendolen Harleth in George Eliot's *Daniel Deronda. Dissertation Abstracts (International), 64 (3-B)*: 1507

Sengun, S. (2001)

Migration as a Transitional Space and Group Analysis. *Group Analysis, 34*: 65-78

Shabad, P.,
Selinger, S. (1995)

Bracing for Disappointment and the Counterphobic Leap into the Future [in Corrigan, E.G., Gordon, P-E. (1995a): 209-228]

Shapiro, E.R. (1998)   Images in Psychiatry: Donald W.
                       Winnicott 1896-1971. *American Journal of
                       Psychiatry, 155*: 421-422

Sheppard, A. (1998)   Princess Diana: what Winnicott Might
                       have Said. *Journal of Melanie Klein
                       Society and Object Relations, 16*: 609-610

Sher, J. (1990)   *Work, Love, Play: Self Repair in the
                       Psychoanalytic Dialogue*: Los Angeles:
                       Doubleday

Sheridan, M.D.   *Play in Early Childhood: From Birth to Six
(1999)   Years*. London: Routledge

Sherman, S.R.   Early Intervention with a Mother-Infant
(2003)   Pair: The Impact of an Enduring and
                       Adaptive Relationship. *Clinical Social
                       Work Journal, 31*: 223-234

Shields, W.S. (2000)   Hope and the Inclination to be
                       Troublesome: Winnicott and the
                       Treatment of Character Disorder in
                       Group Psychotherapy. *International
                       Journal of Group Psychotherapy, 50*: 87-104

Shields, W.S. (2001)   The Subjective Experience of the Self in
                       the Large Group: Two Models for Study.
                       *International Journal of Group
                       Psychotherapy, 51*: 205-223

Shmukler, D.,   The Transitional Object and the
Friedman, M.   Development of the Child Ego State.
(1985)   *Transactional Analysis Journal, 15*: 207-210

Shmukler, D.,   The Developmental Function of Play
Friedman, M.   and its Relevance for Transactional
(1988)   Analysis. *Transactional Analysis Journal,
                       18*: 80-84

Shore, A. (2000)   Child Art Therapy and Parent
                       Consultation: Facilitating Child

Development and Parent Strengths. *Art Therapy, 17*: 14-23

Siebzehner, A.V. (1994) Psychoanalysis of a Child: a Winnicottian Look. *Encounters (Argentina),* 1: 103-108

Siegelman, E.Y. (1990) *Meaning and Metaphor in Psychotherapy* New York: Guilford Press

Silva, E.B. (1996) *Good Enough Mothering? Feminist Perspectives on Lone Motherhood.* London: Routledge

Sinason, V. (2001) Children who Kill their Teddy Bears [in Kahr, B. (2001a): 43-50]

Singer, M. (1989) Giovacchini, P.L. (1986) review. *Psychoanalytic Quarterly, 58*: 111-116

Sjödin, C. (2003) The Significance of Belief for Psychoanalysis. *International Forum of Psychoanalysis, 12*: 44-52

Slavin, M.O. (2000) Hate, Self-Interest and "Good-Enough" Relating. *Psychoanalytic Inquiry, 20*: 441-461

Slochower, J. (1991) Variations in the Analytic Holding Environment. *International Journal of Psychoanalysis, 72*: 709-718

Slochower, J. (1994) The Evolution of Object Usage and the Holding Environment. *Contemporary Psychoanalysis, 30*: 135-151

Slochower, J.A. (1996a) *Holding and Psychoanalysis: A Relational Perspective.* Hillside, NJ: Analytic Press

Slochower, J. (1996b) Holding and the Fate of the Analyst's Objectivity. *Psychoanalytic Dialogues, 6*: 323-353

Slochower, J. (2005)	Holding: Something Old and Something New [in Aron, L., Harris, E. (Eds.). *Relational Psychoanalysis: Innovations and Expansion*, vol. 2: 24-49 Mahwah, NJ: Analytic Press (2005)]
Slochower, J. (2006)	*Psychoanalytic Collisions*. Mahwah, NJ: Analytic Press
Smirnoff, V. (1971)	*The Scope of Child Analysis*. London: Routledge
Smith, B.L. (1989a)	Winnicott and the British Schools [in Fromm, Smith (1989a): 27-51]
Smith, B.L. (1989b)	Winnicott and Self-Psychology [in Fromm, Smith (1989a): 52-87]
Smith, B.L. (1989c)	The Transitional Function of Insight [in Fromm, Smith (1989a): 159-178]
Smith, B.L. (1989d)	Of Many Minds: a Contribution on Many Minds [in Fromm, Smith (1989a): 424-458]
Smith, B.L. (1989e)	The Community as Object [in Fromm, Smith (1989a): 516-534]
Smith, B.L. (1990)	Potential Space and the Rorschach: an Application of Object Relations Theory. *Journal of Personal Assessment*, 55: 756-767
Smith, R.C. (1996)	*The Wounded Jung: Effects of Jung's Relationships on his Life and Work.* Evanston, IL: Northwestern University Press
Smith, T.S. (2002)	*Strong Interaction*. Chicago: Chicago University Press
Sobel, E. (1978)	Rhythm, Sound and Imagery in the Poetry of Gerard Manley Hopkins

	[in Grolnick, Barkin, Muensterberger (1978): 425-446]
Socarides, C. (2001)	D.W. Winnicott and the Understanding of Sexual Perversions [in Kahr, B. (2001a): 95-110]
Solomon, J.C. (1978)	Transitional Phenomena and Obsessive-Compulsive States [in Grolnick, Barkin, Muensterberger (1978): 245-256]
Solow, M.J. (1997)	The Effect of the Holding Environment on the Transition to Parenthood. *Dissertation Abstracts (International), 58 (6-B)*: 3343
Solow, M.J. (2003)	Face and Façade: the Mother's Face as the Baby's Mirror [in Raphael-Leff, J. (1993): 5-17]
Southwood, H.M. (1973)	The Origin of Self Awareness and Ego Behaviour. *International Journal of Psychoanalysis, 54*: 235-239
Speziale-Bagliacci, R. (2004)	*Guilt, Revenge, Remorse and Responsibility after Freud.* London: Routledge
Spezzano, C. (1993)	Rudnytsky, P.L. (1991) review. *Psychoanalytic Books, 4*: 259-264
Spice, N. (2002)	Winnicott and Music [in Caldwell, L. (2002): 193-204]
Spiro, L.H., Devnis, L.E. (1978)	The Use of Onself: from Transitional Object to Illusion in Art [in Grolnick, Barkin, Muensterberger (1978): 238-254]
Spitz, E.H. (1992)	Recycling. *Psychoanalytic Review, 79*: 209-222
Spitz, E.H. (1993)	Picturing the Child's Inner World of Fantasy: on the Dialectic between Image and Word [in Rudnytsky (1993): 261-277]

Spotnitz, H. (1985)   *Modern Psychoanalysis of the Schizophrenic Patient* 2nd ed. New York: Human Science Press

Sprengnether, H. (1993)   Ghost Writing: a M1editation on Literary Criticism as Narrative [in Rudnytsky (1993): 87-98]

Spurling, L. (1991)   Winnicott and the Mother's Face. *Winnicott Studies, 6*: 60-61

Spurling, L. (Ed.) (1993)   *From the Words of my Mouth: Tradition in Psychotherapy.* London: Routledge

Spurling, L. (1996)   Winnicott and the Transference: The Knife-Edge of Belief. *Winnicott Studies, 11*: 51-61

Spurling, L. (1998)   Kahr, B. (1996) review. *Psychodynamic Counselling, 4*: 135-136

Spurling, L. (2003)   On Psychoanalytic Figures as Transference Figures. *International Journal of Psychoanalysis, 84*: 31-43

Steele, R.S. (1988)   Rodman, F.R. (1987) review. *Journal of the History of Behavioral Sciences, 24*: 270-274

Stein, A.A. (1999)   Whose Thoughts are they Anyway? Dimensionally Exploding Bion's "Double Headed Arrow" into Co-Adapting Transitional Space. *Non-Linear Dynamics, Psychology & Life Sciences, 3*: 65-92

Stein, H.F. (1985)   Culture Change, Symbolic Object Loss and Restitutional Process. *Psychoanalysis and Contemporary Thought, 8*: 301-332

Stein, S. (1975)   Consultation Techniques of Winnicott. *South African Medical Journal, 49*: 984-985

Steiner, J. (1991)   *Psychic Retreats: Pathological Organizations in Psychotic, Neurotic and Borderline Patients.* London: Routledge

Stern. D.N. (1985)   *The Interpersonal World of the Infant: a View from Psychoanalysis and Developmental Psychology.* New York: Basic Books (reprinted London: Karnac 1998)

Stevenson, O. (1954)   The First Treasured Possession: a Study of the Part Played by Specially Loved Objects *(preface by Winnicott, D.W.)* and Toys in the Lives of Certain Children. *Psychoanalytic Study of the Child,* 9: 199-217

Stevenson, O. (1971)   Donald Winnicott: an Appreciation. *International Journal of Child Psychology & Psychiatry & Allied Disciplines,* 12: 153-155

Stewart, H. (1992)   *Psychic Experience and Problems of Technique.* London: Routledge

Stewart, H. (1995)   The Development of Mind-as-Object [in Corrigan, E.G., Gordon, P-E. (1995a): 41-54]

Stewart, H. (1996)   *Michael Balint: Object Relations, Pure and Applied.* London: Routledge

Stewart, H. (2004)   Winnicott, Balint and the Independent Tradition. *American Journal of Psychoanalysis, 63*: 207-217

Stone, A.A. (1991)   *Psychoanalytic Explorations* review. *American Journal of Psychiatry, 148*: 259-260

Stout, R.L. (2002)   Object Relations and Winnicott's Conception of Creativity: a Study of the Relationships. *Dissertation Abstracts (International), 62 (12-B)*: 5980

Street, E., Downey, J., Brazier, A. (1991)   The Development of Therapeutic Consultations in Child-focused Family Work. *Journal of Family Therapy,* 13: 311-333

Strenger, C. (1997)   Further Remarks on the Classic and Romantic Visions in Psychoanalysis: Klein, Winnicott and Ethics. *Psychoanalysis and Contemporary Thought,* 20: 207-244

Strozier, C.B. (1997)   Kahr, B. (1996) review. *Psychohistory Review,* 25: 258-260

Sugarman, A., Jaffe, L.S. (1989)   A Developmental Line in Transitional Phenomena [in Fromm, Smith (1979a): 88-129]

Suman, A. (2001)   Interrupted Stories [in Bertolini, M. et al (2001) vol. 2: 173-176]

Summers, F. (1994)   *Object Relations Theories and Psychopathology.* Hillside, NJ: Analytic Press

Summers, F. (1999)   Psychoanalytic Boundaries and Transitional Space Psychoanalytic Psychology 16: 3-20

Summers, F. (2005)   *Self Creation: Psychoanalytic Theory and the Art of the Possible.* Hillside, NJ: Analytic Press

Sussal, C.M. (1991)   Hughes, J.M. (1989) review. *Clinical Social Work Journal,* 19: 435

Sussal, C.M. (1992)   Object Relations Family Therapy as a Model for Practice. *Clinical Social Work Journal,* 20: 313-321

Sutherland, J.D. (1980)   The British Object-Relations Theorists: Balint, Winnicott, Fairbairn, Guntrip. *Journal of the American Psychoanalytical Association,* 28: 829-860

Sutherland, J.D. (1994)   *The Autonomous Self: the Work of John D. Sutherland* (edited Scharff, J.S.). Lanham, MD: Aronson

Sutton, A. (2001)   Dependence and Dependability: Winnicott in a Culture of Symptom Intolerance. *Psychoanalytic Psychotherapy, 15*: 1-19

Symington, N. (1986)   *The Analytic Experience: Lectures from the Tavistock.* London: Free Association Books

Symington, N. (1996)   *Narcissism: a New Theory.* London: Karnac

Symington, N. (1997)   *The Making of a Psychotherapist.* London: Karnac

Szollosy, M. (1998)   Winnicott's Potential Spaces: Using Psychoanalytic Theory to Redress the Crises of Modern Culture. Available on line at *Psyche Matters*

Tallandini, M.A. (1996)   Gaddini, E. (1992) review. *Winnicott Studies, 11*: 82-84

Target, M., Fonagy, P. (1996)   Playing with Reality II: The Development of Psychic Reality from a Theoretical Perspective. *International Journal of Psychoanalysis, 77*: 459-479

Taylor, C. (1989)   *Sources of the Self: The Making of Modern Identity.* Cambridge: Harvard University Press

Taylor, L. (2006)   Kanter, J. (2004b) review. *Journal of American Academy of Child and Adolescent Psychiatry, 45*: 885-887

Teitlebaum, S. (2003)   Playing with Winnicott: a Patient's Account of her Experience Using the Analyst as a Traditional Object. *Canadian Journal of Psychoanalysis, 11*: 435-458

Teurnell. L. (1993)   An Alternative Reading of Winnicott. *International Forum of Psychoanalysis,* 2: 377-382

Thomas, K.R., McGinnis, J.D. (1991)   The Psychoanalytic Theories of D.W. Winnicott as Applied to Rehabilitation. *Rehabilitation, 57*: 63

Ticho, E.A. (1974)   Donald W. Winnicott, Martin Buber and the Theory of Personal Relationships. *Psychiatry, 33*: 240-253

Titchener, J.L. (1990)   Hughes, J.M. (1989) review. *American Journal of Psychotherapy, 44*: 140

Tizard, J.P.M. (1971)   Donald Winnicott. *International Journal of Psychoanalysis, 52*: 226-227 [also in Goldman, D. (1993) with Khan, M.M.R. (1971b): 111-116]

Tizard, J.P.M. (1981)   Donald Winnicott. The President's View of a Past President. *Journal of the Royal Society of Medicine, 74*: 262-274

Tod, R.J.N. (1979)   Publications by Donald W.Winnicott 1962-1978. *International Review of Psychoanalysis, 6*: 377-382

Tolpin, M. (1971)   On the Beginnings of a Cohesive Self: an Application of the Concept of Transmuting Internalization to the Study of Transitional Object and Signa; Anxiety. *Psychoanalytic Study of the Child, 26*: 316-354

Tonnesmann, M. (1993)   The Third Area of Experience in Psychoanalysis. *Winnicott Studies, 8 (Autumn)*: 3-16

Tonnesmann, M. (1995)
Early Emotional Development: Ferenczi to Winnicott. *Bulletin of the British Psychoanalytic Society, 30*: 14-19 [also in Caldwell, (L. 2002a): 45-57]

Tonnesmann, M. (2001)
Discussion of Innes-Smith, J. (2001) [in Bertolini, M. et al (2001) vol. 1: 233-237]

Tonnesmann, M. (2002)
Early Emotional Development: Ferenczi to Winnicott [in Caldwell, L. (2002a): 45-57]

Traub, H.L., Lane, R.C.(2002)
The Case of Ms A. *Clinical Case Studies, 1*: 49-66

Treacher, A. (2002)
"I Like my Life, I Just Like my Life": Narratives of Children of Latency Years [in Caldwell, L. (2002): 177-191]

Trevarthen, C. (1993)
Playing into Reality: Conversations with the Infant Communicator. *Winnicott Studies, 7 (Spring)*: 67-84

Trinci, M. (2001)
With Downcast Eyes: some notes on Magherini, G. (2001) [in Bertolini, M. et al (2001) vol. 2: 228-231]

Trowell, J. (1990)
Babies and their Mothers review. *International Review of Psychoanalysis, 17*: 123-124

Trowell, J. (2002)
The Wider Implications of Infant Observation [in Kahr, B. (2002a): 79-88]

Tuckett, D. (2001)
Reflections on Hernandez, M., Giannakoulas, A (2001) [in Bertolini, M. et al (2001) vol. 1: 160-163]

Turk, C. (1990)
An Inquiry into the Limits of the Psychoanalytic Method [in Giovacchini (1990a): 160-178]

Turner, J.F. (1988)   Wordsworth and Winnicott in the Play Area. *International Review of Psychoanalysis, 15*: 481-496 [also in Rudnytsky (1993): 161-188]

Turner, J.F. (2002)   A Brief History of Illusion: Milner, Winnicott and Rycroft. *International Journal of Psychoanalysis, 83*: 1063-1082

Turp, M. (2000a)   Touch, Enjoyment and Health in Adult Life. *European Journal of Psychotherapy, Counselling & Health, 3*: 61-76

Turp, M. (2000b)   Handling and Self-handling: an Object Relations Perspective on Leisure Exercise. *Psychodynamic Counselling, 6*: 469-487

Turp, M. (2002)   Acting, Feeling and Thinking: Psychoanalytic Psychotherapy with Tracey. *European Journal of Psychotherapy Counselling, 5*: 103-119

Tustin, F. (1972)   *Autism and Child Psychosis.* London: Hogarth Press

Tustin, F. (1980)   Autistic Objects. *International Review of Psychoanalysis, 7*: 27-39

Tustin, F. (1981)   *Autistic States in Children.* London: Routledge

Tustin, F. (1983)   Davis, Wallbridge (1981) review. *Winnicott Studies, 1*: 77-78

Tustin, F. (1985)   The Emergence of a Sense of Self or the Development of "I-ness". *Winnicott Studies, 1*: 36-48 [also in Richards with Wilce (1996): 47-63]

Tustin, F. (1986)   *Autistic Barriers in Neurotic Patients.* London: Karnac

Tustin, F. (1987)   The Rhythm of Safety. *Winnicott Studies, 2*: 19-31

Tustin, F. (1990)   *The Protective Shell in Children and Adults*. London: Karnac

Tyndale, A. (1999)   How Far is Transference Interpretation Essential to Psychic Change? [in Johnson, S., Ruszczynski, S. (1999): 53-72]

Ulanov, A.B. (1985)   A Shared Space. *Quadrant, 18*: 65-80

Ulanov, A.B. (2001)   *Finding Space: Winnicott, God and Psychic Reality*. Louisville, KY: Westminster John Knox Press

Underwood, R.L. (1996)   Primordial Texts: an Object Relations Approach to Biblical Hermeneutics. *Pastoral Psychology, 45*: 181-192

Unwin, C. (2006)   Notes on Integration and Disintegration from Historical and Developmental Perspectives. *Journal of Child Psychotherapy, 32*: 193-213

Urdang, E. (2002)   *Human Behavior in the Social Environment: Interweaving the Inner and Outer Worlds*. Binghamton, NY: Haworth Press

Usuelli, A.K. (1992)   The Significance of Illusion in the Work of Freud and Winnicott: a Controversial Issue. *International Review of Psychotherapy, 19*: 179-187

Vallery, S.K. (1992)   Mentoring in Clinical Supervision of Psychodynamic Psychotherapy: Application of Winnicott's Theory of the Transitional Phenomena. *Dissertation Abstracts (International), 52 (10-B)*: 5551

Van Buskirk, W., McGrath, D. (1999)   Organizational Cultures as Holding Environments: a Psychodynamic Look at Organizational Symbolism. *Human Relations, 52*: 805-832

Vanier, A: (2001)   Some Remarks on Adolescence with Particular Reference to Winnicott and Lacan. *Psychoanalytic Quarterly*, 70: 579-598

Vanier, A. (2002)   Some Remarks on Adolescence with Winnicott and Lacan [in Caldwell, L. (2002): 133-152]

Vellacott, J. (1995)   The Woman Behind Mother. *Winnicott Studies, 10*: 15-24

Vivona, J. (2000)   Autonomous Desire: Women's Worry as Post-œdipal Transitional Object. *Psychoanalytic Psychology, 17*: 243-263

Volkan, D.V., Kavanaugh, J.G. (1978)   The Cat People [in Grolnick, Barkin, Muensterberger (1978): 289-304]

Volkan, D.V. (2001)   Foreword [Kahr, B. (2001a): xix-xxv]

Volmer, F. (1999)   *Agent Casualty.* Dordrecht, Holland: Kluwer Academic

Wakimoto, K. (et al) (1984)   An Approach to Pre-Adolescent Patients Using the "Squiggle Game". *Japanese Journal of Child and Adolescent Psychiatry, 25*: 231-240

Walker, J.S. (1999)   Newman, G.M. (1997) review. *Journal of English and Germanic Philology, 98*: 296

Webber, A.M., Haen, C. (2005)   *Clinical Applications of Drama Therapy in Child and Adolescent Treatment.* London & New York: Brunner-Routledge

Webber, J.A. (2001)   Failure to Hold: An Analysis of School Violence (John Dewey and D.W. Winnicott). *Dissertation Abstracts (International), 62 (6-A)*: 2030

Weich, M.J. (1978)   Transitional Language [in Grolnick, Barkin, Muensterberger (1978): 128-141]

Weich, M.J. (1990) The Good Enough Analyst [in Giovacchini, P. (1990a): 128-141]

Weich, M.J. (1991) *Home is Where You Start From* review. *Journal of the American Psychoanalytic Association, 39*: 259-262

Weisberg, I. (1994) The Facilitating or Inhibiting Environment, Maternal and Psychoanalytic: D.W. Winnicott. *International Journal of Communicative Psychoanalysis and Psychotherapy, 9*: 113-119

Weiss, S. (1997) The Empty Space. *Annual of Psychoanalysis, 25*: 189-199

Welldon, E. (2001) Babies as Transitional Objects [in Kahr, B. (2001a): 19-26]

Wells, D. (2002) Tragedy, Catharsis and Creativity: from Aristotle to Freud to Winnicott. *Free Associations, 52*: 463-478

Werner, S.L (1994) Giovacchini, P.L. (1990a) review. *Journal of the American Academy off Psychoanalysis, 22*: 562-565

Whiteley, J.S. (1994) Attachment, Loss and the Space Between: Personality Disorder in the Therapeutic Community. *Group Analysis, 27*: 359-382

Whiteley, J.S. (1998) Community as Playground: Some Thoughts on the Function of Play in the Therapeutic Community. *International Journal for Therapeutic and Supportive Organizations, 19*: 269-280

Whitty, M.T., Carr, A.N. (2003) Cyberspace as Potential Space: Considering the Web as a playground to Cyber-flirt. *Human Relations, 56*: 869-891

Widdicombe, A. (1997)	Kahr, B. (1996) review. *Journal of Child Psychotherapy, 23*: 161-163
Widlöcher, D. (1970)	On Winnicott's *Maturational Processes and the Facilitating Environment*. *International Journal of Psychoanalysis, 51*: 526-530
Widlöcher, D. (1993)	Freedom of Thought [in Goldman, D. Ed. (1993): 177-183]
Widlocher, D. (2003)	How the Analyst's Person is Affected by and Induces Thought-Transference. *Psychoanalysis in Europe, 57*: 83-90
Wieland, C. (1994)	The Good-Enough Mother and the Use of the Object in Winnicott. *Winnicott Studies, 9*: 25-34
Wilce, G. (1997)	*Thinking About Children* review. *Psychodynamic Counselling, 3*: 230-231
Willbern, D. (1993)	Phantasmagoric *Macbeth* [in Rudnytsky (1993): 101-134]
Wilkin, P. (2006)	In Search of the True Self: a Clinical Journey through the Vale of Soul-making. *Journal of Psychiatric Mental Health Nursing, 13*: 12-18
Williams, G.D. (2002)	Failures Unmended: a Pastoral Psychological Study of a Tragic Vision of Evil in Writings of Winnicott. *Dissertation Abstracts (International), 62 (10-B)*: 4828
Willock, B. (1992)	Projection, Transitional Phenomena and the Rorschach. *Journal of Personality Assessment, 59*: 99-116
Willoughby, R. (2005)	*Masud Khan: the Man and the Reality*. London: Free Association Books

Wilson, S.N. (2005)   The Meanings of Medicating: Pills and Play. *American Journal of Psychotherapy*, *59*: 19-29

Winnicott, C. (1978)   D.W.W.: a Reflection [in Grolnick, Barkin, Muensterberg (1978): 17-33, in Giovacchini (1990a): 3-20 and in Kanter, J. (2004): 237-253]

Winnicott, C. (1980)   Fear of Breakdown: A Clinical Example. *International Journal of Psychoanalysis*, *61*: 351-357

Winnicott, C. (1993)   Interview with Dr. Michael Neve [in Goldman, D. Ed. (1993): 107-110]

Winnicott, D.W. (1962)   Theory of Parent-Infant Relationship: Further Remarks. *International Journal of Psychoanalysis*, *43*: 238-239 [followed by Contributions to the Discussion by: Balint, M., Blau, A., Burlingham, D., Davidson, S., Freud, A., Garma, A., Greenacre, P., James, M., Khan, M.M.R., Lagache, D., Lantos, B., Lebovici, S., Schur, M., Scott, W.C.M., Szekely, L., Winnicott, D.W.]

Winnicott, D.W. (2003)   Preface to Renata Gaddini's translation of *Family and Individual Development*. *Psychoanalysis and History, 5*: 40-52

Wiseman, R.S. (2002)   Toward a Better Understanding of Children's Trichotillomania: an Analysis of Family Treatment. *Dissertation Abstracts (International), 63 (4-B)*: 2081

Wold, M.W., Fromm, M.G. (1979)   Delinquency and Hope: a Clinical Illustration [in Fromm, Smith (1989a): 535-557]

Wolf, R. (1979) — Re-experiencing Winnicott's Environmental Mother: Implications of Art Psychotherapy of Anti-social Youth in Special Education. *Arts in Psychotherapy*, 6: 95-102

Wolman, T. (1994) — Grolnick, S.A. (1990) review. *Psychoanalytic Quarterly*, 63: 367-370

Wolstein, B. (1991) — Schoenewolf, G. (1990) review. *American Journal of Psychotherapy*, 45: 452

Wright, E. (1998) — *Psychoanalytic Criticism: a Reappraisal* London: Polity Press and New York: Routledge

Wright, K. (1990) — *Between Mother and Baby*. London: Free Association Books

Wright, K. (1996) — Looking After the Self [in Richards with Wilce (1996): 65-84]

Wright, K. (1998) — Deep Calling unto Deep: Artistic Creativity and the Maternal Object. *British Journal of Psychotherapy*, 14: 453-467

Wright, K. (2000a) — Face and Façade: the Mother's Face as the Baby's Mirror [in Raphael-Leff, J. (2003): 5-17]

Wright, K. (2000b) — To Make Experience Sing [in Caldwell, L. (2000): 75-96]

Wright, K. (2001) — The Interface Between Mother and Baby [in Bertolini, M. et al (2001) vol. 2: 3-12]

Wright, K. (2006) — Preverbal Experience and the Intuition of the Sacred [in Black, D.M. (2006a): 173-190]

Wyatt-Brown, A.M. (1993)   From the Clinic to the Classroom: D.W. Winnicott, James Britton and the Revolution in Writing Theory [in Rudnytsky (1993): 292-306]

Wynn, F. (1997)   The Embodied Chiasmic Relationship of Mother and Infant. *Human Studies* 20: 253-270

Yates, S. (1932)   *Clinical Notes on the Disorders of Childhood* review. *International Journal of Psychoanalysis, 13*: 242-243

Yates, S. (1997)   Kahr, B. (1996) review. *British Journal of Psychotherapy, 13*: 564

Young, R.M. (2005)   Containment: the Technical and the Tacit in Successful Psychotherapy [in Ryan, J. (2005): 165-286]

Young-Bruehl, E. (2003a)   Rodman, R. (2003) review. *International Journal of Psychoanalysis, 84*: 1661-1666

Young-Bruehl (2003b)   *Where do We Fall when We Fall in Love?* New York: Other Press

Zalidis, S. (2001)   *A General Practitioner, his Patients and their Feelings* London: Free Association Books

Zalidis, S. (2002)   'My Eyes are Misting Over' Therapeutic Consultations in General Practice with a Child Presenting with an Eye Symptom. *Psychoanalytic Psychotherapy, 16*: 1-19

Ziegler, R.G. (1976)   Winnicott's Squiggle Games and its Diagnostic Therapeutic Usefulness. *Art Psychotherapy, 3*: 177-185

Zimmerman, L. (1997)   Against Vanishing: Winnicott and the Modern Poetry of Nothing. *American Imago, 54*: 81-102

Zimmerman, L. (1999)   Public and Potential Space: Winnicott, Ellison and De Lillo. *Centennial Review,* 43: 565-574

Zinkin, L. (1983)   Malignant Mirroring. *Group Analysis,* 16: 113-124

Zucconi, S. (2001)   Psychosis and the Transitional Area: a Clinical Case Study [in Bertolini, M. et al (2001) vol. 2: 103-112]

Zuger, B. (1992)   Grolnick, S.A. (1990) review. *Journal of the American Academy of Psychoanalysis,* 20: 157-158

PART II

Complete listing in three sections

Articles

Aaltonen, J., Räkkökäinen. V (1987)	The Paradox and the Dissolution of the Œdipus Complex. *Scandinavian Psychoanalytic Review, 10*: 117-132
Ablon, S.L. (2001)	Continuities of Tongues: a Developmental Perspective on the Role of Play in Child and Adult Psychoanalytic Process. *Journal of Clinical Psychoanalysis, 10*: 345-365
Abramowitz, S.A. (1995)	Killing the Needy Self: Women Professionals and Suicide (a Critique of Winnicott's False-self Theory). *Progress in Self Psychology, 11*: 177-188
Adams, W.W. (2006)	Love, Open Awareness and Authenticity: a Conversation with William Blake and D.W. Winnicott. *Journal of Humanistic Psychology, 46*: 9-35
Adler, G. (1989)	Transitional Phenomena, Projective Identification and the Essential Ambiguity of the Psychoanalytic Situation. *Psychoanalytic Quarterly, 58*: 61-104

Aguayo, J. (2002)   Reassessing the Clinical Affinity Between Melanie Klein and D.W. Winnicott, 1935-1951: Klein's Unpublished "Notes on Baby" in Historical Context. *International Journal of Psychoanalysis, 83*: 1135-1152

Aiken, S.C., Herman, T. (1997)   Gender, Power and Crib Geography: Transitional Spaces and Potential Places. *Gender, Place and Culture, 4*: 63-88

Albiston, R.K. (1984)   The Advent of Object Representation: a Piagetian Critique of the British School Theorists Klein, Fairbairn, Winnicott and Guntrip. *Dissertation Abstracts (International), 44 (10-B)*: 3185

Alford, C.F. (2000)   Levinas and Winnicott: Motherhood and Responsibility. *American Imago, 57*: 235-260

Alford, C.F. (2002a)   Levinas, Winnicott and the Ethics of Ruthlessness. *Journal for the Psychoanalysis of Culture and Society, 7*: 39-42

Alphandary, I. (2002)   The Subject of Autonomy and Fellowship in Maupassant, Winnicott and Conrad. *Dissertation Abstracts (International), 62 (10A)*: 3376

Altman, N. (1994)   A Perspective on Child Psychoanalysis. *Psychoanalytic Psychology, 11*: 383-395

Alvarez, A. (1996)   The Clinician's Debt to Winnicott. *Journal of Child Psychotherapy, 22*: 377-382

Anderson, J.W. (2003)   Recent Psychoanalytic Theorists and their Relevance to Psychobiography: Winnicott, Kernberg and Kohut. *Annual of Psychoanalysis, 31*: 79-96

Anderson, J.W. (2004)
The Most Influential Psychoanalyst since Freud. *PsycCRITIQUES, 49*

Applegate, J.S. (1990)
Theory, Culture and Behavior: Object Relations in Context. *Child and Adolescent Social Work Journal, 7*: 85-100

Applegate, J.S. (1993)
Winnicott and Clinical Social Work: a Facilitating Partnership. *Child and Adolescent Social Work Journal, 10*: 3-19

Applegate, J.S. (1997b)
The Holding Environment: an Organizing Metaphor for Social Work Theory and Practice. *Smith College Studies in Social Work, 68*: 7-29

Applegate, J.S. (1999)
Winnicott and the Paradoxes of Intersubjectivity. *Smith College Studies in Social Work, 69*: 203-220

Applegate, J.S. (2002)
Parallel Paths: a Personal Journey to Winnicott and Beyond. *Psychoanalytic Inquiry, 22*: 510-518

Aron, L. (1992)
Interpretation as Expression of the Analyst's Subjectivity. *Psychoanalytic Psychology, 11*: 383-395

Arthern, J., Madill, A. (1999)
How do Transitional Objects Work?: The Therapist's View. *British Journal of Medical Psychology, 72*: 1-21

Athanassiou, C. (1991)
Construction of a Transitional Space in an Infant Twin Girl. *International Review of Psychoanalysis, 18*: 53-63

Babits, M. (2001)
Using Therapeutic Metaphor to Provide a Holding Environment: the Inner Edge of Possibility. *Clinical Social Work Journal, 29*: 21-33

Bacal, H.A. (1987)   British Object Relations Theorists and
                          Self-psychology: Some Clinical
                          Reflections. *International Journal of
                          Psychoanalysis, 68*: 81-98

Bacon, R.J.E. (2002)   Winnicott Revisited: a Point of View.
                          Free Associations, 50: 250-170

Bacon-Greenberg, K.   Winnicott: the Man and his Theory.
(2004)   *PsyART, 8*

Bank, R. (1999)   Mythic Perspectives and Perspectives
                          on Truth: Approaching Winnicott by
                          Way of Comparisons between Kohut
                          and Freud. *Psychoanalytic Review,
                          86*: 109-136

Barak, Y.,   Gestalt Elements in Winnicott's
Rabinowitz, G.   Psychoanalytic Technique. *Gestalt
(1995)   Journal, 18*: 87-91

Belger, A.W. (2002)   Theory as Holding Environment: Using
                          Winnicott to Explore the Beginning
                          Psychoanalytic Psychotherapist's
                          Relationship to Theory. *Dissertation
                          Abstracts (International), 63 (2-B)*: 1009

Benjamin, J. (1990)   An Outline of Subjectivity: The
                          Development of Recognition.
                          Psychoanalytic Psychology, 7/Supp: 33-46

Benjamin, J. (1993)   Reply to Burack (1993) on Donald
                          Winnicott. *Psychoanalysis and
                          Contemporary Thought, 16*: 447-454

Berg, D.F. (1999)   Pluralism, Religious Bias and
                          Pathologizing: the Interpretation and
                          Use of Winnicott's Theories in the
                          Psychoanalytic Study of Religion.
                          *Dissertation Abstracts (International),
                          59 (10-A)*: 3849...

Berger, B. (1999)   Deprivation and Abstinence in Psychoanalytic Psychotherapy. *Israel Journal of Psychiatry and Related Sciences*, 3: 164-173

Berger, L.R. (1980)   The Winnicott Squiggle Game: a Vehicle for Communicating with the School-aged Child *Pediatrics*, 66: 921-924

Berman, E. (1997)   Relational Psychoanalysis: a Historical Background. *American Journal of Psychotherapy*, 51: 185-203

Berman, E. (2003)   On Joseph Aguayo "Reassessing the Clinical Affinity between Melanie Klein and D.W. Winnicott (Aguayo 2002). *International Journal of Psychoanalysis*, 84: 445-446

Bethelard, F., Young-Bruehl, (1999)   The Wise Baby as the Voice of the True Self. *Psychoanalytic Quarterly*, 68: 585-610 E.

Beyda, A. (2006)   Playing and Ultimate Reality: Dialectics of Experience in Jung and Winnicott. *Dissertation Abstracts (International)*, 66 (9-B): 5977

Bingley, A. (2003)   In Here and Out There: Sensations between and Landscape. *Social and Cultural Geography*, 4: 329-345

Blass, R. (2001)   On the Ethical and Evaluative Nature of Developmental Models in Psychoanalysis. *Psychoanalytic Study of the Child*, 56: 193-218

Blum, H.P., Ross, J.M. (1993)   The Clinical Relevance of the Contribution of Winnicott. *Journal of the American Psychoanalytic Association*, 41: 219-235

Blum, H.P. (1997) Clinical and Developmental dimensions of Hate. *Journal of the American Psychoanalytic Society, 45*: 358-375

Blumenson, S.R. (1986) The Application of Modern Psychoanalytic Techniques of Winnicott's Concept of the Holding Environment: a Linear Study of Three Emotionally Deprived Pre-œdipal Patients. *Dissertation Abstracts (International), 47 (5-B)*: 2150...

Bodin, G. (1994) A comparison of Concepts in Self-Psychology and Winnicott's Theory of the Development of the Self. *Scandinavian Psychoanalytic Review, 17*: 40-58

Bonamino, V. (1991) D.W. Winnicott and the Position of the Analyst and the Analysand in the Psychoanalytic Situation. *Rivista di Psicoanalisi, 37*: 626-667

Borden, W. (1998) The Place and Play of Theory in Practice: a Winnicottian Perspective. *Journal of Analytic Social Work, 5*: 25-40

Boyer, L.B. (1997) The Verbal Squiggle Game in Treating the Seriously Disturbed Patient. *Psychoanalytic Quarterly, 64*: 603-606]

Boynton, R. (2002) The Return of the Repressed: the Strange Case of Masud Khan. *Boston Review, 27(6)*: 23-29

Boz, S. et al (1994) Articulations between Antisocial Tendency and Depression. *Encounters (Argentina), 1*: 87-93

Brafman, A.H. (1997)   Winnicott's *Therapeutic Consultations* Revisited. *International Journal of Psychoanalysis, 8*: 773-787

Brafman, A.H. (2000)   The Child is Still Ill – How are the Parents? *Psychoanalytic Psychotherapy, 14*: 123-162

Brandchaft, B. (1986)   19 British Object Relations: Theory and Self-Psychology. *Progress in Self-Psychology, 2*: 245-272

Brody, H.S. (2001)   Paul Klee: Art, Potential Space and the Transitional Process. *Psychoanalytic Review, 82*: 369-392

Brody, S. (1980)   Transitional Objects: Idealization of a Phenomenon. *Psychoanalytic Quarterly, 49*: 561-605

Bronstein, A.A. (1992)   The Fetish, Transitional Objects and Illusion. *Psychoanalytic Review, 79*: 239-260

Brusset, B. (2003)   The Intersubjective Relation and Psychoanalytic Work. *Psychoanalysis in Europe Bulletin, 57*: 62-69

Buckley, P. (1994)   Self Psychology, Object-Relation Theory and Supportive Psychotherapy. *American Journal of Psychotherapy, 48*: 519-524

Burack, C. (1993)   Love, Rage and Destruction: Donald Winnicott and Social Theory. *Psychoanalysis and Contemporary Thought, 16*: 429-446

Bürgin, D. (2004)   Winnicott's Squiggle Game in Practice. *International Journal of Psychoanalysis, 85*: 1297-1303

Burns-Smith, J. (1999)
Theology and Winnicott's Object Relations Theory. *Journal of Psychology and Theology, 27*: 3-19

Busch, F. (1974)
Dimensions of the First Transitional Object. *Psychoanalytic Study of the Child, 29*: 215-230

Busch, F., McKnight, J. (1977)
Theme and Variations of First Transitional Object. *International Journal of Psychoanalysis, 58*: 479-486

Caldwell, L. (2003)
The Outrageous Prince: Winnicott's Uncure of Masud Khan [intro. to Goldman, D. (2003)]. *British Journal of Psychotherapy, 19*: 483-485

Canter, H.M. (1995)
The Imagination of Peace: A Winnicottian Relations Understanding. *Dissertation Abstracts (International), 55 (11-B)*: 5060

Caradoc-Davies, G. (1995)
A Return Journey to the Concept of Top-Dog/Under-Dog Travelling with Winnicott and Others. *British Gestalt Journal, 4*: 129-133

Carr, A., Downs, A. (2004)
Transitional and Quasi-objects in Organization Studies: Viewing Enron from the Object Relations World of Winnicott and Serres. *Journal of Organisational Change Management, 17*: 352-364

Carter, L. (2000)
The Analyst and his Personality: Winnicott analyzing Guntrip as a Case in Point. *Journal of Analytic Psychology, 45*: 487-488

Casement, P.J. (1982) Samuel Beckett's Relationship to his Mother-tongue. *International Review of Psychoanalysis, 9*: 35-44 [also in Rudnytsky (1993): 229-246]

Casement, P.J. (2000) The Issue of Touch: a Retrospective Overview. *Psychoanalytic Inquiry, 20*: 160-184

Casement, P.J. (2002b) Learning from Life. *Psychoanalytic Inquiry, 22*: 519-533

Castelloe, M. (2004) The Good-enough Setting of Anna Deveare Smith: Restaging Crown Heights. *Psychoanalysis, Culture and Society, 9*: 207-218

Castro, C. (1996) A First Approach to Clinical Work Taken by the Hand of Winnicott. *Winnicott Studies, 11*: 62-70

Cedillo, J.C.S. (2001) A Story of Losses and the Creation of an Alternate World. *International Forum of Psychoanalysis, 10*: 64-71

Charles, M. (1998) On Wondering: Creating Openings into the Analytic Space. *Journal of Melanie Klein and Object Relations, 16*: 367-387

Charles, M. (1999) *The Piggle*: Confrontations with Non-Existence in Childhood. *International Journal of Psychoanalysis, 80*: 783-795

Chazan, S.E. (1997) Ending Child Psychotherapy: Continuing the Cycle of Life. *Psychoanalytic Psychology, 14*: 221-238

Chescheir, M.W. (1985) Some Implications for Winnicott's Concept for Clinical Work Practice. *Clinical Social Work Journal, 13*: 218-233

Chescheir, M.W., Schultz, K.H. (1989) — The Development of a Capacity for Concern in Anti-Social Children: Winnicott's Concept of Human Relatedness. *Clinical Social Work Journal*, 17: 24-39

Claman, L. (1980) — The Squiggle Drawing Game in Child Psychotherapy. *American Journal of Psychotherapy*, 34: 414-425

Coco, J.H. (1999) — Exploring the Frontier from the Inside Out: John Sloan's Nude Studies. *Journal of the American Psychoanalytic Association*, 47: 1335-1376

Cooper, J. (1993a) — Different Ways of Structuring the Frame: According to Winnicott, Khan and Langs. *Bulletin of the British Association of Psychotherapy*, 24: 23-35

Cooper, S.H., Adler, G. (1990) — Toward a Clarification of the Transitional Object and Self-objects in the treatment of the Borderline Patient. *Annual of Psychoanalysis*, 18: 133-152

Coppolillo, H.P. (1967) — Maturational Aspects of the Transitional Phenomenon. *International Journal of Psychoanalysis*, 48: 237-246

Coppolillo, H.P. (1976) — The Transitional Phenomenon Revisited. *Journal of the American Academy of Child Psychiatry*, 15: pp. 36-47

Cornell, W.F. (1997) — If Reich had Met Winnicott. *Energy and Character*, 28: 50-60

Cornell, W.F. (2000) — If Berne Met Winnicott: Transactional Analysis and Relational Analysis. *Transactional Analysis Journal*, 30: 270-275

Coyote, A.L. (2000) — Two Perspectives on Selfhood: Donald Woods Winnicott M.D. and Dvaita Yoga

Philosophy. *Dissertation Abstracts (International), 61 (3-B)*: 1663

Crastnopol, M. (1999) The Analyst's Personality: Winnicott Analyzing Guntrip as a Case in Point. *Contemporary Psychoanalysis, 35*: 271-300

Crème, P. (1994) The Playing Spectator: a Study on the Applicability of the Theories of D.W. Winnicott to Contemporary Concepts of the Viewer's Relationship to Film. *Ph.D. Thesis*: Kent 45-9182

Crewdson, F. (1996) The False Self as Explored in a Long-term Psychoanalysis. *Journal of the American Academy of Psychoanalysis, 24*: 29-43

Daehnert, C. (1998) The False Self as a Means of Disidentification: A Psychoanalytic Case Study. *Contemporary Psychoanalysis, 34*: 241-271

Dajani, K.G. (2003) Psychological Resilience: a Theoretical Contribution - Georg Wilhelm, Friedrich Hegel, D.W. Winnicott. *Dissertation Abstracts (International), 63 (10-B)*: 4080

Daniel, P. (2001) Masud Khan and Winnicott. *Bulletin of the British Psychoanalytical Society, 37*: 30-33

Davar, E. (2001) The Loss of the Transitional Object – some Thoughts about Transitional and "pre-transitional" Phenomena. *Psychodynamic Counselling, 7*: 5-26

Davis, M.E.V. (1985) Some Thoughts on Winnicott and Freud. *Bulletin of the British Association of Psychotherapy, 16*: 57-71

Davis, M.E.V. (1987) The Writing of D.W. Winnicott. *International Review of Psychoanalysis, 14*: 491-501

Davis, M.E.V. (1990) Play and Symbolism in Lowenfeld and Winnicott. *Free Associations, 3 vol. 2/3*: 395-422

Davis, M.E.V. (1993a) Destruction as an Achievement in the Work of Winnicott. *Winnicott Studies, 8 (Spring)*: 85-92

Davis, M.E.V. (1993b) Winnicott and the Spatula Game (edited and abridged by Sievers, R.). *Winnicott Studies, 8 (Autumn)*: 57-67

Davis, M.E.V. (1995) Winnicott and Object Relations (edited and abridged by Sievers, R.). *Winnicott Studies, 10*: 33-45

Davis, M.R., Irving, H. (1985) The Holding Environment in the In-Patient Treatment of Adolescents. *Adolescent Psychiatry, 12*: 434-443

Daws, D. (1996) The Spatula, The Electric Socket and the Spoon. *Journal of Child Psychotherapy, 22*: 392-393

De Canteros, N.L. (1994) Winnicott and Clinical Practice in Psychosomatics, Narcissistic Hypersensitivity and its Vicissitudes. *Encounters (Argentina), 1*: 61-69

De Goldstein, R.Z. (1994) The Child as Transitional Object of the Mother: Reverted Dependence Demand. *Encounters (Argentina), 1*: 11-23

De Greif, L.M.V. (1994) Illusion, Paradox and Metaphor in Psychoanalytic Practice. *Encounters (Argentina), 1*: 51-59

De Groba, A.M.S. (1994)   Some Vicissitudes of Displaying: The Capacity to be One's Own. *Encounters (Argentina),* 1: 95-101

De Schvartzman, A.R. (1994)   Initial Interviews with Adolescents. *Encounters (Argentina),* 1: 79-86

De Wet, V. (1990)   "Holding" as Therapeutic Manœuvre in Family Therapy. *Journal of Family Therapy,* 12: 189-194

Dockar-Drysdale, B. (1974)   My Debt to Donald Winnicott. *Journal of Association of Workers for Maladjusted Children,* 2: 2-5

Doron, A., Mendlovic, S. (1999)   Hypnosis and Winnicott's Transitional Phase. *Contemporary Hypnosis,* 16: 36-39

Downey, T.W. (1978)   Transitional Phenomena in the Analysis of Early Adolescent Males. *Psychoanalytic Study of the Child,* 33: 19-46

Dwyer, S. (2006)   Some Thoughts on the Work of D.W. Winnicott for Present-day Social Work Practice with Adults. *Journal of Social Work Practice,* 20: 83-89

Eddowes, L. (1997)   Sidemarkers and Teddy Bears: an Application of Winnicott's Ideas in Pædiatric Radography. *Psychodynamic Counselling,* 3: 195-207

Ehrenberg, D.B. (1976)   The "Intimate Edge" and the "Third Area". *Contemporary Psychoanalysis,* 12: 489-496

Ehrlich, R. (2004)   Winnicott's Response to Klein. *Psychoanalytic Quarterly,* 73: 453-484

Eigen, M. (1980a)   On the Significance of the Face. *Psychoanalytic Review, 67*: 426-444 [also in Eigen (1993): 49-60]

Eigen, M. (1980b)   Instinctual Fantasy and Ideal Images. *Contemporary Psychoanalysis, 16*: 119-137 [also in Eigen, (1993): 61-75]

Eigen, M. (1981a)   The Area of Faith in Winnicott, Lacan and Bion. *International Journal of Psychoanalysis, 62*: 413-433 [also in Eigen (1993) 09-138]

Eigen, M. (1981b)   Guntrip's Analysis with Winnicott – A Critique of Glatzer. Evans (1977). *Contemporary Psychoanalysis, 17*: 103-111 [also in Eigen (1993): 139-146]

Eigen, M. (1985)   The Sword of Grace: Flannery O'Connor, Wilfred R. Bion and D.W. Winnicott. *Psychoanalytic Review, 72*: 337-346

Eigen, M. (1992)   The Fire that Never Goes Out. *Psychoanalytic Review, 79*: 271-287

Eigen, M. (1998a)   Soundproof Sanity and Fear of Madness. *Journal of Melanie Klein and Object Relations, 16*: 411-423 [also in Eigen (1999): 171-185]

Eisenstein-Naveh, A.R. (2003)   The Center for Children and Families at Risk: a Facilitating Environment. *Family Journal, 11*: 19

Eklund, M. (2000)   Applying Object Relations Theory to Psychosocial Occupational Therapy: Empirical and Theoretical Considerations. *Occupational Therapy and Mental Health, 15*: 1-26

Ekstrom, S.R. (1984) Self-theory and Psychoanalysis: The Evolution of the Self-concept and its Use in the Clinical Theories of C.G. Jung, D.W. Winnicott and Heinz Kohut. *Dissertation Abstracts (International)*, 45 (1-B): 347

Elmhirst, S.I. (1980) Transitional Objects in Transition. *International Journal of Psychoanalysis*, 61: 367-373

Endoh, T. (1990) An Examination into Transitional Object Origins: Transitional Object and Maternal Care. *Japanese Journal of Developmental Psychology*, 1: 59-69

Endoh, T. (1991) Stress within Mother Infant Interactions as a Determinant of the Occurrence of Infant's Attachment to a Transitional Object. *Japanese Journal of Educational Psychology*, 39: 243-252

Epstein, M. (2005b) A Strange Beauty: Emmanuel Ghent and the Psychologies of East and West. *Psychoanalytic Dialogues*, 15: 125-138

Faber, M.D. (1988) The Pleasure of Rhyme: a Psychoanalytic Note. *International Review of Psychoanalysis*, 15: 375-380

Farhi, N. (1996) The Squiggle Foundation. *Journal of Child Psychotherapy*, 22: 404-406

Farhi, N. (2003a) Introduction to the Gaddini-Winnicott Correspondence. *Psychoanalysis and History*, 5: 3-12

Farhi, N. (2003b) In Her Mother's Name. *Contemporary Analysis*, 39: 75-87

Favero, M.,
Ross, D.R. (2003)
Words and Transitional Phenomena in Psychotherapy. *American Journal of Psychotherapy, 57*: 287-299

Field, N. (1991)
Projective Identification: Mechanism of Mystery? *Journal of Analytic Psychology, 36*: 93-109

Fielding, J. (1985)
'To be or not to be': Hamlet, Culture and Winnicott. *Winnicott Studies, 1*: 58-67

Fielding, J. (1987)
The Creature there Never has Been: 'Alice' and Winnicott. *Winnicott Studies, 2*: 87-100

Fielding, J. (1988)
'Prove True, Imagination': Keats, Coleridge and Winnicott. *Winnicott Studies, 3*: 4-12

Fielding, J. (1991)
'Men Children Only': Adolescence, Fighting and Self-Definition. *Winnicott Studies, 6*: 48-59

Fintzy, R.T. (1971)
Vicissitudes of the Transitional Object in a Borderline Child. *International Journal of Psychoanalysis, 52*: 107-114

Fishman, E.A. (2003)
An Integrative Approach to Parent-child Attachment through the Work of Bowlby, Ainsworth, Winnicott and Kohut. *Dissertation Abstracts (International), 64 (6-B)*: 2914

Flynn, C.,
Stirtzinger, R. (2001)
Understanding a Regressed Adolescent Boy through Story Writing and Winnicott's Intermediate Area. *Arts in Psychotherapy, 28*: 299-309

Fogel, G.I. (1992)
Winnicott's Antitheory and Winnicott's Art: his Significance for Adult Analysis

Psychoanalytic Study of the Child,
42: 205-222

Fonsera, V.R. (1999)   The Phenomenon of Object-Presenting
and its Implications for Development.
International Journal of Psychoanalysis,
80: 885-897

Formaini, H. (2004)   Peering into One of Winnicott's "Blank
Spots". *American Imago, 61:* 527-538

Fowler, C.,   Assessing Transitional Phenomena with
Hilsenroth, M.J.   the Transitional Object Memory Probe.
Handler, L. (1998)   *Bulletin of the Menninger Clinic,*
62: 455-474

Fowler, J.C. (2005)   Transitional Relating and the Capacity
for Play in Treatment. *Journal of*
Personality Assessment, 72: 218-223

Fox, R.P. (1977)   Transitional Phenomena in the
Treatment of a Psychotic Adolescent.
International Journal of Psychiatric
Psychotherapy, 6: 147-164

Frankel, R. (2002b)   Fantasy and Imagination in Winnicott's
Work. *British Journal of Psychotherapy,*
19: 3-20

Fraser, M.L (1997)   The Use of Transitional Space in
Pastoral Counselling: Psychological and
Theological Meaning Making.
Dissertation Abstracts (International),
57 (11-B): 7263

Frazier, R.T. (1993)   Space and Holding: Beginning Pastoral
Counselling with Incest Victims. *Pastoral*
Psychology, 42: 81-94

Frederickson, J.   From Delusion to Play. *Clinical Social*
(1991)   *Work Journal, 19:* 349-362

French, R. (1999)   The Importance of Capacities in
                     Psychoanalysis and the Language of
                     Human Development. *International
                     Journal of Psychoanalysis, 80*: 1215-1226

Fujii, K. (1985)   A Developmental Study on Transitional
                     Objects. *Japanese Journal of Educational
                     Psychology, 33*: 106-114

Fuller, P. (1987)   Mother and Child in Henry Moore and
                     Winnicott. *Winnicott Studies, 2*: 49-70

Gaddini, R. with   Transitional Objects and the Process of
Gaddini, E. (1970)   Individuation: a Study in Three
                     Different Social Groups. *Journal of the
                     American Academy of Child Psychiatry,
                     9*: 347-365

Gaddini, R. (1981)   Bion's "Catastrophic Change" and
                     Winnicott's "Breakdown". *Rivista di
                     Psicoanalisi, 27*: 610-625

Gaddini, R. (1985)   The Precursors of Transitional Objects
                     and Phenomena. *Winnicott Studies,
                     1*: 49-57 (also in *Psychoanalysis and
                     History, 5*: 53-62)

Gaddini, R. (1987)   Early Care and the Roots of
                     Internalization. *International Review of
                     Psychoanalysis, 14*: 321-332

Gaddini, R. (1993)   On Autism. *Psychoanalytic Inquiry,
                     13*: 134-143

Gaddini, R. (1996)   Lullabies and Rhymes in the Emotional
                     Life of Children and No-Longer
                     Children *Winnicott Studies, 11*: 28-40

Gaddini, R. (2003a) Correspondence between Donald
                     Winnicott and Renata Gaddini.
                     Psychoanalysis and History, 5: 13-48

Gaddini, R. (2003b)   The Precursors of Transitional Objects and Phenomena. *Psychoanalysis And History, 5*: 53-61

Gaddini, R. (2003c)   Creativity and the 'Nebulous' in Winnicott (2000). *Psychoanalysis and History, 5*: 63-70

Gaddini, R. (2004)   Thinking about Winnicott and the Origins of the Self. *Psychoanalysis and History, 6*: 225-235

Galligan, A.C. (2000)   That Place where we Live: the Discovery of Self through the Creative Play Experience. *Journal of Child and Adolescent Psychiatric Nursing, 13*: 169-176

Gargiulo, G.J. (1992a)   Sublimation: Winnicottian Reflections. *Psychoanalytic Review, 79*: 327-340

Gargiulo, G.J. (2003)   Hidden Boundaries/Hidden Spaces. *Psychoanalytic Review, 90*: 381-392

Garland, C. (1982)   Group Analysis: Taking the Non-Problem Seriously. *Group Analysis, 15*: 4-14

Gau, J.V. (1991)   The Theological and Psychological Foundations of Adult Faith as Seen in Hans Urs von Balthasar, Melanie Klein and D.W. Winnicott. *Dissertation Abstracts (International), 51 (7-A)*: 2422

Gerity, J.A. (2001)   Josie, Winnicott and the Hungry Ghosts. *Art Therapy, 18*: 35-40

Gerrard, J. (1990)   Use and Abuse in Psychotherapy. *British Journal of Psychotherapy, 7*: 121-128

Gerson, G. (2004)   Winnicott, Participation and Gender. *Feminism and Psychology, 14*: 561-582

Gerson, G. (2005)   Individuality, Deliberation and Welfare
                       in Donald Winnicott. *History of the
                       Human Sciences, 18*: 107-126

Ghent, E. (1990)   Masochism, Subjection, Surrender:
                       Masochism as a Perversion of
                       Surrender. *Contemporary Psychoanalysis,
                       26*: 108-136

Ghent, E. (1992)   Paradox and Process. *Psychoanalytic
                       Dialogues, 2*: 135-139

Gibson, M. (2004)   Melancholy Objects. *Mortality,
                       9*: 285-299

Gillespie, W.H   Donald W. Winnicott. *International
(1971)   Journal of Psychoanalysis, 52*: 227-228

Ginot, E. (2001)   The Holding Environment and
                       Intersubjectivity. *Psychoanalytic
                       Quarterly, 70*: 414-445

Giovacchini, P.L.   Dangerous Transitions and the
(2001b)   Traumatized Adolescent. *American
                       Journal of Psychoanalysis, 61*: 7-22

Glatzer, H.T.,   On Guntrip's Analysis with Fairbairn
Evans, W.N. (1977)   and Winnicott. *International Journal of
                       Psychoanalytic Psychotherapy, 6*: 81-98

Glatzer, H.T. (1985)   Early Mother-Child Relationships:
                       Notes on the pre-œdipal Fantasy.
                       Dynamic Psychotherapy, 3: 27-37

Glenn, L. (1987)   Attachment Theory and Group
                       Analysis: The Group Matrix as a Secure
                       Base. *Group Analysis, 20*: 109-117

Godley, W. (2001a)   Saving Masud Khan. *London Review of
                       Books* (Feb. 22)

Godley, W. (2001b)   My Lost Hours on the Couch. *The
                       (London)Times* (Feb. 23)

Godley, W. (2004)   Commentary on Sandler, A.M. (2004). *International Journal of Psychoanalysis*, *85*: 42-44

Goetzmann, L. (2004)   "Is it Me or isn't it?" – Transplanted Organs and their Donors as Transitional Objects. *American Journal of Psychoanalysis, 64*: 279-289

Goldberg, B. (1999)   Spatial Transitions: Contesting the Limits of Social and Psychic Space. *Psychoanalysis and Contemporary Thought, 22*: 315-341

Golden, G.K. (1991)   A Token of Loving: from Melancholia to Mourning. *Clinical Social Work Journal, 19*: 23

Golden, G.K., Hill, M.A. (1994)   Only Sane: Autistic Barriers in "Boring" Patients. *Clinical Social Work Journal, 22*: 9-26

Goldman, D. (1993a)   In Search of the Real: The Origins and Originality of D.W. Winnicott. *Dissertation Abstracts (International), 54 (4-B)*: 2200...

Goldman, D. (1996)   An Exquisite Corpse: the Strain of Working in and out of Potential Space. *Contemporary Psychoanalysis, 32*: 339-358

Goldman, D. (1998a)   Surviving as Scientist and Dreamer: Winnicott and "The Use of an Object". *Contemporary Psychoanalysis, 34*: 359-368

Gomer, G.M. (1994)   Embodiment as a Central Theme in the Work of D.W. Winnicott. *Dissertation Abstracts (International), 55 (3-A)*: 592

Green, A. (1975)   The Analyst, Symbolization and
                    Absence in the Analytic Setting (on
                    Change in Analytic Practice and
                    Analytic Experience). In Memory of
                    D.W. Winnicott). *International Journal of
                    Psychoanalysis, 56*: 1-22

Green, A. (1997)   The Intuition of the Negative in *Playing
                    and Reality. International Journal of
                    Psychoanalysis, 78*: 1071-1084 [also in
                    Abram, J.(2000a): 85-106, and in
                    Kohon, G. (1999): 205-221 and in
                    Bertolini, M. et al (2001) vol. 1: 43-58]

Green, A. (2004)   Thirdness and Psychoanalytic Concepts.
                    Psychoanalytic Quarterly, 73: 99-135

Green, L.B. (2006) The Value of Hate in the
                    Countertransference. *Clinical Social Work
                    Journal, 34*: 187

Greenacre, P. (1962) Theory of the Parent-Infant
                    Relationship: Further Remarks.
                    *International Journal of Psychoanalysis,
                    43*: 235-237

Greenacre, P. (1969) The Fetish and the Transitional Object.
                    *Psychoanalytic Study of the Child,
                    24*: 144-164

Greenacre, P. (1970) The Transitional Object and the Fetish
                    with Special Reference to the Role of
                    Illusion. *International Journal of
                    Psychoanalysis, 51*: 447-456

Groarke, S. (2000) Winnicott and the Government of the
                    Environment. *Free Associations,
                    46*: 74-104

Groarke, S. (2003) A Life's Work: on Rodman's *Winnicott.
                    Free Associations, 50*: 472-497

Guntrip, H. (1975)   My Experience of Analysis with
                       Fairbairn and Winnicott. *International
                       Review of Psychoanalysis, 2*: 145-15
                       (reprinted with editorial Introduction
                       (1996). *International Journal of
                       Psychoanalysis, 77*: 739-754) [also in
                       Goldman, D. (1993): 139-158]

Gustafson, J.,   Winnicott and Sullivan in the Brief
Dichter, H. (1983)   Psychotherapy Clinic. Part I – Possible
                       Activity and Passivity. Part II – The
                       Necessity for New Theory and Practice.
                       Part III (joint author Kaye, D.) – The
                       Organization of the Clinic and its
                       Unsolved Problems. *Contemporary
                       Psychoanalysis, 19*: 624-672

Hägglund, T-B.   On the Psychoanalytical Conception
(1976)   of D.W. Winnicott. *Psychiatria Fennica*:
                       105-111

Hägglund, T-B.   On the Creative Experience in
(1997)   Psychoanalysis. *Scandinavian
                       Psychoanalytic Review, 20*: 58-74

Hagood, L. (2006)   Awakening to Dreams. *Journal of
                       Religion and Health, 45*: 160-170

Hamalainen, O.   Some Consideration on the Capacity
(1999)   to be Alone. *Scandinavian Psychoanalytic
                       Review, 22*: 33-47

Hamilton, V. (1987)   Rhythm and Interpretation in Maternal
                       Care and Psychoanalysis. *Winnicott
                       Studies, 2*: 32-47

Hamilton, V.   On the Otherness of Being: Winnicott's
(1996a)   Ideas on 'Object Usage' and 'the
                       Experience of Externality'. *Journal of
                       Child Psychotherapy, 22*: 383-391

Hanchett, S., Casale, L. (1976)
The Theory of Transitional Phenomena and Cultural Symbols. *Contemporary Psychoanalysis, 12:* 496-507

Hand, N. (1995)
D.W. Winnicott: the Creative Vision. *Annual Conference Proceedings,* 24: 167-170 (International Association of School Librarianship)

Handler, L. (1999)
Assessment of Playfulness: Hermann Rorschach Meets D.W. Winnicott. *Journal of Personality Assessment,* 72: 208-217

Hanna, E. (1992)
False-Self Sensitivity to Countertransference: Anatomy of a Single Session. *Psychoanalytic Dialogues,* 2: 369-382

Hansen, D., Drowdahl, R. (2006)
The Holding Power of Love: John Wesley and D.W. Winnicott in Conversation. *Journal of Psychology and Christianity, 25:* 54-63

Hardy, D.S. (2000)
Re-describing Relationships in Christian Spiritual Direction using Winnicott's Psychoanalytic Object Relations Theory. *Dissertation Abstracts (International), 60 (12-B):* 6398

Hardy, D.S. (2003)
Finding Spaces: Winnicott, God and Psychic Reality. *International Journal for the Psychology of Religion, 15:* 287-289

Harris, A.L. (2005)
The Holding Environment: Considerations for Healthy Birthing Care. *Dissertation Abstracts (International), 66 (1-B):* 554

Harwood, I. (1986)
The Need for Optimal, Available Caretakers: Moving Towards Extended

	Self-Object Experience. *Group Analysis,* 19: 291-302
Harwood, I. (2005)	Distinguishing Between the Facilitating and the Self-serving Charismatic Group Leader. *Group,* 27: 121-129
Hausner, R. (1985)	Medication and Transitional Phenomena. *International Journal of Psychoanalytic Psychotherapy,* 11: 375-407
Hayman, A. (1997)	Winnicott on Infancy. *Psychoanalytic Psychotherapy in South Africa,* 5: 23-34
Hazell, J. (1991)	Reflections on my Analysis with Guntrip. *Contemporary Psychoanalysis,* 27: 148-166
Healy, K.C. (2004)	Looking at the one we have Pierced: Repentance, Resurrection and Winnicott's "Capacity for Concern". *Pastoral Psychology,* 53: 53-62
Heard, D.H. (1978)	From Object Relations to Attachment Theory: a Basis for Family Therapy. *British Journal of Medical Psychology,* 51: 67-76
Hearst, L. (1981)	Emergence of the Mother in the Group. *Group Analysis,* 14: 25-32
Henderson, J. (1973)	Community Transference: with Notes on the Counter Response. *Bulletin of the Menninger Clinic,* 37: 258-269
Henderson, J. (1974)	Community Transference Reviewed: with Notes on the Clinic Community Interface. *Journal of the American Academy of Psychoanalysis,* 2: 113-128
Henderson, J. (1984)	Play in the Psychotherapy of Self-object Relating. *Canadian Journal of Psychiatry,* 29: 417-424

Henriques, M. (1993)	'Sum, I Am'. *Winnicott Studies, 8 (Autumn)*: 47-49
Hernandez, M. (1998)	Winnicott's "Fear of Breakdown": on and Beyond. *Trauma Diacritics, 28*: 134-143
Hirsch, A.T. (1986)	Predicting Child Adjustment from Early Mothering Behavior: A Longitudinal Examination of Winnicott's Theory. *Dissertation Abstracts (International), 46 (8-B)*: 2816
Hobson, P. (1998)	On Relationships and Relatedness: Winnicott's Set Situation. *Infant Behaviour and Research, 21*: 135
Hobson, P. et al (2005)	Personal Relatedness and Attachment in Infants and Mothers with Borderline Personality Disorder. *Development and Psychopathology, 17*: 329-347
Hoffman, M. (2004)	From Enemy Combatant to Strange Bedfellow: The Role of Religious Narratives in the Work of W.R.D. Fairbairn and D.W. Winnicott. *Psychoanalytic Dialogues, 14*: 769-784
Hoffmann, J.M. (2000)	There is Such a Thing as an Infant. *Infant Mental Health Journal, 21*: 42-51
Hogan, P.C. (1992)	The Politics of Otherness in Clinical Psychoanalysis: Racism as Pathogen in a Case of D.W. Winnicott. *Literature and Psychology, 38*: 36-43
Hopkins, B. (1984)	Keats' Negative Capability and Winnicott's Creative Play. *American Imago, 41*: 85-100
Hopkins, B. (1989)	Jesus and Object-use: a Winnicottian Account of the Resurrection Myth.

International Review of Psychoanalysis,
16: 93-100

Hopkins, B. (1997)   Winnicott and the Capacity to Believe.
                       International Journal of Psychoanalysis,
                       78: 485-498 [also in *PsyART, 7,* 2003
                       (June-Sept)]

Hopkins, B. (2004)   Wordsworth, Winnicott and the Claims
                       of the "Real". *PsyART, 8*

Hopkins, B. (2005)   Winnicott and Imprisonment. *American
                       Imago, 62*: 269-284

Hopkins, J. (1996)   The Dangers and Deprivations of
                       Too-Good Mothering: a Type of Spoiling
                       Observed by Winnicott. *Journal of Child
                       Psychotherapy, 22*: 407-422 (also in
                       *Educational Therapy & Therapeutic
                       Teaching, 9,* 2000: 6-17)

Hopkins, L.B.   D.W. Winnicott's Analysis of Masud
(1998)   Khan: a Preliminary Study of Failures of
                       Object Usage. *Contemporary
                       Psychoanalysis, 34*: 5-47

Hopkins, L.B.   Masud Khan's Application of
(2000)   Winnicott's "Play" Techniques to
                       Analytic Consultation and Treatment of
                       Adults. *Contemporary Psychoanalysis,
                       36*: 639-663

Hopkins, L.B.   Red Shoes, Untapped Madness and
(2004a)   Winnicott on the Cross: an Interview
                       with Marion Milner. *Annual of
                       Psychoanalysis, 14*: 233-244

Hopkins, L.B   How Masud Khan Fell into
(2004b)   Psychoanalysis. *American Imago,
                       61*: 483-494

Hutter, A.D. (1982)   Poetry in Psychoanalysis: Hopkins, Rossetti, Winnicott. *International Review of Psychoanalysis, 9*: 303-316 [also in Rudnytsky (1993): 63-86]

Hyllienmark, G. (1986)   Smoking as a Transitional Object. *British Journal of Medical Psychology, 59*: 263-267

Irvine, E. (1973)   The Role of Donald Winnicott: Healing, Teaching, Nurture. *British Journal of Social Work, 3*: 383-390

Issroff, J. (1983)   A Reaction to reading *Boundary and Space: an Introduction to the Work of D.W. Winnicott* by Madeleine Davis and David Wallbridge. *International Review of Psychoanalysis, 10*: 231-235

Issroff, J. (1991)   The Healthy Adolescent and his Creativity. *Psychiatriki, 2*: 118-130

Issroff, J. (1993)   Kitchen Therapy: Remembering the 'Theory of Salivation' and Advocating Cooking as an Aid in Psychoanalytic Child Psychotherapy with Latency Age Children. *Winnicott Studies, 7 (Spring)*: 67-84

Issroff, J. (1995)   D.W. Winnicott's Ability to Facilitate Turning Points Voices. *Art and Science of Psychotherapy, 31*: 4-10

Jackson, J. (1996)   An Experimental Investigation of Winnicott's Set Situation: a Study of South African White, Black and Institutionalized Infants aged 7 to 9 moths old. *Journal of Child Psychotherapy, 27*: 343-361

Jallinsky, S. (1994)   Donald Winnicott, the Illusionist of Psychoanalysis. *Encounters (Argentina), 1*: 41-49

James, D.C. (1984)   Bion's 'Containing' and Winnicott's "Holding" in the Context of the Group Matrix. *International Journal of Group Psychotherapy, 34*: 201-213

James, M. (1962)   Infantile Narcissistic Trauma – Observations on Winnicott's Work in Infant Care and Child Development. *International Journal of Psychoanalysis, 43*: 69-80

James, M. (1985)   The Essential Contribution of D.W. Winnicott. *Winnicott Studies, 1*: 26-35

Jarmon, H. (1990)   The Supervisory Experience: An Object Relations Perspective. *Psychotherapy, 27*: 195-201

Jemstedt, A. (1993)   A Comment on Teurnell's "The Piggle – a Sexually Abused Girl". *International Forum of Psychoanalysis, 2*: 145-148

Jemstedt, A. (2000)   Potential Space: The Place of Encounter between Inner and Outer Reality. *International Forum of Psychoanalysis, 9*: 124-131

Jerry, P.A. (1994)   Winnicott's Therapeutic Consultation and the Adolescent Patient. *Crisis Intervention and Time-limited Treatment, 1*: 61-72

Johns, J. (1996)   The Capacity to be Alone. *Journal of Child Psychotherapy, 22*: 373-376

Johnson, S. (2005)   D.W.Winnicott: "The Aims of Psychoanalytical Treatment". *Journal of the British Association of Psychotherapists, 43*: 124-128

Jones, J.W. (1992)   Knowledge in Transition: Toward a Winnicottian Epistomology. *Psychoanalytic Review, 79*: 223-237

Jones, K. (2005)   The Role of Father in Psychoanalytic
                          Theory: Historical and Contemporary
                          Trends. *Smith College Studies in Social
                          Work, 75*: 7-28

Jordan, M.J. (1998)   Winnicott's Contribution to the Concept
                          of Patient Care in Medicine. *Dissertation
                          Abstracts (International), 59 (5-B)*: 2104

Kafka, J.S. (1969)   The Body as Transitional Object: a
                          Psychoanalytic Study of A Self-
                          mutilating Patient. *British Journal of
                          Medicine, 43*: 207-212

Kahn, E.M. (1986)   The Discovery of the True Self. *Clinical
                          Social Work Journal, 14*: 310-320

Kahne, M.J. (1967)   On the Persistence of Transitional
                          Phenomena into Adult Life. *International
                          Journal of Psychoanalysis, 48*: 247-258

Kahr, B. (1996a)   Donald Winnicott and the Foundations
                          of Child Psychotherapy. *Journal of Child
                          Psychotherapy, 22*: 327-42

Kahr, B. (1999a)   Winnicott's Boundaries. *Journal of
                          Communicative Psychoanalysis and
                          Psychotherapy, 12*: 66-70

Kahr, B. (2000a)   Ethical Dilemmas of the Psycho-
                          analytical Biographer: the Case of
                          Donald Winnicott. *Free Associations, 8*:
                          105-120

Kahr, B. (2003b)   Masud Khan's Analysis with Donald
                          Winnicott: on the Hazards of
                          Befriending a Patient. *Free Associations,
                          10*: 190-222

Kahr, B. (2004)   Rodman, R. 1934-2004. *American Imago,
                          61*: 539-542

Kanter, J. (1990)   Community-based Management of
                     Psychotic Clients: the Contributions of
                     D.W. and Clare Winnicott. *Clinical Social
                     Work Journal, 18*: 23-41

Kanter, J. (2000)   The Untold Story of Clare and Donald
                     Winnicott: How Social Work Influenced
                     Modern Psychoanalysis. *Clinical Social
                     Work Journal, 28*: 245-262

Kanter, J. (2004a)   "Let's Never Ask him what to Do":
                     Clare Britton's Transformative Impact
                     on Donald Winnicott. *American Imago,
                     61*: 457-482

Karnac, H. (1991)   On Psychoanalytic Bookselling
                     1950-1989 (paper presented at a meeting
                     of the Applied Section of the British
                     Psychoanalytic Society 26th June, 1991)

Kegerreis, D. (1999) A Benevolently Dangerous Growth:
                     Surviving the Trauma of Change with
                     Borderline Patients in Group
                     Psychotherapy. *Group Analysis,
                     32*: 427-438

Kennard, D. (1989)   The Therapeutic Community Impulse:
                     What Makes it Grow? *International
                     Journal of Therapeutic Communities,
                     10*: 155-163

Kerr, A. (1991)   The Unmet-Need: Can Severely
                     Disturbed Children Become Good-
                     Enough Parents? *Winnicott Studies,
                     6*: 21-38

Khan, M.M.R.   Obituary: D.W. Winnicott. *British
(1971a)   Journal of Medical Psychology,
                     44*: 387-388

Khan, M.M.R. (1971b) Donald Winnicott. *International Journal of Psychoanalysis, 52*: 225-226 [also in Goldman, D. (1993) with Tizard, J.P.M. (1971): 111-116]

King, L. (1994) 'There is No Such Thing as a Mother'. *Winnicott Studies, 9*: 18-24

Kingsbury, P. (2003) Psychoanalysis, a Gay Spatial Science? *Social and Cultural Geography, 4*: 347-367

Kinst, J.M. (2003) Trust, Emptiness and the Self in the Practice of Soto Zen Buddhism: an Exploration including the Insights of Self-psychology – Erik Erikson and D.W. Winnicott. *Dissertation Abstracts (International), 64 (6-A)*: 2122

Kirshner, L.A. (1991) The Concept of the Self in Psychoanalytic Theory and its Philosophical Foundations. *Journal of the American Psychoanalytic Association, 39*: 157-182

Kluzer, A.U. (1992) The Significance of Illusion in the Work of Freud and Winnicott: a Controversial Issue. *International Review of Psychoanalysis, 19*: 179-187

Knauss, W. (1999) The Creativity of Destructive Fantasies. *Group Analysis, 32*: 397-411

Koepele, K.C., Teixeira. M.A. (2000) Annihilation Anxiety: a Metapsychological Exploration of D.W. Winnicott's The Piggle. *Psychoanalysis and Psychotherapy, 17*: 229-256

Konigsberg, I. (1996) Transitional Phenomena, Transitional Space, Creativity and Spectatorship in Film. *Psychoanalytic Review, 83*: 865-889

Kristovich, D. (2002)
Late Adolescents' Use of Music as Transitional Space. *Dissertation Abstracts (Internatonal), 62 (8-A)*: 2883

Kuhns, R. (1992)
Loss and Creativity: Notes on Winnicott and Nineteenth Century American Poets. *Psychoanalytic Review, 79*: 197-208

Kulka, R. (1995)
Revolutionary Evolution in Psychoanalysis. *Israel Journal of Psychotherapy, 9*: 100-110

Kuriloff, E. (1998)
Winnicott and Sullivan: Playing with the Interpersonal Model in a Transitional Space. *Contemporary Psychoanalysis, 34*: 379-388

Kwawer, J.S. (1981)
Object Relations and Interpersonal Theories. *Contemporary Psychoanalysis, 17*: 276-288

Kwawer, J.S. (1998)
On Using Winnicott. *Contemporary Psychoanalysis, 34*: 389-396

Lambert, K. (1987)
Some Religious Implications of the Work of Freud, Jung and Winnicott. *Winnicott Studies, 2*: 49-70

Lamothe, R. (1995)
Messengers of Hate: a Psychoanalytic and Theological Analysis of Intransigence in Religion. *Dissertation Abstracts (International), 56 (1-B)*: 0557

Lamothe, R. (2000)
The Birth of Reality: Psychoanalytic Developmental Considerations. *American Journal of Psychotherapy, 54*: 355-371

Lamothe, R. (2005a)
Creating Space: the Fourfold Dynamics of Potential Space. *Psychoanalytic Psychology, 22*: 207-233

Lanyado, M. (1996)   Winnicott's Children: the Holding
                       Environment and Thepautic
                       Communication in Brief and
                       Non-intensive Work. *Journal of Child
                       Psychotherapy, 22*: 423-443

Lanyado, M. (2003)   The Emotional Tasks of Moving from
                       Fostering to Adoption: Transitions,
                       Attachment, Separation and Loss.
                       *Clinical Child Psychology and Psychiatry,
                       8*: 337-349

Larkin, J. (1987)   The Judicious Use of 'Good Enough'
                       Therapy in the Treatment of Borderline
                       and Narcissistic Disorders. *International
                       Journal of Partial Hospitalization,
                       4*: 227-234

Larson, R.,   The Capacity to be Alone as a Stress
Lee, M. (1996)   Buffer. *Journal of Social Psychology,
                       136*: 5-16

Last, J.M. (1988)   Transitional Relatedness and
                       Psychotherapeutic Growth.
                       Psychotherapy, 25: 185-190

Lavender, J. (1992)   Winnicott's Mind Psyche and its
                       Treatment. *American Journal of Dance
                       Therapy, 14*: 31-39

Lee, C. (1985)   The Good-Enough Family. *Journal of
                       Psychology and Theology, 13*: 182-189

Leiman, M. (1992)   The Concept of Sign in the Work of
                       Vygotsky, Winnicott and Bakhtin:
                       Further Integration of Object Relation
                       Theory and Activity Theory. *British
                       Journal of Medical Psychology, 65*: 209-221

Lemma, A. (2005)   The Many Faces of Lying. *International
                       Journal of Psychoanalysis, 86*: 737-753

Lerner, P.M. (1985)   The False Self Concept and its
                       Measurement. *Ontario Psychologist, 17*: 3-6

Lerner, P.M. (2005)   On Developing a Clinical Sense of Self.
                       Journal of Personality Assessment, 84: 21

Le Roux, E.E. (2001)   Loneliness in the Therapeutic Dialogue:
                       the Concepts of Winnicott and
                       Heidegger. *Dissertation Abstracts
                       (International), 61 (9-B)*: 4991

Levinge, A. (1999)   Music Therapy and the Theories of
                       Donald Winnicott. *Ph.D. Thesis*:
                       Birmingham 51-10071

Levy. E.,   D.W. Winnicott in the Literature
Campbell, K.J.   Classroom. *Teaching English in the
(2000)   Two Year College, 27*: 320-328

Litt, C.J. (1986)   Theories of Transitional Object
                       Attachment: an Overview. *International
                       Journal of Behavioral Development,
                       9*: 383-399

Little, M.I. (1985)   Winnicott Working in Areas where
                       Psychotic Anxieties Predominate: a
                       Personal Record. *Free Associations,
                       3*: 9-42

Little, M.I. (1987)   On the Value of Regression to
                       Dependence. *Free Associations, 10*: 7-22

Lombardie, K.L.   When a Body Meets a Body:
(2006)   a Neo-Kleinian View of Language and
                       Bodily Experience. *Psychoanalytic
                       Review, 93*: 379-390

Lonie, I. (1985)   From Humpty Dumpty to Rapunzel:
                       Theoretical Formulations Concerning
                       Borderline Personality Disorders.
                       *Australian and New Zealand Journal of
                       Psychiatry, 19*: 372-381

Lonie, I. (1992) The Winnicott Baby. *Australian Journal of Psychotherapy, 11*: 11-18

Lopez-Corvo, R.E. (2006) The Forgotten Self: with the Case of Bion's Theory of Negative Links. *Psychoanalytic Review, 93*: 363-377

Luborsky, E.B. (2001) "No Talking": the Possibility of Play. *Journal of Clinical Psychoanalysis, 10*: 445-459

Lucas, T., Hughes, P.M. (1988) Holding and Holding-on: Using Winnicott's Ideas in Group Psychotherapy with twelve- to thirteen-year-olds. *Group Analysis, 21*: 135-151

Luepnitz, D. (2005) Orwell, Winnicott and Lacan: Notes of a Psychoanalyst from Project H.O.M.E. *Psychoanalysis, Culture and Society, 10*: 328-334

MacAskill, N.D. (1982) The Theory of Transitional Phenomena and its Application to the Psychotherapy of the Borderline Patient. *British Journal of Medical Psychology, 55*: 349-360

McCarthy, J.B. (1995) Adolescent Character Formation and Psychoanalytic Theory. *American Journal of Psychotherapy, 55*: 245-267

McCarthy, J.B. (2003) Disillusionments and Devaluation in Winnicott's Analysis of Masud Khan. *American Journal of Psychotherapy, 63*: 81-92

McDonald, M. (1970) Traditional Tunes and Musical Development. *Psychoanalytic Study of the Child, 25*: 503-520

McDougall, J. (1993) Of Sleep and Dream. *International Forum of Psychoanalysis, 2*: 204-218

McDougall, J. (1999)   Violence and Creativity. *Scandinavian Psychoanalytic Review,* 22: 207-217

Madden, K. (1997)   The Dark Interval: Inner Transformation Through Mourning and Memory. *Journal of Religion and Health,* 36: 29-52

Magro, E.P. (2001)   The Role of Imagination in Catechesis in Light of D.W. Winnicott's Theory of Emotional Development. *Dissertation Abstracts (International), 61 (11-A)*: 4422

Marlkillie, R. (1996)   Guntrip's Analysis with Fairbairn and Winnicott. *International Journal of Psychoanalysis,* 77: 763-771

Martellock, A.K. (2003)   She who is Not: a Psychobiography of Catherine of Siena Using the Theories of D.W. Winnicott. *Dissertation Abstracts (International), 64 (1-B)*: 1910

Meares, R. (1986)   On the Ownership of Thought: an Approach to the Origins of Separation Anxiety. *Psychiatry, 49*: 80-91

Mednick, R.A. (1982)   Guntrip's "Diary": Resistance or Mirroring? *Hillside Journal of Clinical Psychiatry, 4*: 235-249

Meissner, W.W. (1992)   Religious Thinking as Transitional Conceptualization. *Psychoanalytic Review, 79*: 175-196

Meline, C.W. (2004)   The Creative Dimension of Subjectivity in Lacan, Freud and Winnicott. *Dissertation Abstracts (International), 65 (4-A)*: 1398

Mendelsohn, E. (2002)   The Analyst's Bad-Enough Participation. *Psychoanalytic Dialogues, 12*: 331-358

Mesas, B.C. (1991) The Brief Psychoanalytic Psychotherapy technique of D.W. Winnicott. *Dissertation Abstracts (International)*, *52 (4-B)*: 2307-2308

Mezan, P. (1985) Beyond the Reality Principle: An Enquiry into the Ego Psychology of D.W. Winnicott. *Dissertation Abstracts (International)*, *46 (8-B)*: 1693-1694

Mikardo, J. (1996) Hate in the Countertransference. *Journal of Child Psychotherapy*, *22*: 398-401

Mikics, D. (2006) Psychoanalytic Criticism of Shakespeare. *Literature Compass*, *3*: 529-546

Milivojevic, L., Strakali, I.S. (2004) Importance of Object Relations for Development of Capacity for Normal Love. *Croatian Medical Journal*, *45*: 18-24

Miller, M.C. (1992) Winnicott Unbound: The Fiction of Philip Roth and the Sharing of Potential Space. *International Review of Psychoanalysis*, *19*: 445-456

Minsky, R. (1995) Reaching Beyond Denial – sight and insight – a Way Forward? (drawing on the theory of Freud, Klein, Winnicott, Lacan and Kristeva). *Free Associations*, *5*: 326-351

Mirella-Back, J. (2000) The Relationship between Maternal History of Victimization, Arrests, Social Supports and Abusive Parenting Behavior: a Winnicottian Perspective. *Dissertation Abstracts (International)*, *60 (9-A)*: 3528

Mitchell, G. (2002) An Introduction to the Work of D.W. Winnicott. *Representing Children*, *14*: 251-273

Mitchell, L. (2000)   Attachment to the Missing Object:
                      Infidelity and the Missing Love. *Journal of
                      Applied Psychoanalytic Studies*, 2: 383-395

Modell, A.H. (1970)   The Transitional Object and the Creative
                      Act. *Psychoanalytic Quarterly*, 39: 240-250

Modell, A.H. (1975)   A Narcissistic Defence against Affects
                      and the Illusion of Self-sufficiency.
                      International Journal of Psychoanalysis,
                      56: 275-282

Modell, A.H. (1985)   The Works of Winnicott and the
                      Evolution of his Thought. *Journal of the
                      American Psychoanalytic Association*,
                      33(S): 1133-137

Mody, Z.R.,   Milieu for Change: the Therapeutic
Bucchold, E.S.   Education of a Mother-Child
(1988)   Relationship. *Journal of Child
                      Psychotherapy*, 14: 81-97

Montreal Winnicott   A Note on What Winnicott Might have
Study Group (2003)   Said about the Terrorist Attack on the
                      World Centre, in New York 11
                      September 2001. *Free Associations*,
                      54: 190-202

Morey, J.R. (2005)   Winnicott's Splitting Headache:
                      Considering the Gap between Jungian
                      and Object Relations Concepts. *Journal
                      of Analytic Psychology*, 50: 330-350

Morse, S.J. (1972)   Structure and Reconstruction: a Critical
                      Comparison of Michael Balint and D.W.
                      Winnicott. *International Journal of
                      Psychoanalysis*, 53: 487-50

Murray, L. (1989)   Winnicott and the Developmental
                      Psychology of Infancy. *British Journal of
                      Psychotherapy*, 5: 333-348

Murray, L. (1996)   Winnicott: a Research Perspective.
                     Journal of Child Psychotherapy, 22: 362-372

Nayowith, S.A.   The Development of a "Good-enough
(2000)   Shelter" and a "Secure Base".
                    Dissertation Abstracts (International),
                    61 (2-A): 770

Neri, C. (2005)   What is the Function of Faith and Trust
                    in Psychoanalysis? *International Journal
                    Of Psychoanalysis, 86*: 79-98

Newman, A. (1985)   D.W. Winnicott and Friendship or
                    Where is Playing? *Winnicott Studies*,
                    1: 68-76

Newman, A. (1988)   The Breakdown that Was: Winnicott and
                    the Fear of Breakdown. *Winnicott
                    Studies*, 3: 36-47

Newman, A. (1991)   The Breakdown That Was, part two:
                    'There is No Such Thing as a Baby'
                    Winnicott Studies, 6: 39-47

Newman, K. (1999)   The Usable Analyst: the Role of the
                    Affective Engagement of the Analyst in
                    Reaching Usability. *Annual of
                    Psychoanalysis, 26*: 175-194

Newman, K.M.   Winnicott Goes to the Movies:
(1996)   the False Self in Ordinary People.
                    Psychoanalytic Quarterly, 65: 787-807

Nickman, S.L. (2004) The Holding Environment in Adoption.
                     *Journal of Infant Child and Adolescent
                     Psychotherapy, 3*: 329-341

Nolasco, R.R. (2002) Interpreting the Transforming Function
                     of Eucharist using Winnicott's Object
                     Relations Theory and Neville's Theory
                     of Religious Symbols. *Dissertations
                     Abstracts (International), 63 (3-A)*: 1007

Nutkevitch, I.V. (1987) The Transitional Object and Transitional Phenomena: Winnicott Revisited. *Dissertation Abstracts (International), 47 (9-B)*: 3966

Ochsner, J.K. (2000) Behind the Mask: A Psychoanalytic Perspective on Interaction in the Design Studio. *Journal of Architectural Education, 53*: 194-206

Ogden, T.H. (1979) On Projective Identification. *International Journal of Psychoanalysis, 60*: 357-373

Ogden, T.H. (1983) The Concept of Internal Object Relations. *International Journal of Psychoanalysis, 64:* 227-241

Ogden, T.H. (1985a) On Potential Space. *International Journal of Psychoanalysis, 66*: 129-141 [also in Giovacchini, P. (1990a): 90-112 and in Goldman, D. (1993): 223-240]

Ogden, T.H. (1985b) The Mother, The Infant and the Matrix: Interpretations of Aspects of the Work of Donald Winnicott. *Contemporary Psychoanalysis, 21*: 346-371

Ogden, T.H. (1987) The Transitional œdipal Relationship in Female Development. *International Journal of Psychoanalysis, 68*: 485-498 [also in Ogden, T.H. (1989a): 109-140]

Ogden, T.H. (1988) Misrecognitions and the Fear of Not Knowing. *Psychoanalytic Quarterly, 57*: 643-666

Ogden, T.H. (1989c) On the Concept of an Autistic-Contiguous Position. *International Journal of Psychoanalysis, 70*: 127-140 [also in Ogden, T.H. (1989a): 47-81]

Ogden, T.H. (1991)   Some Theoretical Concepts on Personal
                      Isolation. *Psychoanalytic Dialogues,*
                      1: 377-390 [also in Ogden, T.H. (1994):
                      167-181]

Ogden, T.H. (1992)   The Dialectically Constituted/
                      Decentred Subject of Psychoanalysis, II:
                      the Contributions of Klein and
                      Winnicott. *International Journal of*
                      Psychoanalysis, 73: 613-626 [also in
                      Ogden, T.H. (1994): 33-60]

Ogden, T.H. (1995)   Analyzing Forms of Aliveness and
                      Deadness of the Transference Counter-
                      transference *International Journal of*
                      Psychoanalysis, 76: 695-709 [also in
                      Ogden, T.H. (1997a): 23-63]

Ogden, T.H.   Reading Winnicott. *Psychoanalytic*
(2001b)   *Quarterly, 70*: 299-324 [also in Ogden,
                      T.H. (2001b): 205-235]

Ogden, T.H. (2004)   On Holding and Containing, Being and
                      Dreaming. *International Journal of*
                      Psychoanalysis, 86: 737-753

Olvin, M.,   The Pre-Conscious and Potential
Lombardi, K.L.   Space. *Psychoanalytic Review,*
(1990)   *77*: 573-587

Orbach, S. (1995)   Countertransference and the False Body.
                      Winnicott Studies, 10: 3-13

Ornstein, A. (1984)   The Function of Play in the Process of
                      Psychotherapy. *Annual of Psychoanalysis,*
                      12: 349-366

Ornston, D. (1978)   Projective Identification and Maternal
                      Impingement. *International Journal of*
                      Psychoanalytic Psychotherapy, 7: 508-532

Padel, J. (1988)	An Appreciation of John Turner's Paper "Wordsworth and Winnicott in the Play Area". *International Review of Psychoanalysis, 15*: 497-498

Padel, J. (1991)	The Psychoanalytic Theories of Melanie Klein and Donald Winnicott and their Interaction in the British Society of Psychoanalysis. *Psychoanalytic Review, 78*: 324-345

Padel, J. (1996)	The Case of Harry Guntrip. *International Journal of Psychoanalysis, 77*: 755-761

Pang, L.B. (1997)	The Psychological Meaning of Playing: a Phenomenological Exploration of the Subjective Experience of Adults. *Dissertation Abstracts (International), 58 (5-B)*: 2722

Parker, R. (1994)	Maternal Ambivalence. *Winnicott Studies, 9*: 3-17

Parsons, Marianne (1999)	The Logic of Play in Psychoanalysis. *International Journal of Psychoanalysis, 80*: 871-884

Pass, S.F. (1997)	The Relationship between Mother's Response to Children's Developing Autonomy and Children's Utilization of Symbolic Play. *Dissertation Abstracts (International), 57 (7-B)*: 4749

Pedder, J.R. (1977)	The Role of Space and Location in Psychotherapy, Play and Theatre. *International Review of Psychoanalysis, 4*: 215-223

Pedder, J.R. (1982)	Failure to Mourn, and Melancholia. *British Journal of Psychiatry, 141*: 329-337

Peltz, R. (2005)   The Manic Society. *Psychoanalytic Dialogues*, *15*: 347-366

Phillips, A. (1989)   Winnicott: an Introduction. *British Journal of Psychiatry*, *155*: 612-618

Pinkney, T.A. (1982)   An Interpretation of Some Aspects of the Work of T.S. Eliot in the Light of the Psychoanalysis of Melanie Klein and D.W. Winnicott. *M. Litt. Thesis* Oxford 32-363

Pizer, S.A. (1992)   The Negotiation of Paradox in the Analytic Process. *Psychoanalytic Dialogues*, *2*: 215-240

Pontalis, J.-B. (2006)   Noble Encounters. *American Imago*, *63*: 145-157

Posner, B.M. et al   In Search of Winnicott's Aggression.
(2001)   *Psychoanalytic Study of the Child*, *56*: 171-192

Pound, K.S. (2002)   The Challenges for Self-disclosure for Student Therapists and the Development of the Provisional Clinical Self. *Dissertation Abstracts (International)*, *63 (4-B)*: 2069

Price, A. (1994)   Effects of Maternal Deprivation on the Capacity to Play: a Winnicottian Perspective on Work with Inner City Children. *Psychoanalytic Psychology*, *11*: 341-355

Priel, B. (1999)   Bakhtin and Winnicott: On Dialogue, Self and Cure. *Psychoanalytic Dialogues*, *9*: 487-504

Prodgers, A. (1990)   The Dual Nature of the Group as Mother: the Uroboric Container. *Group Analysis*, *23*: 17-30

Propato, N.C. (1994)   The Third Space: its Theoretical
                       Fundamentation and its Application in
                       Psychoanalytical Practice (the Thematic
                       of the Psychic Spaces). *Encounters
                       (Argentina)*, 1: 71-77

Pullen, N.C. (2002)   Layers of Self: Extending Winnicott's
                       Theory on the Self. *Dissertation Abstracts
                       (International)*, 62 (11-B): 5387

Rafferty, M.A. (2000) A Conceptual Model for Clinical
                       Supervision in Nursing and Health
                       Visiting Based on Winnicott's (1960)
                       Theory of the Parent-Infant
                       Relationship. *Journal of Psychiatric and
                       Mental Health Nursing*, 7: 153-161

Ratner, D.G. (2006)   A Buddhist Interpretation of
                       D.W. Winnicott. *Dissertation Abstracts
                       (International)*, 66 (9-B): 5072

Reardon, D.B. (2002)   Erotic Play and Live Dreaming.
                       Dissertation Abstracts (International),
                       63 (4-B): 2070

Rees, C. (1995)   The Dialectic between Holding and
                       Interpreting in Winnicott's
                       Psychotherapy. *Psychoanalytic
                       Psychotherapy in South Africa*, 3: 13-30

Reeves, C. (1993)   The Role of Milieu Therapy in the
                       Treatment of Sexually Abused Children.
                       Child and Youth Care Forum, 22: 111-124

Reeves, C. (1996a)   Interview with Barbara Dockar-
                       Drysdale. *Journal of Child Psychotherapy*,
                       22: 402-403

Reeves, C. (1996b)   Transition and Transience: Winnicott on
                       Leaving and Dying. *Journal of Child
                       Psychotherapy*, 22: 444-455

Reeves, C. (2002) A Necessary Conjunction: Docker-Drysdale and Winnicott. *Journal of Child Psychotherapy, 28*: 3-28

Reeves, C. (2003) Creative Space: a Winnicottian Perspective on Child Psychotherapy in Britain - Past, Present and Future. *Insikten, 4 (Sweden)*: 22-29

Reeves, C. (2004a) On Being "Intrinsical": a Winnicott Enigma. *American Imago, 61*: 427-456

Reiland, P.H. (2004) The Object beyond Objects and the Sacred: Reflection on Freud's and Winnicott's Contribution to the Psychology of Religion. *Scandinavian Psychoanalytical Review, 27*: 78-86

Reis, B.E. (2004) You are Requested to Close your Eyes. *Psychoanalytic Dialogues, 14*: 349-371

Resch, R.C. et al (1988) The Later Creation of a Transitional Object. *Psychoanalytical Psychology, 5*: 369-387

Rich, W. (2001) Grace and Imagination: from Fear to Freedom. *Journal of Religion and Health, 40*: 213-230

Richards, V. (1993) Time-Sickness. *Winnicott Studies, 8 (Autumn)*: 17-29

Richards, V. (1994) Mothers, Mirrors and Masks. *Winnicott Studies, 9*: 35-48

Ringel, S. (2003) Play and Impersonation: Finding the Right Intersubjective Rhythm. *Clinical Social Work Journal, 31*: 371-381

Romano, E. (1994) Time for Encounter, Regression and Creativity in Winnicott. *Encounters (Argentina), 1*: 25-39

Rosegrant, J. (2002)   Rhymes and Animals: Aspects of the Development of Play. *Journal of the American Psychoanalytic Society,* *50 (4)*: 1321-1328

Rosorea, B.P. (2004)   Abstinence and Neutrality Revisited: an Examination of Two Child Therapy Cases – Axline's Dibs and Winnicott's Piggle. *Dissertation Abstracts (International), 65 (6-B)*: 3181

Ross, M. (2000)   "Good-enough" isn't so Bad: Thinking about Success and Failure in Ethnic Conflict Management. *Journal of Peace Psychology, 6*: 37-47

Rudnytsky, P. (1988)   Redefining the Revenant: Guilt and Sibling Loss in Guntrip and Freud. *Psychoanalytical Study of the Child, 43*: 423-432

Rudnytsky, P. (1989)   Winnicott and Freud. *Psychoanalytical Study of the Child, 44*: 331-350

Russell, J. (2003)   Differance and Psychic Space. *American Imago, 60*: 501

Russo, L. (1991)   Some Notes on the Letters of D.W. Winnicott. *Rivista di Psicoanalisi, 37*: 668-693

Rycroft, C. (1970)   Symbolism and its Relation to Primary and Secondary Sources. *Rivista di Psicanalisi, 27*: 365-392

Sabbadini, A. (2003)   Encounter with Renata Gaddini. *Psychoanalysis and History, 5*: 1-2

Samuels, L. (1996)   A Historical Analysis of Winnicott's "The Use of an Object". *Winnicott Studies, 11*: 41-50

Sandbank, T. (1993) Psychoanalysis and Maternal Work – some Parallels. *International Journal of Psychoanalysis*, 4: 15-727

Sandler, AM. (2004) Institutional Responses to Boundary Violations: the Case of Masud Khan. *International Journal of Psychoanalysis*, 85: 38-41

Sayers, J. (2002) Marion Milner, Mysticism and Psychoanalysis. *International Journal of Psychoanalysis*, 83: 105-120

Sayers, J. (2004a) Intersubjective Winnicott. *American Imago*, 61: 519-526

Sayers, J. (2004c) Robert Rodman: a Memorial Tribute. *American Imago*, 61: 519-525

Schacht, L. (1972) Psychoanalytic Facilitation into the "Subject-Uses-Subject" Phase of Maturation. *International Journal of Child Psychotherapy*, 1: 71-88

Schacht, L. (1988) Winnicott's Position in Regard to the Self with Special Reference to Childhood. *International Review of Psychoanalysis*, 15: 515-529

Schacht, L. (2003) The Paradox of Creativity. *Psychoanalysis in Europe*, 57: 54-62

Scharff, J.S. (2003) The British Object Relation Theorists: Fairbairn, Winnicott, Balint, Guntrip, Sutherland and Bowlby. [Paper read at a symposium "Understanding Dissidence and Controversy in the History of Psychoanalysis" – published 2004 New York: Other Press: 175-200]

Schlachet, P.J. (1986) The Concept of Group Space. *International Journal of Group Psychotherapy*, 36: 33-53

Schlauch, C.R. (1990) Illustrating Two Complementary Enterprises at the Interface of Psychology and Religion through Reading Winnicott. *Pastoral Psychology*, 39: 47-63

Schlierf, C. (1983) Transitional Objects and Object Relations in a Case of Anxiety Neurosis. *International Review of Psychoanalysis*, 10: 319-332

Schneider, E. (1996) Holding and Caring: a Borderline Patient in a New Psychotherapy Group. *Group Analysis*, 29: 125-126

Schneiderman, L. (1999) Willa Cather: Transitional Object and Creativity. *Imagination, Cognition and Personality*, 19: 131-147

Schreuder, B.J.N. (2001) The Violation of Inner and Outer Boundaries in Political Persecution. *Journal of Applied Psychoanalytic Studies*, 3: 231-242

Schwartz. M.M. (1992) Introduction: D.W. Winnicott's Cultural Space. *Psychoanalytic Review*, 79: 169-174

Scurlock, A. (2005) Early Disillusionment. *Dissertation Abstracts (International)*, 65 (11-B): 6058

Selvin, J. (2003) Winnicottian Reading of Gwendolen Harleth in George Eliot's *Daniel Deronda. Dissertation Abstracts (International)*, 64 (3-B): 1507

Sengun, S. (2001)   Migration as a Transitional Space and
                       Group Analysis. *Group Analysis,*
                       34: 65-78

Shapiro, E.R. (1998)   Images in Psychiatry: Donald W.
                       Winnicott 1896-1971. *American Journal of*
                       Psychiatry, 155: 421-422

Sheppard, A. (1998)   Princess Diana: what Winnicott Might
                       have Said. *Journal of Melanie Klein and*
                       Object Relations, 16: 609-610

Sherman, S.R. (2003)   Early Intervention with a Mother-Infant
                       Pair: The Impact of an Enduring and
                       Adaptive Relationship. *Clinical Social*
                       Work Journal, 31: 223-234

Shields, W.S. (2000)   Hope and the Inclination to be
                       Troublesome: Winnicott and the
                       Treatment of Character Disorder in
                       Group Psychotherapy. *International*
                       Journal of Group Psychotherapy,
                       50: 87-104

Shields, W.S. (2001)   The Subjective Experience of the Self in
                       the Large Group: Two Models for Study.
                       International Journal of Group
                       Psychotherapy, 51: 205-223

Shmukler, D.,   The Transitional Object and the
Friedman, M. (1985)   Development of the Child Ego State.
                       Transactional Analysis Journal, 15: 207-210

Shmukler, D.,   The Developmental Function of Play
Friedman, M. (1988)   and its Relevance for Transactional
                       Analysis. *Transactional Analysis Journal,*
                       18: 80-84

Shore, A. (2000)   Child Art Therapy and Parent
                       Consultation: Facilitating Child

	Development and Parent Strengths. *Art Therapy*, 17: 14-23
Siebzehner, A.V. (1994)	Psychoanalysis of a Child: a Winnicottian Look. *Encounters (Argentina)*, 1: 103-108
Sjödin, C. (2003)	The Significance of Belief for Psychoanalysis. *International Forum of Psychoanalysis*, 12: 44-52
Slavin, M.O. (2000)	Hate, Self-Interest and "Good-Enough" Relating. *Psychoanalytic Inquiry*, 20: 441-461
Slochower, J. (1991)	Variations in the Analytic Holding Environment. *International Journal of Psychoanalysis*, 72: 709-718
Slochower, J. (1994)	The Evolution of Object Usage and the Holding Environment. *Contemporary Psychoanalysis*, 30: 135-151
Slochower, J. (1996b)	Holding and the Fate of the Analyst's Objectivity. *Psychoanalytic Dialogues*, 6: 323-353
Smith, B.L. (1990)	Potential Space and the Rorschach: an Application of Object Relations Theory. *Journal of Personal Assessment*, 55: 756-767
Solow, M.J. (1997)	The Effect of the Holding Environment on the Transition to Parenthood. *Dissertation Abstracts (International)*, 58(6-B): 3343
Southwood, H.M. (1973)	The Origin of Self Awareness and Ego Behaviour. *International Journal of Psychoanalysis*, 54: 235-239
Spitz, E.H. (1992)	Recycling. *Psychoanalytic Review*, 79: 209-222

Spurling, L. (1991)   Winnicott and the Mother's Face.
                       Winnicott Studies, 6: 60-61

Spurling, L. (1996)   Winnicott and the Transference: The
                       Knife-Edge of Belief. *Winnicott Studies,
                       11*: 51-61

Spurling, L. (2003)   On Psychoanalytic Figures as
                       Transference Figures. *International
                       Journal of Psychoanalysis, 84*: 31-43

Stein, A.A. (1999)   Whose Thoughts are they Anyway?
                       Dimensionally Exploding Bion's
                       "Double Headed Arrow" into
                       Co-Adapting Transitional Space.
                       *Non-Linear Dynamics, Psychology and Life
                       Sciences, 3*: 65-92

Stein, H.F. (1985)   Culture Change, Symbolic Object Loss
                       and Restitutional Process. *Psychoanalysis
                       and Contemporary Thought, 8*: 301-332

Stein, S. (1975)   Consultation Techniques of Winnicott.
                       South African Medical Journal, 49: 984-985

Stevenson, O. (1954)   The First Treasured Possession: a Study
(preface by   of the Part Played by Specially Loved
Winnicott, D.W.)   Objects and Toys in the Lives of Certain
                       Children. *Psychoanalytic Study of the
                       Child, 9*: 199-217

Stevenson, O. (1971)   Donald Winnicott: an Appreciation.
                       *International Journal of Child Psychology
                       and Psychiatry and Allied Disciplines,
                       12*: 153-155

Stewart, H. (2004)   Winnicott, Balint and the Independent
                       Tradition. *American Journal of
                       Psychoanalysis, 63*: 207-217

Stout, R.L. (2002)   Object Relations and Winnicott's
                       Conception of Creativity: a Study of the

Relationships. *Dissertation Abstracts (International), 62(12-B)*: 5980

Street, E., Downey, J., Brazier, A. (1991)
The Development of Therapeutic Consultations in Child-focused Family Work. *Journal of Family Therapy, 13*: 311-33

Strenger, C. (1997)
Further Remarks on the Classic and Romantic Visions in Psychoanalysis: Klein, Winnicott and Ethics. *Psychoanalysis and Contemporary Thought, 20*: 207-244

Summers, F. (1999)
Psychoanalytic Boundaries and Transitional Space Psychoanalytic Psychology 16: 3-20

Sussal, C.M. (1992)
Object Relations Family Therapy as a Model for Practice. *Clinical Social Work Journal, 20*: 313-321

Sutherland, J.D. (1980)
The British Object-Relations Theorists: Balint, Winnicott, Fairbairn, Guntrip. *Journal of the American Psychoanalytic Association, 28*: 829-860

Sutton, A. (2001)
Dependence and Dependability: Winnicott in a Culture of Symptom Intolerance. *Psychoanalytic Psychotherapy, 15*: 1-19

Szollosy, M. (1998)
Winnicott's Potential Spaces: Using Psychoanalytic Theory to Redress the Crises of Post-modern Culture. Available on line at *Psyche Matters*

Target, M., Fonagy, P. (1996)
Playing with Reality II: The Development of Psychic Reality from a Theoretical Perspective. *International Journal of Psychoanalysis, 77*: 459-479

Teitlebaum, S. (2003) Playing with Winnicott: a Patient's Account of her Experience Using the Analyst as a Traditional Object. *Canadian Journal of Psychoanalysis*, 11: 435-458

Teurnell. L. (1993) An Alternative Reading of Winnicott. *International Forum of Psychoanalysis*, 2: 377-382

Thomas, K.R., McGinnis, J.D. (1991) The Psychoanalytic Theories of D.W. Winnicott as Applied to Rehabilitation. *Rehabilitation, 57*: 63

Ticho, E.A. (1974) Donald W. Winnicott, Martin Buber and the Theory of Personal Relationships. *Psychiatry, 33*: 240-253

Tizard, J.P.M. (1971) Donald Winnicott. *International Journal of Psychoanalysis, 52*: 226-227 [also in Goldman, D. (1993) with Khan, M.M.R. (1971b): 111-116]

Tizard, J.P.M. (1981) Donald Winnicott. The President's View of a Past President. *Journal of the Royal Society of Medicine, 74*: 262-274

Tod, R.J.N. (1979) Publications by Donald W. Winnicott 1962-1978. *International Review of Psychoanalysis, 6* pp. 377-382

Tolpin, M. (1971) On the Beginnings of a Cohesive Self: an Application of the Concept of Transmuting Internalization to the Study of Transitional Object and Signal Anxiety. *Psychoanalytic Study of the Child, 26*: 316-354

Tonnesmann, M. (1993) The Third Area of Experience in Psychoanalysis. *Winnicott Studies, 8 (Autumn)*: 3-16

Tonnesmann, M. (1995)
Early Emotional Development: Ferenczi to Winnicott. *Bulletin of the British Psychoanalytic Society, 30*: 14-19 [also in Caldwell, (L. 2002a): 45-57]

Traub, H.L., Lane, R. C. (2002)
The Case of Ms. A. *Clinical Case Studies, 1*: 49-66

Trevarthan, C. (1993)
Playing into Reality: Conversations with the Infant Communicator. *Winnicott Studies, 7 (Spring)*: 67-84

Turner, J.F. (1988)
Wordsworth and Winnicott in the Play Area. *International Review of Psychoanalysis, 15*: 481-496 [also in Rudnytsky, (1993): 161-188]

Turner, J.F. (2002)
A Brief History of Illusion: Milner, Winnicott and Rycroft. *International Journal of Psychoanalysis, 83*: 1063-1082

Turp, M. (2000a)
Touch, Enjoyment and Health in Adult Life. *European Journal of Psychotherapy, Counselling and Health, 3*: 61-76

Turp, M. (2000b)
Handling and Self-handling: an Object Relations Perspective on Leisure Exercise. *Psychodynamic Counselling, 6*: 469-487

Turp, M. (2002)
Acting, Feeling and Thinking: Psychoanalytic Psychotherapy with Tracey. *European Journal of Psychotherapy Counselling, 5*: 103-119

Tustin, F. (1980)
Autistic Objects. *International Review of Psychoanalysis, 7*: 27-39

Tustin, F. (1985)
The Emergence of a Sense of Self. *Winnicott Studies, 1*: 36-48 [also in Richards with Wilce (1996): 47-63]

Tustin, F. (1987) The Rhythm of Safety. *Winnicott Studies*, 2: 19-31

Ulanov, A.B. (1985) A Shared Space. *Quadrant, 18*: 65-80

Underwood, R.L. (1996) Primordial Texts: an Object Relations Approach to Biblical Hermeneutics. *Pastoral Psychology, 45*: 181-192

Unwin, C. (2006) Notes on Integration and Disintegration from Historical and Developmental Perspectives. *Journal of Child Psychotherapy, 32*: 193

Usuelli, A.K. (1992) The Significance of Illusion in the Work of Freud and Winnicott: a Controversial Issue. *International Review of Psychotherapy, 19*: 179-187

Vallery, S.K. (1992) Mentoring in Clinical Supervision of Psychodynamic Psychotherapy: Application of Winnicott's Theory of the Transitional Phenomena. *Dissertation Abstracts (International), 52(10-B)*: 5551

Van Buskirk, W., McGrath, D. (1999) Organizational Cultures as Holding Environments: a Psychodynamic Look at Organizational Symbolism. *Human Relations, 52*: 805-832

Vanier, A. (2001) Some Remarks on Adolescence with Particular Reference to Winnicott and Lacan. *Psychoanalytic Quarterly, 70*: 579-598

Vellacott, J. (1995) The Woman Behind Mother. *Winnicott Studies, 10*: 15-24

Vivona, J. (2000) Autonomous Desire: Women's Worry as Post-œdipal Transitional Object. *Psychoanalytic Psychology, 17*: 243-263

Wakimoto, K. (et al) (1984) An Approach to Pre-Adolescent Patients Usinf the "Squiggle Game".

Japanese Journal of Child and Adolescent Psychiatry, 25: 231-240

Webber, J.A. (2001)   Failure to Hold: An Analysis of School Violence (John Dewey and D.W. Winnicott). *Dissertation Abstracts (International), 62 (6-A)*: 2030

Weisberg, I. (1994)   The Facilitating or Inhibiting Environment, Maternal and Psychoanalytic: D.W. Winnicott. *International Journal of Communicative Psychoanalysis and Psychotherapy, 9*: 113-119

Weiss, S. (1997)   The Empty Space. *Annual of Psychoanalysis, 25*: 189-199

Wells, D. (2002)   Tragedy, Catharsis and Creativity: from Aristotle to Freud to Winnicott. *Free Associations, 52*: 463-478

Whiteley, J.S. (1994)   Attachment, Loss and the Space Between: Personality Disorders in the Therapeutic Community. *Group Analysis, 27*: 359-382

Whiteley, J.S. (1998)   Community as Playground: Some Thoughts on the Function of Play in the Therapeutic Community. *International Journal for Therapeutic and Supportive Organizations, 19*: 269-280

Whitty, M.T., Carr, A.N. (2003)   Cyberspace as Potential Space: Considering the Web as a playground to Cyber-flirt. *Human Relations, 56*: 869-891

Widlöcher, D. (1970)   On Winnicott's *Maturational Processes and the Facilitating Environment. International Journal of Psychoanalysis, 51*: 526-530

Widlöcher, D. (2003)	How the Analyst's Person is Affected by and Induces Thought-Transference. *Psychoanalysis in Europe, 57*: 83-90
Wieland, C. (1994)	The Good-Enough Mother and the Use of the Object in Winnicott. *Winnicott Studies, 9*: 25-34
Wilkin, P. (2006)	In Search of the True Self: a Clinical Journey through the Vale of Soul-making. *Journal of Psychiatric and Mental Health Nursing, 13*: 12-18
Williams, G.D. (2002)	Failures Unmended: a Pastoral Psychological Study of a Tragic Vision of Evil in Writings of Winnicott. *Dissertation Abstracts (International), 62(10-B)*: 4828
Willock, B. (1992)	Projection, Transitional Phenomena and the Rorschach. *Journal of Personality Assessment, 59*: 99-116
Wilson, S.N. (2005)	The Meanings of Medicating: Pills and Play. *American Journal of Psychotherapy, 59*: 19-29
Winnicott, C. (1980)	Fear of Breakdown: a Clinical Example. *International Journal of Psychoanalysis, 61*: 351-357
Winnicott, D.W. (1962)	Theory of Parent-Infant Relationship: Further Remarks. *International Journal of Psychoanalysis, 43*: 238-239 [followed by Contributions to the Discussion by: Balint, M., Blau, A., Burlingham, D., Davidson, S., Freud, A., Garma, A., Greenacre, P., James, M., Khan, M.M.R., Lagache, D., Lantos, B., Lebovici, S., Schur, M., Scott, W.C.M., Szekely, L., Winnicott, D.W.]

Winnicott, D.W. (2003) Preface to Renata Gaddini's translation of *Family and Individual Development. Psychoanalysis and History, 5*: 40-52

Wiseman, R.S. (2002) Toward a Better Understanding of Children's Trichotillomania: an Analysis of Family Treatment. *Dissertation Abstracts (International), 63(4-B)*: 2081

Wolf, R. (1979) Re-experiencing Winnicott's Environmental Mother: Implications of Art Psychotherapy of Anti-social Youth in Special Education. *Arts in Psychotherapy, 6*: 95-102

Wright, K. (1998) Deep Calling unto Deep: Artistic Creativity and the Maternal Object. *British Journal of Psychotherapy, 14*: 453-467

Wynn, F. (1997) The Embodied Chiasmic Relationship of Mother and Infant. *Human Studies, 20*: 253-270

Zalidis, S. (2002) 'My Eyes are Misting Over' Therapeutic Consultations in General Practice with a Child Presenting with an Eye Symptom. *Psychoanalytic Psychotherapy, 16*: 1-19

Ziegler, R.G. (1976) Winnicott's Squiggle Games and its Diagnostic Therapeutic Usefulness. *Art Psychotherapy, 3*: 177-185

Zimmerman, L. (1997) Against Vanishing: Winnicott and the Modern Poetry of Nothing. *American Imago, 54*: 81-102

Zimmerman, L. (1999) Public and Potential Space: Winnicott, Ellison and De Lillo. *Centennial Review, 43*: 565-574

Zinkin, L. (1983) Malignant Mirroring. *Group Analysis, 16*: 113-124

Books

Abadi, S. (2001)	Explorations: Losing and Finding Oneself in the Potential Space [in Bertolini, M. et al (2001) vol. 1: 79-87]
Abend, S. (Ed.) (1996)	*The Place of Reality in Psychoanalytic Theory and Technique.* New York: Aronson
Abram, J. (1996)	*The Language of Winnicott.* London: Karnac (reprint, New York: Aronson 2004)
Abram, J. (Ed.) (2000a)	*André Green at the Squiggle Foundation.* London: Karnac for the Squiggle Foundation
Abram, J. (2000b)	A Kind of French Winnicott [editor's foreword in Abram, A. (2000a): xi-xviii]
Abrams, S., Neubauer, P. (1978)	Transitional Objects: Animate and Inanimate [in Grolnick, Barkin, Muensterberger (1978): 133-144]
Aite, P. (2001)	Between C.G. Jung and D.W. Winnicott [in Bertolini, M. et al (2001) vol. 2: 242-244]
Alby, J-M. (1993)	Being English and a Psychoanalyst [in Goldman, D. ed. (1993): 159-164]
Alford, C.F. (2002b)	*Levinas, The Frankfurt School and Psychoanalysis.* New York: Wesleyan University Press
Alford, C.F. (2006)	*Psychology and the Natural Law of Reparation.* Cambridge: Cambridge University Press

Aliprandi, M.T. (2001)
Antisocial Acting-out as a Substitute for the Spontaneous Gesture in Adolescence [in Bertolini, M. et al (2001) vol. 2: 133-138]

Alizade, A.M. (Ed.) (2006)
Motherhood in the Twenty-first Century. London: Karnac

Altman, N. et al (2002)
Relational Child Psychotherapy. New York: Other Press

Altman, N. (2005)
Relational Perspectives on the Therapeutic Action of Psychoanalysis [in Ryan, J. (2005): 15-50]

Alvarez, A. (1992)
Live Company: Psychoanalytic Therapy with Autistic, Abused and Borderline Psychotic Children. London: Routledge

Amado, G., Vansina, L. (Eds.) (2005)
The Transitional Approach in Action London: Karnac

André, J. (2002)
Separation [in Widlöcher, D. ed. (2002). *Infantile Sexuality and Attachment.* London: Karnac: 123-131]

Andrews, J.C. (2001)
Manic Defence and its Place in Therapy [in Bertolini, M. et al (2001) vol. 1: 255-256] (see also Neri, F. (2001) for discussion)

Anthony, E.J. (2002)
Memories of Donald Winnicott [in Kahr (2002a): 137-140]

Anzieu, D. (1989)
The Skin Ego: A Psychoanalytic Approach to the Self. New York & London: Yale University Press

Anzieu, D. (Ed.) (1990)
Psychic Envelopes. London: Karnac

Applegate, J.S.,
Bonovitz, J.M.
(1995)
The Facilitating Environment: a Winnicottian Approach for Social Workers and other Helping Professions. Northvale, NJ: Aronson

Applegate, J.S.
(1996)
The Good-enough Social Workers: Winnicott Applied [in Sanville, J.B. Ed. (1996). *Fostering, Healing and Growth: a Psychoanalytic Social Work Approach*: 77-96 Lanham, MD: Aronson]

Armellini, M. (2001)
The Father as Function, Environment and Object [in Bertolini, M. et al (2001) vol. 2: 37-46

Atwood, G.E.,
Stolorow, R.D.
(1984)
Structures of Subjectivity: Explorations in Psychoanalytic Phenomenology. Hillside, NJ and London: Analytic Press

Azevedo, R. (2001)
Fetish-object, Transitional Object [in Bertolini, M. et al (2001) vol. 1: 204-209]

Bacal, H.A. (1989)
Winnicott and Self Psychology: Remarkable Reflections [in Dettrick, D.W. & S.P.(1989): 259-271]

Bacal, H.A.,
Newman, K. (1990)
Theories of Object Relations: Bridges to Self Psychology. New York: Columbia University Press

Balint, E. (2000)
The Broken Couch [in Rudnytsky (2000): 1-26]

Barkin, L. (1978)
The Concept of the Transitional Object [in Grolnick, Barkin, Muensterberger (1978): 511-536]

Barnett, B. (2001)
A Comparison of the Thought and Work of Donald Winnicott and Michael Balint [in Bertolini, M. et al (2001) vol. 2: 185-188] (see also Dreyfus, P. (2003) for discussion)

Barrat, B.B. (1984) *Psychic Reality and Psychoanalytic Knowing* Hillside, NJ: Analytic Press

Bassin, D., Honey, M. Kaplan, M.M.(Eds.) (1994) *Representations of Motherhood* New Haven, CT and London: Yale University Press

Benjamin, J. (2000) Reparative Projects [in Rudnytsky (2000): 233-275]

Bergmann, M.S. (Ed.) (2004a) *Understanding Dissidence and Controversy in the History of Psychoanalysis* New York: Other Press

Bergmann, M.S. (2204b) Rethinking Dissidence and Change in the History of Psychoanalysis [in Bergmann, M.S. (2004a): 1-110]

Bertolini, M., Giannakoulas, A., Hernandez, M., Molino, A. (Eds.) (2001a) *Squiggles and Spaces: Revisiting the Work of D.W. Winnicott* London & Philadelphia: Whurr (Wiley)

Bertolini, M. (2001b) Central Masturbatory Fantasy, Fetish and Transitional Phenomena [in Bertolini, M et al (2000) vol. 1: 210-217]

Bertolini, M., Neri, F.(2005) Sex as a Defence against Sexuality [in Caldwell, L. (2005): 105-120]

Black, D.M. (Ed.) (2006a) *Psychoanalysis and Religion in the 21st Century: Competitors or Collaborators?* Hove, Sussex: Routledge (in association with the Institute of Psychoanalysis, London)

Black, D.M. (2006b) The Case for a Contemplative Position [in Black, D.M. (2006a): 63-80]

Blass, R.B. (2006)   Beyond Illusion: Psychoanalysis and the
                      Question of Religious Truth [in Black,
                      D.M. (2006a): 23-42]

Bollas, C. (1986)   The Transformational Object [in Kohon,
                      (1986): 83-100]

Bollas, C. (1987)   *The Shadow of the Object: Psychoanalysis
                      of the Unthought Known*. London: Free
                      Association Books

Bollas, C. (1989)   *Forces of Destiny: Psychoanalysis and
                      Human Idiom*. London: Free Association
                      Books

Bollas, C. (1993a)   *Being a Character, Psychoanalysis and
                      Self-Experience*. London: Routledge

Bollas, C. (1993b)   The Æsthetic Movement and the Search
                      for Transformation [in Rudnytsky
                      (1993): 40-49]

Bolognini, S. (2001) The 'Kind-hearted' versus the Good
                      Analyst: Empathy and Hatred in
                      Countertransference [in Bertolini, M.
                      et al (2001) vol. 2: 120-129]

Bomford, R. (2006)   A Simple Question? [in Black, D.M.
                      (2006a): 252-269]

Bonamino, V.,   Creativity, Dreaming, Living:
Di Renzo, M.   Overlapping Circles in the Work of
(2000)   Marion Milner and D.W. Winnicott [in
                      Caldwell. L. (2000): 97-112]

Bonaminio, V.   Through Winnicott to Winnicott
(2001)   [in Bertolini, M. et al (2001) vol. 1: 88-98]

Bowie, M. (2000)   Psychoanalysis and Art: the Winnicott
                      Legacy [in Caldwell, L. (2000): 11-29]

Bowlby, R. (2004)   *Fifty Years of Attachment Theory* (with
                      contributions from Kahr, B. and King, P.)

	London: Karnac on behalf of the Winnicott Clinic of Psychotherapy
Boyer, L.B. (1990a)	Regression in Treatment: On Early Object Relations [in Giovacchini (1990a): 200-225]
Boyer, L.B., Giovacchini, P. (Eds.) (1990b)	*Master Technicians on Treating the Regressed Patient.* Northvale, NJ: Aronson
Boyer, L.B. (1990c)	Psychoanalytic Intervention in Treating the Regressed Patient [introduction to Boyer and Giovacchini (1990b): 1-33]
Brafman, A.H. (2001a)	*Untying the Knot: Working with Children and Parents.* London: Karnac
Brafman, A.H. (2001b)	What About the Parents? [in Bertolini, M. et al (2001) vol. 2: 30-36]
Brazelton, T.B., Cramer, B.G. (1990)	*The Earliest Relationship: Parents, Infants and the Drama of Early Attachment.* Reading, MA: Addison-Wesley reprinted London: Karnac 1991
Burgin, V. (2004)	*The Remembered Film.* London: Reaktion Books
Caldwell, L. (Ed.) (2000)	*Art, Creativity, Living.* London: Karnac for the Squiggle Foundation
Caldwell, L. (Ed.) (2002a)	*The Elusive Child.* London: Karnac for the Squiggle Foundation
Caldwell, L. (2002b)	Introduction [Caldwell, L. (2002a): 1-13]
Caldwell, L. (Ed.) (2005)	*Sex and Sexuality: Winnicottian Perspectives.* London: Karnac for the Squiggle Foundation
Cameron, K. (1996)	Winnicott and Lacan: Selfhood and Subjecthood [in Richards with Wilce (1996): 37-45]

Campbell, D. (2001)   On Pseudo-normality: a Contribution to the Psychopathology of Adolescence [in Kahr, B. (2001a): 61-72]

Carratelli, T.I. (2001)   On De Goldstein, R.Z. (2001) [in Bertolini, M. et al (2001) vol. 1: 241-246

Casas de Pereda, M. (2001)   Adolescent Resignification [in Bertolini M. et al (2001) vol. 1: 218-227]

Casement, P. (1985)   *On Learning from the Patient.* London: Routledge

Casement, P. (1990)   *Further Learning from the Patient.* London: Routledge

Casement, P. (2002a)   *On Learning from our Mistakes.* London: Routledge

Casement, P.J. (2002c)   Foreword to Kahr, B. (2002a): xxi-xxix

Cassidy, J. (1999)   *Handbook of Attachment: Theory, Research and Clinical Applications.* New York: Guilford Press

Chagas-Bovet, A.M. (2001)   Exploring the Pathways of Illusion [in Bertolini, M. et al (2001) vol. 1: 126-133]

Clancier, A., Kalmanovitch, J. (1987)   *Winnicott and Paradox: from Birth to Creation* London, Tavistock

Clancier, A., Kalmanovitch, J. (1990)   A Splash of Paint in his Style [in Giovacchini, P. (1990a): 41-59]

Coles, P. (Ed.) (2006)   *Sibling Relationships.* London: Karnac

Cooper, J. (1993b)   *Speak of Me as I am: The Life and Work of Masud Khan.* London: Karnac

Coppolillo, H.O. (1987)   *Psychodynamic Psychotherapy of Children.* Madison CO, International Universities Press

Corrigan, E.G., Gordon, P-E. (Eds.) (1995a)   *The Mind Object: Precocity and Pathology of Self-Sufficiency.* London: Karnac

Corrigan, E.G., Gordon, P-E. (Eds.) (1995b)   The Mind as an Object [in Corrigan, E.G., Gordon, P-E. (1995a): 1-23]

Cowan-Jenssen, S. (1995)   Primal Psychotherapy [in Ryan, J. (2005): 137-163]

Cox, M. (2001)   On the Capacity for Being Inside Enough [in Kahr, B. (2001a): 111-120]

Cunningham, M. (2006)   Vedanta and Psychoanalysis [in Black, D.M. (2006a): 234-251]

Curtis, R.C. (Ed.) (1991)   *The Relational Self: Theoretical Convergences in Psychoanalysis and Social Psychiatry.* New York: Guilford

Dalley, T. (1992)   *Handbook of Art Therapy.* London: Routledge

Dauber, A.B. (1993)   Thomas Traherne and the Poetics of Object Relations [in Rudnytsky (1993): 133-160]

Davids, M.F. (2006)   'Render unto Caesar what is Caesar's': is there a Realm of God in the Mind? [in Black, D.M. (2006a): 45-62]

Davis, M.E.V., Wallbridge, D. (1981)   *Boundary and Space: An Introduction to the Work of D.W. Winnicott* London: Karnac & New York: Brunner-Mazel (revised edition London: Karnac 1991)

Davoin, F. (1989)   Potential Space and the Space between Two Deaths [in Fromm, Smith (1989a): 581-603]

192

Daws, D.,
Boston, M. (Eds.)
(1977)
The Child Psychotherapist and Problems of Young People. London: Routledge (revised edition 1981. Reprinted 1988, London: Karnac)

De Astis, G. (2001)
The Influence of Winnicott on Francis Tustin's Thinking [in Bertolini, M. et al (2001) vol. 2: 189-195]

De Goldstein, R.Z.
(2001)
The Matrix of the Psyche-soma [in Bertolini, M. et al (2001) vol. 1: 172-183] (see also Carratelli (2001) for discussion)

DeLaCour. E.P.
(1989)
Fear of Breakdown: A Case with Multiple Psychotic Episodes [in Fromm, Smith (1989a): 558-580]

Denzler, B. (2001)
Empathy: Love or Skill? [in Bertolini, M. et al (2003) vol. 2: 232-235

Deri, S. (1978)
Transitional Phenomena: Vicissitudes of Symbolization and Creativity [in Grolnick, Barkin, Muensterberger (1978): 43-60]

Deri, S. (1984)
Symbolization and Creativity. New York: International Universities Press

De Silvestris, P.
(2001)
Interminable Illusion [in Bertolini, M. et al (2001) vol. 2: 59-64

Detrick, D.W. & S.P.
(Eds.) (1989)
Self Psychology: Comparisons and Contrasts. Hillside, NJ: Analytic Press

Diamond, N. (2005)
When Thought is not Enough [in Ryan, J. (2005): 113-136]

Di Cintro, M. (2002)
"Ordered Anarchy": Writing as Transitional Object in *Moise and the World of Reason*. *Tennessee Williams Annual Review, 5*

Dickes, R. (1978)   Parents, Transitional Objects and
                           Childhood Fetishes [in Grolnick, Barkin,
                           Muensterberger (1978): 305-320]

Dinnage, R. (1978)   A Bit of Light [in Grolnick, Barkin,
                           Muensterberger (1978): 363-378]

Doane, J.,   *From Klein to Kristeva: Psychoanalytic*
Hodges, D. (1992)   *Feminism and the Search for the 'Good*
                           Enough Mother' Ann Arbor: Michigan
                           University Press

Dockar-Drysdale, B.   *The Provision of Primary Experience:*
(1990)   *Winnicottian Work with Children and*
                           Adolescents. London: Free Association
                           Books

Dockar-Drysdale, B.   *Therapy and Consultation in Child Care.*
(1993)   London: Free Association Books

Douglas, A.,   *Care and Coping: A Guide to Social*
Philpot, T. (1998)   *Services.* London: Routledge

Drapeau, P. (2002)   From Freud to Winnicott: an Encounter
                           between Mythical Children [in
                           Caldwell, L. (2002): 15-44]

Dreyfus, P. (2001)   A Discussion of Barnett, B. (2001) [in
                           Bertolini, M. et al (2001)
                           vol. 2: 236-241]

Eigen, M.,   Object Relations and Expressive
Robbins, A.   Symbolism: Some Structures and
(1980c)   Functions of Expressive Therapy [in
                           Robbins, A. (Ed.) *Expressive Therapy: A*
                           Creative Arts Approach to Depth-Oriented
                           Treatment. New York: Human Sciences
                           Press (1980): 73-94]

Eigen, M. (1986a)   *The Psychotic Core.* New York: Aronson.
                           (reprinted London: Karnac 2004)

Eigen, M. (1986b)   Aspects of Mindlessness-Selflessness: A Common Madness [in Travers, J.A. (Ed.) *Psychotherapy and the Selfless Patient*. New York: Haworth Press (1986): 75-82] (*Psychotherapy and the Selfless Patient* also published in *The Psychotherapy Patient*, *Vol. 2 No. 2*)

Eigen, M. (1989)   Aspects of Omniscience [in Fromm, Smith (1989a): 604-628]

Eigen, M. (1991)   Winnicott's Area of Freedom [in Schwartz-Salant, N., Stein, M. (Eds.) (1991) *Liminality and Transitional Phenomena* Wilmette, IL: Chiron Publications: 67-88]

Eigen, M. (1993)   *The Electrified Tightrope* New York: Aronson (reprinted London: Karnac 2004)

Eigen, M. (1995)   Mystical Precocity and Psychic Short-Circuits [in Corrigan, E.G., Gordon, P-E. (1995a): 109-134]

Eigen, M. (1996)   *Psychic Deadness* New York: Aronson (reprinted London: Karnac 2004)

Eigen, M. (1998b)   *The Psychoanalytic Mystic* London: Free Association Books

Eigen, M. (1999)   *Toxic Nourishment*. London: Karnac

Eigen, M. (2001)   *Damaged Bonds*. London: Karnac

Eigen, M. (2004)   *The Sensitive Self*. Middletown, CT: Wesleyan University Press

Elkind, S.N. (1992)   *Resolving Impasses in Therapeutic Relationships*. New York: Guilford Press

Epstein, L., Feiner, A.H. (1979)   *Countertransference*. Northdale NJ: Aronson

Epstein, L. (2001)   Further Thoughts on the Winnicott-Khan Analysis [in Petrucelli and Stuart (2001): 375-384]

Epstein, M. (1998)   *Going to Pieces without Falling Apart* New York: Broadway Books

Epstein, M. (2002)   *Going on Being.* New York: Broadway Books

Epstein, M. (2005a)   *Open to Desire: Embracing a Lust for Life Instincts from Buddhism and Psychotherapy.* New York: Gotham Books

Epstein, M. (2006)   The Structure of No-structure: Winnicott's Concept of Unintegration and the Buddhist Notion of No-self [in Black, D.M. (2006a): 223-233]

Erlicher, P., Quarantini, A.Z. (2001)   Reparation in Respect of Mother's Organized Defence Against Depression [in Bertolini, M. et al (2001) vol. 2: 24-29]

Farhi, N. (1993)   Winnicott and Personal Tradition [in Spurling, L. (Ed.) (1993). London: Routledge: 78-105]

Farhi, N. (2001)   Psychotherapy and the Squiggle Game: a Sophisticated Game of Hide-and-Seek [in Bertolini, M. et al (2001) vol. 2: 65-75] (see also Giannini (2003) for discussion]

Farrell, E. (2001)   Vomit as a Transitional Object [in Kahr, B. (2002a): 73-82]

Feinsilver, D.B. (1989)   Transitional Play with Regressed Schizophrenic Patients [in Fromm, Smith (1989a): 205-237]

Fielding, J. (1997)   "So Rare a Wonder'd Father": Winnicott's Negotiation of the Paternal [in Richards with Wilce (1997): 59-72]

Fielding, J. (2000)   "I Thought so Then": *Othello* and the
                         Unknown Thought [in Caldwell, L.
                         (2000): 49-62]

Firman, J. (1997)   *The Primal Wound: a Transpersonal View
                         of Trauma, Addiction and Growth.* Albany,
                         NY: State University of New York Press

Firman, J.,   *Psychosynthesis: a Psychology of the Spirit*
Gilla, A. (2002)   Albany, NY: State University of New
                         York Press

First, E. (1994)   Mothering, Hate and Winnicott [in
                         Bassin, Honey, Kaplan (1994): 147-161]

Flax, J. (1990)   *Thinking Fragments: Psychoanalysis,
                         Feminism and Post-modernism in the
                         Contemporary West.* Berkeley: University
                         of California Press

Flew, A. (1978)   Transitional Objects and Transitional
                         Phenomena: Comments and
                         Interpretation [in Grolnick, Barkin,
                         Muensterberger (1978): 483-502]

Forcey, L.R. (1987)   *Mothers of Sons: Toward an Understanding
                         of Responsibility.* Westport, CT: Praeger

Ford, D.H.,   *Contemporary Models of Psychotherapy:*
Urban, H.B. (1998)   *A Comparative Analysis.* New York: Wiley

Fordham, M. (1985)   *Explorations into the Self.* London,
                         Academic Press (new edition London:
                         Karnac 2002)

Forrester, J. (1997)   On Holding as Metaphor: Winnicott
                         and the Figure of St. Christopher [in
                         Richards with Wilce (1997): 41-58]

Frankel, R. (Ed.)   *The Adolescent Psyche: Jungian and
(1998)   Winnicottian Perspectives.* London and
                         New York: Routledge

Frankel, R. (2002a)   A Winnicottian View of an American
                        Tragedy [in Caldwell (2002): 153-175]

Fromm, M.G.,   *The Facilitating Environment: Clinical*
Smith, B.L. (Eds.)   *Applications of Winnicott's Theory.*
(1989a)   Madison, CO: International Universities
                        Press

Fromm, M.G.   Winnicott's Work in Relation to Classical
(1989b)   Psychoanalysis and Ego Psychology
                        [in Fromm, Smith (1989a): 3-26]

Fromm, M.G.   Impasse and Transitional Relatedness
(1989c)   [in Fromm, Smith (1989a): 179-204]

Fromm, M.G.   Photography as Transitional
(1989d)   Functioning [in Fromm, Smith (1989a):
                        279-316]

Fromm, M.G.   Dreams Represented in Dreams:
(1989e)   a Discussion of the True Self/False Self
                        Duality [in Fromm, Smith
                        (1989a): 459-488]

Fromm, M.G.   Disturbances of the Self in the
(1989f)   Psychoanalytic Setting [in Fromm,
                        Smith (1989a): 489-515]

Gaddini, E. (1992)   *A Psychoanalytic Theory of Infantile*
                        Experience (Ed. Limentani. A.). London:
                        Routledge/Institute of Psychoanalysis

Gaddini, R. (1978)   Transitional Object Origins and the
                        Psychosomatic Symptom [in Grolnick,
                        Barkin, Muensterberger (1978): 109-132]

Gaddini, R. (1990)   Regression and its Uses in Treatment: an
                        Elaboration in the Thinking of Winnicott
                        [in Giovacchini, P.L. (1990a): 182-199] also
                        in Boyer and Giovacchini (1990b): 227-244]
                        and in Goldman, D. (1993): 257-272]

Gaddini, R. (2001)   The Psyche-soma Matrix: *Through Pædiatrics to Psychoanalysis* [in Bertolini, M. et al (2001) vol. 1: 167-171]

Gallo, P., Nacinovitch, R. (2001)   Primary Maternal Preoccupation: Pregnancy and Child-rearing [in Bertolini, M. et al (2001) vol. 2: 155-160]

Garanzini, M. (1988)   *The Attachment Circle: an Object Relations Approach to the Healing Ministries.* New York: Paulist Press

Gargiulo, G.J. (1998)   Winnicott's Psychoanalytic Playground [in Marcus, P. and Rosenberg, A. (Eds.). *Philosophies of Life and their Impact.* New York: New York University Press (1998): 140-146]

Gee, H. (2002)   My Experience of Winnicott [in Kahr (2002a): 141-145]

Geissmann, C., Geissmann, P. (1998)   *A History of Child Analysis.* London and New York: Routledge

Giannakoulas, A. (2005)   Childhood Sexual Theories and Childhood Sexuality: the Primal Scene and Parental Sexuality [in Caldwell, L. (2005): 55-68)]

Giannini, G. del C. (2001)   Reflections on Farhi, C. (2001) [in Bertolini, M. et al (2001) vol. 2: 223-227]

Giannotti, V. et al (2001)   From the Æsthetics of External Objects to the Quality of Internal Objects: On the Diagnosis of Alopecia in Childhood and Adolescence [in Bertolini, M. et al (2001) vol. 2: 161-168]

Gibeault, A. (2001)   Art in Prehistory: a Potential Space for Play [in Bertolini, M. et al (2001) vol. 1: 136-145]

Giovacchini, P.L. (1978)   The Impact of Delusion and the Delusion of Impact: Ego Defect and the Transitional Phenomenon [in Grolnick, Barkin, Muensterberger (1978): 321-344]

Giovacchini, P.L. (1984)   *Character Disorders and Adaptive Mechanisms*. New York: Aronson

Giovacchini, P.L. (1986)   *Developmental Disorders: the Transitional Space in Mental Breakdown and Creative Imagination*. Northvale, NJ: Aronson

Giovacchini, P.L. (1989)   *Countertransference Triumphs and Catastrophes*. Northvale, NJ: Aronson

Giovacchini, P.L. (Ed.) (1990a)   *Tactics and Techniques in Psychoanalytic Therapy III: The Implications of Winnicott's Contributions*. Northvale, NJ: Aronson

Giovacchini, P.L. (1990b)   Interpretations, an Obscure Technical Area: Winnicott's 'Interpretation in Psychoanalysis' [in Giovacchini (1990a): 71-89]

Giovacchini, P.L. (1990c)   Absolute and Not Quite Absolute Dependence [in Giovacchini (1990a): 142-159 and in Goldman, D. (1993): 241-256]

Giovacchini, P.L. (1990d)   Regression, Reconstruction and Resolution: Containment and Holding 4 [in Giovacchini, (1990a): 226-264]

Giovacchini, P.L. (2001a)   Transitional Objects in Treatment of Primitive Mental States [in Kahr (2001a): 83-94]

Goldberg, P. (1990)   The Holding Environment: Conscious and Unconscious Elements in the Building of a Therapeutic Framework [in Boyer and Giovacchini (1990b): 271-301]

Goldman, D. (1993b)
In Search of the Real: The Origins and Originality of D.W. Winnicott. Northvale, NJ: Aronson

Goldman, D. (Ed.) (1993c)
In One's Bones: The Clinical Genius of Winnicott. Northvale, NJ: Aronson

Goldman, D. (2001)
The Outrageous Prince: Winnicott's Uncure of Masud Khan [in Petrucelli and Stuart (2001): 359-374. Also in *British Journal of Psychotherapy*, 19: 486-501]

Gordon, R. (2001)
Psychosomatics in Jung and Winnicott [in Bertolini, M. et al (2001) vol. 2: 169-172]

Green, A. (1978)
Potential Space in Psychoanalysis: the Object in the Setting [in Grolnick, Barkin, Muensterberger, (1978): 167-190]

Green, A. (1986)
On Private Madness. London: Hogarth Press

Green, A. (1993)
Analytic Play and its Relationship to the Object [in Goldman, D. (Ed.) (1993): 213-222

Green, A. (1999)
The Fabric of Affect in the Psychoanalytic Discourse. London and New York: Routledge

Green, A. (2000a)
Andre Green at the Squiggle Foundation (Ed.) Abram, J. London: Karnac

Green, A. (2000b)
Experience and Thinking in Analytic Practice [in Green, A. (2000a): 1-15]

Green, A. (2000c)
Object(s) and Subject [in Green, A. (2000a): 17-37]

Green, A. (2000d)
On Thirdness [in Green, A. (2000a): 39-68]

Green, A. (2000e)   The Posthumous Winnicott: on *Human Nature* [in Green, A. (2000a): 69-83]

Green, A. (2001)   The Intuition of the Negative in *Playing and Reality* [in Bertolini, M. et al (2001) vol. 1: 43-58]

Green, A. (2003)   The Dead Mother Complex [in Raphael-Leff, J. (2003): 162-174]

Green, A. (2005a)   *Play and Reflection in Donald Winnicott's Writings.* London: Karnac on behalf of the Winnicott Clinic of Psychotherapy

Green, A. (2005b)   Conjectures about Winnicott's Unconscious Countertransference in the Case of Masud Khan, in the Light of the Wynne Godley Case. [in Green, A. (2005a): 29-38]

Green, A. (2005c)   Winnicott at the Start of the Millennium [in Caldwell, L. (2005): 11-31]

Green, A., Kohon, G. (2005e)   *Love and its Vicissitudes.* Hove, Sussex: Routledge

Green, A. (2005f)   To Love or not to Love: Eros and Eiris [in Green, A., Kohon, G. (2005e): 1-39]

Greenbaum, T. (1978)   The 'Analyzing' and the 'Transitional Object' [in Grolnick, Barkin, Muensterberger, (1978): 191-202]

Greenberg, J., Mitchell, S. (1983)   *Object Relations Theory in Psychoanalytic Theory.* Boston, MA & London: Harvard University Press. pp.188-232

Greenhalgh, P. (1994)   *Emotional Growth and Learning.* London: Routledge

Greenson, R.R. (1978)   On Traditional Objects and Transference [in Grolnick, Barkin, Muensterberger, (1978): 203-210]

Grier, F. (2006) Reflections on the Phenomenon of Adoration in Relationships, both Human and Divine [in Black, D.M. (2006a): 154-172]

Grieve, P. (2001) On Schacht, L. (2001) [in Bertolini, M. et al (2001) vol. 1: 238–240]

Grimaldi, S. (2001) Winnicott in Italy [in Bertolini, M. et al (2001) vol. 2: xvii-xix]

Grolnick, S.A., Barkin, L., Muensterberger, W. (Eds.) (1978) *Between Reality and Fantasy: Transitional Objects and Phenomena* New York: Aronson

Grolnick, S.A. (1978a) Dreams and Dreaming as Transitional Phenomena [in Grolnick, Barkin, Muensterberger (1978): 211-232]

Grolnick, S.A., Lengyel, A. (1978b) Etruscan Burial Symbols and the Transitional Process [in Grolnick, Barkin, Muensterberger (1978): 379-410]

Grolnick, S.A. (1990) *The Work and Play of Winnicott.* New York: Aronson

Grolnick, S. (1993) How to Do Winnicottian Therapy [in Goldman, D. (Ed.) (1993): 185-212]

Grotstein, J.S. (1989) Winnicott's Importance in Psychoanalysis [in Fromm, Smith (1989a): 130-158]

Grotstein, J.S. (1990) Invariants in Primitive Emotional Disorders [in Boyer and Giovacchini (1990b); 139-164]

Guntrip, H. (1961) *Personality Structure and Human Interaction: the Developing Synthesis of Psychodynamic Theory.* London: Hogarth Press (reprinted London: Karnac 1995)

Guntrip, H. (1968)   *Schizoid Phenomena, Object Relations and the Self.* London: Hogarth Press (reprinted London: Karnac 1992)

Guntrip, H. (1971)   *Psychoanalytic Theory, Therapy and the Self.* London: Hogarth Press and New York: Basic Books (reprinted London: Karnac 1985)

Guntrip, H. (1994)   *Personal Relations Therapy: the Collected Papers* (edited Hazell, J.) Lanham, MD: Aronson

Gutierres-Green, L. (2001)   'Had I only been Born a Woman...': the Feminine Element in Men [in Bertolini, M. et al (2001) vol. 1: 184-197]

Hagman, G. (2005)   *Æsthetic Beauty: Beauty, Creativity and the Search for the Ideal.* Amsterdam and New York: Rodopi

Hamilton, V. (1982)   *Narcissus and Œdipus: the Children of Psychoanalysis.* London: Routledge and Kegan Paul

Hamilton, V. (1996b)   *The Analyst's Pre-Conscious.* Hillside, NJ: Analytic Press

Harwood, I.H. (1987)   The Evolution of the Self: an Integration of Winnicott's and Kohut's Concepts [in Honess, T. and Yardley, K (Eds.) (1987) *Self and Identity: Perspectives Across the Lifespan.* New York and London: Routlledge: 55-76]

Hauptman, B. (2005)   Reflections on Donald Winnicott and John Bowlby [in Issroff, J., (2005): 101-113]

Hazell, J. (1996)   *H.J.S. Guntrip: a Psychoanalytical Biography.* London: Free Association Books

Hedges, L. (1992)   *Interpreting the Countertransference.*
                      Northvale, NJ: Aronson

Hernandez, M.,   On the Construction of Potential Space
Giannakoulos, A.   [in Bertolini, M. et al (2001)
(2001)   vol. 1: 146-159]

Hills, M. (2002)   *Fan Cultures.* London and New York:
                      Routledge

Hinshelwood, R.,   Orestes and Democracy [in Coles, P.
Winship, G. (2006)   (2006): 75-96]

Hoey, B. (1996)   *Who Calls the Tune?: a Psycho-dramatic
                      Approach to Child Therapy.* London:
                      Routledge

Holbrook, D. (1972)   *Sex and Dehumanization.* London: Pitman
                      Publishing (new ed. Brunswick, NJ:
                      Transaction 1997)

Holbrook, D. (1993)   Lawrence's False Solution [in
                      Rudnytsky (1993): 189-215]

Holbrook, D. (1994)   *Creativity and Popular Culture.* Cranbury,
                      NJ: Associated University Press

Holbrook, D. (2002)   D.W. Winnicott [in Kahr, B. (2002a):
                      146-150]

Hollins, S. (2006)   Young People with Learning Disabilities
                      and Challenging Behaviour: a
                      Winnicottian Perspective [in Morgan
                      and Hollins (2006): 21-35]

Holmes, J. (1993)   *Between Art and Science: Essays on
                      Psychiatry and Psychotherapy.* London:
                      Tavistock/Routledge

Holmes, J. (2001)   *The Search for the Secure Base: Attachment
                      Theory and Psychoanalysis.* Hove, Sussex
                      and New York: Brunner-Routledge

Hood, C. (1975)   *Child Care and Development*. London: Mills and Boon

Hopkins, J. (2002)   From Baby Games to Let's Pretend: the Achievement of Playing [in Kahr, B. (2002): 91-99]

Hopkins, L.B. (2001)   Masud Khan's Descent into Alcoholism [in Petrucelli and Stuart (2001): 319-346]

Hopkins, L.B. (2006b)   *False Self: The Life of Masud Khan*. New York: Other Press

Horn, A. (1999)   *Handbook of Child and Adolescent Psychotherapy*. Hove, Sussex: Routledge

Horton, P.C. (1981)   *Solace*. Chicago: University of Chicago Press

Hudak, G.M. (2001)   On what is Labelled 'Playing': Locating the 'True' in Education [in Hudak, G.M., Kihn, P. (2001). *Labelling: Pedagogy and Politics*: 9-26 London and New York: Routledge-Falmer]

Hughes, J.M. (1989)   *Reshaping the Psychoanalytic Domain: The Work of Melanie Klein, W.R.D. Fairbairn and D.W. Winnicott*. Berkeley: California University Press

Hurry, A. (Ed.) (1998a)   *Psychoanalysis and Developmental Therapy*. London: Karnac

Hurry, A. (1988b)   Psychoanalysis and Developmental Therapy [in Hurry (1998a): 32-73]

Innes-Smith, J. (2001)   Breakdown, Madness and Health [in Bertolini, M. et al (2001) vol. 1: 18-30] (see also Tonnesmann, M. (2001) for discussion)

Issroff, J. (1975)   Adolescence and Creativity [in Meyerson, S. (Ed.). *Adolescence: The Crisis of Adjustment – a Study of Adolescence by Members of the Tavistock Clinic and other British Experts*. 143-164. London: George Allen & Unwin]

Issroff, J. (1988)   Suicide Provoked by Pathological Mourning in Families: the Dynamics and Dangers of Feeling 'Not Being Wanted Enough' or 'Not Being Good Enough' [in Chigler, E. (Ed.). *Counselling and Therapy in Grief and Bereavement*: 197-212 Tel Aviv: Freund]

Issroff, J. (2001)   Reflections on *Playing and Reality* [in Bertolini, M. et al (2001 vol. 1): 59-70]

Issroff, J. (2005)   *Donald Winnicott and John Bowlby: Personal and Professional Perspectives.* London: Karnac

Jacobs, M. (1995)   *D.W. Winnicott.* London & New Delhi: Sage

Jacobs, T.J. (1991)   *The Use of the Self: Countertransference and Communication in the Analytic Situation.* Madison, CT: International Universities Press

Jacoby, M. (1990)   *Individuation and Narcissism: the Psychology of Self in Jung and Kohut.* London: Routledge

Jenkyn, S.M. (1997)   *The Play's the Thing.* London: Routledge

Johns, J. (2001a)   Winnicott: a Beginning [in Kahr, B. (2001a): 11-18]

Johns, J. (2001b)   Personalisation [in Bertolini, M. et al (2001) vol. 1: 99-102]

Johnson, S.
Ruszczynski, S.
(Eds.) (1999)

Psychoanalytic Psychotherapy in the Independent Tradition.
London: Karnac

Johnson, S. (1999a)

Who and Whose I am: the Emergence of the True Self [in Johnson, S., Ruszczynski, S. (1999): 9-26]

Johnson, S. (1999b)

The Move from Object-relating to Object-usage: a Clinical Example [in Johnson, S., Ruszczynski, S. (1999): 111-132]

Jones, J.W. (1997)

Playing and Believing: the Uses of D.W. Winnicott in the Psychology of Religion [in Capps, D. (Ed.) (1997). *Religion, Society and Psychoanalysis:* 106-126] Boulder, CO: Westview Press

Jones, J.W. (2002)

Terror and Transformation: The Ambiguity of Religion in Psychoanalytic Perspective.
London and New York: Routledge

Josselson, R. (1992)

The Space Between Us: Exploring Dimensions of Human Relationships. San Francisco: Jossey Bass

Kahane, C. (1993)

Gender and Voice in Transitional Phenomena [in Rudnytsky (1993): 278-291]

Kahn, W.A. (2004)

Holding Fast: the Struggle to Create Resilient, Care-giving Organizations.
London & New York: Brunner/Routledge

Kahr, B. (1996c)

D.W. Winnicott: A Biographical Portrait.
London: Karnac

Kahr, B. (Ed.) (2001a)

Forensic Psychotherapy and Psychopathology: Winnicottian Perspectives. London: Karnac

Kahr. B. (2001b) Winnicott's Contribution to the Study of Dangerousness [intro. Kahr, B. (2001a): ix-xxiv]

Kahr, B. (Ed.) (2002a) *The Legacy of Winnicott: Essays on Infant and Child Mental Health.* London: Karnac

Kahr, B. (2002b) Donald Woods Winnicott: the Cartographer of Innocence [in Kahr, B. (2002a): 1-12]

Kahr, B. (2002c) Winnicottiana: Some Hitherto Unpublished Documents [in Kahr (2002a): 151-160]

Kahr, B. (2003a) On the Memorialisation of Donald Winnicott [in McDougall (2003) (foreword): 9-14]

Kahr, B. (2005) The Fifteen Key Ingredients to Good Psychotherapy [in Ryan, J. (2005): 1-14]

Kahr, B. (2006) Winnicott's Contribution to the Study of Dangerousness [appendix to Morgan and Hollins (2006): 39-47]

Kalsched, D. (1996) *The Inner World of Trauma: Archetypal Defenses of the Personal Spirit.* London: Routledge

Kaminer, H. (1978) Transitional Object Components in Self and Other Relationships [in Grolnick, Barkin, Muensterberger (1978): 233-244]

Kanter, J. (Ed.) (2004b) *Face to Face with Children: the Life and Work of Claire Winnicott.* London: Karnac

Kernberg, O. (1980) *Internal World and External Reality: Object Relations Theory Applied.* New York: Aronson

Kestemberg, E. (1993)	A Yeast for Thought [in Goldman, D. (Ed.) (1993): 1165-170]
Kestenberg, J.S. (1978)	Transsensus-outgoingness and Winnicott's Intermediate Zone [in Grolnick, Barkin, Muensterberger (1978): 61-74]
Kestenberg, J.S., Weinstein, J. (1978)	Transitional Object and Body Image Formation [in Grolnick, Barkin, Muensterberger (1978): 75-96]
Khan, M.M.R., Davis, J.A., Davis, M.E.V. (1974)	The Beginning and Fruition of the Self: an Essay on D.W. Winnicott [in Davis, J.A., Dutting, J. *The Scientific Foundations of Pædiatrics:* 274-289. London: Heinemann Medical Books (1974)]
Khan, M.M.R. (1975)	*The Privacy of the Self: Papers on Psychoanalytic Theory and Technique.* London: Hogarth Press (reprinted London: Karnac 1996)
Khan, M.M.R. (1979)	*Alienation in Perversions.* London: Hogarth Press (reprinted London: Karnac 1989)
Khan, M.M.R. (1983)	*Hidden Selves: Between Theory and Practice in Psychoanalysis.* London: Hogarth Press (reprinted London: Karnac 1989)
Khan, M.M.R. (1988)	*When Spring Comes: Awakenings in Clinical Psychoanalysis.* London: Chatto and Windus (published as *The Long Wait* New York: Summit Books 1989)
Killick, K., Schaverein, J. (1997)	*Art, Psychotherapy and Psychosis.* London: Routledge
King, P. (2001)	Remembering Winnicott [in Bertolini, M. et al (2001) vol. 1: 268]

King, P. (2005)   *Time Present and Times Past: Selected Papers.* London: Karnac

Kirschner, S.R. (1996)   *The Religious and Romantic Origins of Psychoanalysis, Individuation and Integration in Post-Freudian Theory.* Cambridge: Cambridge University Press

Klein, J. (1987)   *Our Need for Others and its Roots in Infancy.* London: Routledge.

Klein, J. (1995)   *Doubts and Certainties in the Practice of Psychotherapy.* London: Karnac

Klein, R.S. (1990)   *Object Relations and the Family Process.* Westport, CT: Praeger

Kluzer, A.U. (2001)   Illusion and Reality in the Work of D.W. Winnicott [in Bertolini, M. et al (2001) vol. 2: 49-58]

Kohon, G. (Ed.) (1986)   *The British School of Psychoanalysis: the Independent Tradition.* New Haven, CT: Yale University Press and London: Free Association Books

Kohon, G. (Ed.) (1999)   *The Dead Mother: The Work of André Green.* Hove, London and New York: Routledge

Kohon, G. (2005)   Love in a Time of Madness [in Green, A., Kohon, G. (2005e): 41-100]

Kotowicz, A. (1993)   Tradition, Violence and Psychotherapy [in Spurling, L. (Ed.) (1993): 132-157]

Kumin, I. (1997)   *Pre-Object Relatedness: Early Attachment and the Psychoanalytic Situation.* New York: Guilford Press

Lally, E. (2002)   *At Home with Computers.* Oxford and
New York: Berg

Lambert, K. (1981)   *Analysis, Repair and Individuation.*
London: Academic Press (New edition
London: Karnac 1994)

Lamothe, R. (2005b)   *Becoming Alive: Psychoanalysis and
Vitality.* Hove, Sussex and New York:
Routledge

Langs, R. (2002)   D.W. Winnicott: the Traditional Thinker
[in Kahr (2002a): 13-22]

Lanza, A.M.,   Self-States and the Maternal Integration
Bucci, S.P.,   Function [in Bertolini, M. et al (2001)
Chagas-Bovet, A.M.   vol. 2: 13-23]
(2001)

Laufer, M. (2001)   Reflection on Central Masturbation
Fantasy, the Fetish and Transitional
Objects [in Bertolini, M. et al (2001)
vol. 1: 201-203]

Lawler, S. (2000)   *Mothering the Self: Mothers, Daughters,
Subjects.* London and New York:
Routledge

Lebovici, S. (1993)   An Inimitable Genius [in Goldman, D.
(Ed.) (1993): 1171-176]

Lee, G. (1997)   Alone Among Three: The Father and
the Œdipus Complex [in Richards with
Wilce (1997): 73-87]

Lemma, A. (2003)   *Introduction to Practice of Psychoanalytic
Psychotherapy.* Chichester: Wiley

Lewin, R.A.,   *Losing and Fusing: Borderline Transitional
Schultz, G. (1992)   Object and Self Relations.* Northvale,
NJ: Aronson

Little, M. (1981)   *Transference Neurosis and Transference Psychosis.* Northvale, NJ: Aronson & London: Free Association Books

Little, M.I. (1990)   *Psychotic Anxieties and Containment: a Personal Record of an Analysis with Winnicott.* Hillside, NJ: Aronson

Little, M.I. (1993)   Psychotherapy with D.W.W. [in Goldman, D. (Ed.) (1993): 123-138]

Lomas, P. (1973)   *True and False Experience.* London: Allen Lane

Lomas, P. (1981)   *The Case for a Personal Psychotherapy.* Oxford: Oxford University Press

Lomas, P. (1987)   *The Limits of Psychoanalysis: What's Wrong with Psychoanalysis?* Harmondsworth: Penguin Books

Lomas, P. (1998)   *Personality Disorder and Family Life.* New Brunswick, NJ: Transaction Publishers

Lomas, P. (2000)   An Independent Streak [in Rudnytsky (2000): 51-62]

Lorenzer, A., Orban, P. (1987)   Transitional Objects and Phenomena: Socialization and Symbolization [in Grolnick, Barkin, Muensterberger (1987): 469-482]

Lubbe, T. (2000)   *The Borderline Psychotic Child: a Selective Integration.* London: Routledge

McDougall, J. (1986)   *Theatres of the Mind: Illusion and Truth in the Psychoanalytic Stage.* New York: Norton & London: Free Association Books

McDougall, J. (1987)   *Theatres of the Body.* New York: Norton & London: Free Association Books 1989

McDougall, J. (2003)   *Donald Winnicott the Man: Reflections and Recollections*. The Donald Winnicott Memorial Lecture. London: Karnac (on behalf of the Winnicott Clinic of Psychotherapy)

Machado, L.M. (2001)   Transitional Phenomena, Potential Space and Creativity [in Bertolini, M. et al (2001) vol. 1: 71-75]

MacIntyre, A. (2004)   *The Unconscious: A Conceptual Analysis.* London: Routledge

McMahon, L. (1992)   *The Handbook of Play Therapy.* Hove, Sussex: Routledge

McWilliam, N. (2004)   *Psychoanalytic Psychotherapy: a Practitioner's Guide.* London and New York: Guilford

Maffei, G. (2001)   C.G. Jung's *Memories, Dreams, Reflections*: Notes on the Review by D.W. Winnicott [in Bertolini, M. et al (2001) vol. 2: 196-203]

Magherini, G. (2001)   The Parent-Child Relationship in Italian Renaissance Painting: External and Internal Realities in Giovanni Bellini's 'Families' [in Bertolini, M. et al (2991) vol. 2: 76-88] (see also Trinci, M. (2003) for further notes)

Mariotti, P. (2001)   Cumulative Trauma: When All Does Not Go Well in the Everyday life of the Infant [in Bertolini, M. et al (2001) vol. 2: 93-102]

Martin-Cabrè, L.J. (2001)   Winnicott and Ferenczi: Trauma and the Maternal Analyst [in Bertolini, M. et al (2001) vol. 2: 179-184]

Meares, R. (1992)   *The Metaphor of Play: The Self, The Secret and the Borderline Experience*. Melbourne: Hill of Content

Meares, R. (1993)   *The Metaphor of Play: Disruption and Restoration in the Borderline Experience*. Northvale, NJ: Aronson. 3rd edition (1995). Hove, Sussex and New York: Routledge

Meares, R. (2005)   *The Metaphor of Play: Origin and Breakdown of Personal Being*. Hove, Sussex: Routledge (Updated edition of Meares, R. (1992) and Meares, R. 1993)

Meisel, P., Kendrick, W. (Eds.) (1986)   *Bloomsbury/Freud: The Letters and Times of James and Alix Strachey 1925-1925*. London: Chatto and Windus

Meissner, W.W. (1984a)   *Psychoanalysis and Religious Experience*. New Haven, CT: Yale University Press

Meissner, W.W. (1984b)   *The Borderline Spectrum and Developmental Issues*. Hillside, NJ: Aronson

Meissner, W.W. (1988)   *Treatment of Patients in the Borderline Spectrum*. Hillside, NJ: Aronson

Miller, J.C. (2004)   *The Transcendent Function: Jung's Model of Psychological Growth*. Albany, NY: State University of New York Press

Miller, R. (1978)   Poetry as a Traditional Object [in Grolnick, Barkin, Muensterberger (1987): 447-468]

Milligan, J. (2001)   Deprivation and Delinquency in the Treatment of the Adolescent Forensic Patient [in Kahr, B.(2001a): 44-50]

Mills, J. (Ed.) (2002)   *A Pedagogy of Becoming*. Amsterdam and New York: Rodopi

Milner, M. (1969)   *The Hands of the Living God: an Account of a Psychoanalytic Treatment.* London: Hogarth Press

Milner, M. (1977)   Winnicott and Overlapping Circles [in Milner, M. (1987): pp. 287-298]

Milner, M. (1978)   D.W. Winnicott and the Two-way Journey [in Grolnick, Barkin, Muensterberger (1978): 35-42 also in Goldman, D. (1993): 117-122]

Milner, M. (1987)   *The Suppressed Madness of Sane Men.* London: Tavistock

Milner, M. (2001)   On Winnicott [in Bertolini, M. et al (2001) vol. 1: 265-267]

Mitchell, J. (2001)   Femininity from the Margins [in Bertolini, M. et al (2001) vol. 1: 247-254

Mitchell, J. (2006)   Sibling Trauma: a Theoretical Consideration [in Coles, P. (2006): 155-174]

Mitchell, S.A. (2000)   Between Philosophy and Politics [in Rudnytsky (2000): 101-136]

Modell, A.H. (1990a)   The Roots of Creativity and the Use of an Object [in Giovacchini (1990a): 113-127]

Modell, A.H. (1990b)   *Other Times, Other Realities: Toward a Theory of Psychoanalytic Treatment.* Cambridge, MA and London: Harvard University Press

Modell, A.H. (1993)   "The Holding Environment" and the Therapeutic Action of Psychoanalysis [in Goldman, D. (Ed.) (1993): 273-290]

Momigliano, L.N. (1992)   *Continuity and Change in Psychoanalysis* (especially chapter 2). London: Karnac

Montgomery, J.D.   Chronic Patienthood as an Iatrogenic

(1989)	False Self [in Fromm, Smith (1989a): 345-364]
Morgan, R., Hollins, C. (contributors) (2006)	*Young People and Crime – Improving Provision for Children who offend* The Donald Winnicott Lecture. London: Karnac on behalf of The Winnicott Clinic of Psychotherapy
Muensterberger, W. (1978)	Between Reality and Fantasy [in Grolnick, Barkin, Muensterberger (1978): 3-14]
Natterson, J. (1991)	*Beyond Countertransference: the Therapist's Subjectivity in the Therapeutic Process.* New York: Aronson
Neri, F. (2001)	Discussion of Andrews, J.C. (2001) [in Bertolini, M. et al (2001) vol. 1: 257-261]
Neu, J. (2000)	*A Tear is an Intellectual Thing: the Meanings of Emotion.* Oxford: Oxford University Press
Newirth, J. (2003)	*Between Emotion and Cognition: The Generative Unconscious.* New York: Other Press
Newman, A. (1995)	*Non-Compliance in Winnicott's Words: A Companion to the Work of D.W. Winnicott.* London: Free Association Books
Newman, G.M. (1997)	*Locating the Romantic Subject: Novalis with Winnicott.* Detroit: Wayne State University Press
Nicolò, A.M. (2001)	Antisocial Acting-out as a Defence Against Breakdown [in Bertolini, M. et al (2001) vol. 2: 139-144]
Noonan, E. (1993)	Tradition in Training [in Spurling, L. (Ed.) (1993): 18-39]

Nussbaum, M.C.
(2001)

Upheavals of Thought: the Intelligence of Emotions. Cambridge: Cambridge University Press

Nussbaum, M.C.
(2004)

Hiding from Humanity: Disgust, Shame and the Law. Princeton, NJ: Princeton University Press

O'Connor, P.A.
(2000)

Facing the Fifties: from Denial to Reflection. London: Allen & Unwin

Ogden, T.H. (1986)

The Matrix of the Mind: Object Relations and the Psychoanalytic Dialogue. New York: Aronson (reprinted London: Karnac 1992)

Ogden, T.H. (1989a)

The Primitive Edge of Experience. New York: Aronson (reprinted London: Karnac 1992)

Ogden, T.H. (1989b)

Playing, Dreaming and Interpreting Experience: Comments on Potential Space [in Fromm, Smith (1989a): 255-278]

Ogden, T.H. (1990)

On Potential Space [in Giovacchini, P. (1990a): 90-112

Ogden, T.H. (1993)

The Electrified Tightrope. Northvale, NJ: Aronson (reprinted London: Karnac 2004)

Ogden, T.H. (1994)

Subjects of Analysis. London: Karnac

Ogden, T.H. (1996)

Psychic Deadness. Northvale, NJ: Aronson (reprinted Karnac 2004)

Ogden, T.H. (1997)

Reverie and Interpretation. Northvale, NJ: Aronson (reprinted London: Karnac 1999)

Ogden, T.H. (1999)

Toxic Nourishment. London: Karnac

Ogden, T.H. (2001a)	*Conversations at the Frontiers of Dreaming.* London: Karnac
Orbach, S. (2002)	The False Self and the False Body [in Kahr (2002a): 124-134]
Padel, J. (2001a)	Nothing so Practical as a Good Theory [in Bertolini, M. et al (2001) vol. 1: 3-17]
Padel, J. (2001b)	Winnicott's Thinking [in Bertolini, M. et al 2001 vol. 1: 269]
Painceira, A.J. (2001)	The Capacity to Be Alone [in Bertolini, M. et al (2001) vol. 1: 107-111]
Parrish, D. (1978)	Transitional Objects and Phenomena in a Case of Twinship [in Grolnick, Barkin, Muensterberger (1978): 271-288]
Parsons, Michael (2000)	*The Dove that Returns, the Dove that Vanishes: Paradox and Creativity in Psychoanalysis.* London: Routledge
Parsons, Michael (2006)	Ways of Transformation [in Black, D.M. (2006a): 117-131]
Pasquale, G. (2001)	A Clinical Approach to Empathy [in Bertolini, M. et al (2001) vol. 2: 115-119]
Pearson, J. (Ed.) (2004)	*Analyst of the Imagination: The Life and Work of Charles Rycroft* London: Karnac
Peña, S. (2001)	The Presence of Winnicott in Me [in Bertolini, M. et al (2001) vol. 1: 31-37]
Petrucelli, J., Stuart, C. (Eds.) (2001)	*Hungers and Compulsions.* Northvale, NJ: Aronson
Phillips, A. (1988)	*Winnicott* [Fontana Modern Masters Series] London: Collins (reprinted Cambridge, MA: Harvard University Press 1988)

Phillips, A. (1995)   The Story of the Mind [in Corrigan,
                      E.G., Gordon, P-E. (1995a):
                      229-240]

Phillips, A. (1998)   *The Beast in the Nursery*. London: Faber

Phillips, A. (2000)   Winnicott's Hamlet [in Caldwell, L.
                      (2000): 31-47]

Phillips, A. (2005)   Talking Nonsense, and Knowing When
                      to Stop [in Caldwell, L.
                      (2005): 145-161]

Piontelli, A. (1992) *From Fœtus to Child: an Observational and
                      Psychoanalytic Study*. London and New
                      York: Tavistock/Routledge

Poirier, R. (1993)   Frost, Winnicott, Burke [in Rudnytsky
                      (1993): 216-228]

Pontalis, J.-B. (1981) *Frontiers in Psychoanalysis: Between the
                        Dream and Psychic Pain*. London:
                        Hogarth Press

Pruyser, P.W. (1983) *The Play of Imagination: Toward a
                      Psychoanalysis of Culture*. New York:
                      International Universities Press

Raphael-Leff, J.   Primary Maternal Persecution
(2001)   [in Kahr, B. (2001a): 27-42]

Raphael-Leff, J.   *Parent-Infant Psychodynamics: Wild
(Ed.) (2003)   Things, Mirrors and Ghosts*. London:
                      Whurr

Rayner, E. (1971)   *Human Development*. London: Allen and
                      Unwin (3rd ed. 1986)

Rayner, E. (1990)   *The Independent Mind in British
                      Psychoanalysis*. London: Free Association
                      Books

Redfearn, J. (1988)   *Myself, My Many Selves*. London:
                      Academic Press (new edition London:
                      Karnac 1994)

Reeves, C. (2005a)   Singing the Same Tune?: Bowlby and
                        Winnicott on Deprivation and
                        Delinquency [in Issroff, J. (2005): 71-100]

Reeves, C. (2005b)   A Duty to Care: Reflections on the
                        Influence of Bowlby and Winnicott on
                        the 1948 Children Act [in Issroff, J.
                        (2005): 179-207]

Reeves, C. (2005c)   Postscript: From Past Impact to Present
                        Influence [in Issroff, J. (2005): 209-215]

Retallack, J. (2003)   *The Poetical Wager.* Berkeley, CA:
                        University of California Press

Richards, B. (Ed.)   *Capitalism and Infancy: Essays on
(1984)   Psychoanalysis and Politics.* London: Free
                        Association Books

Richards, J. (1999)   The Concept of Internal Cohabitation
                        [in Johnson, S., Ruszczynki, S. (1999):
                        27-52]

Richards, V. with   *The Person Who is Me: Contemporary
Wilce, G. (Eds.)   Perspectives on the True and False Self.*
(1996a)   London: Karnac for the Squiggle
                        Foundation

Richards, V. (1996b)   Hunt the Slipper [in Richards with
                        Wilce (1996a): 23-35]

Richards, V. with   *Fathers, Families and the Outside World.*
Wilce, G. (Eds.)   London: Karnac for the Squiggle
(1997a)   Foundation

Richards, V. (1997b)   Papa Versus Pooh [in Richards with
                        Wilce (1997a): 1-8]

Richards, V. (1997c)   "If Father Could Be Home —" [in
                        Richards with Wilce (1997a): 89-97]

Richards, V. (2005)   *The Who you Dream Yourself: Playing and Interpretation in Psychotherapy and Theatre.* London: Karnac

Rizzuto, A-M. (1979)   *The Birth of the Living God: Psychoanalytic Study.* Chicago: Chicago University Press

Roazen, P. (2002)   A Meeting with Donald Winnicott in 1965 [in Kahr (2002a): 23-35]

Robinson, H.T. (2005)   Adult Eros in D.W. Winnicott [in Caldwell, L. (2005): 83-103]

Rodman, F.R. (Ed.) (1987)   *The Spontaneous Gesture: Selected Letters of Donald Winnicott.* Cambridge, MA: Harvard University Press and London: Karnac

Rodman, F.R. (1990)   Insistence on Being Himself [in Giovacchini (1990a): 21-40]

Rodman, F.R. (1999)   Winnicott's Laughter [in Barron, J.W. (Ed.) (1999). *Humor and Psyche: Psychoanalytic Perspectives.* Hillside, N.J: Analytic Press: 177-202]

Rodman, F.R. (2003)   *Winnicott: Life and Work.* Cambridge, MA: Perseus

Rogers, R. (1991)   *Self and Other: Object Relations in Psychoanalysis and Literature.* New York: New York University Press

Rollin, L., West, M.I. (1999)   *Psychoanalytic References to Children's Literature.* Jefferson, NC: McFarland

Rosen, M. (2001)   Winnicott's Complex Relationship to Hate and Hatefulness [in Petrucelli and Stuart (2001): 347-358]

Rubin, J.B. (1998) *A Psychoanalysis for Our Time: Exploring the Blindness of the Seeing I.* New York and London: New York University Press

Rubin, J.B. (2006) Psychoanalysis and Spirituality [in Black, D.M. (2006a): 132-153]

Rudnytsky, P. (1991) *The Psychoanalytic Vocation: Rank, Winnicott and the Legacy of Freud.* New Haven, CT and London: Yale University Press

Rudnytsky, P. (Ed.) (1993) *Transitional Objects and Potential Spaces: Literary Uses of D.W. Winnicott.* New York: Columbia University Press

Rudnytsky, P. (2000) *Psychoanalytic Conversations: Interviews with Clinicians, Commentators and Critics.* Hillside, NJ: Analytic Press

Ryan, J. (Ed.) (2005) *How Does Psychotherapy Work?* London: Karnac

Rycroft, C. (1985) *Psychoanalysis and Beyond.* London: Chatto and Windus

Rycroft, C. (1991) *Viewpoints.* London: Hogarth Press

Rycroft, C. (2000) A Science of the Mind [in Rudnystsky (2000): 63-80]

Sacksteder, J.L. (1989) Personalization as an Aspect of the Process of Change in 'Anorexia Nervosa' [in Fromm, Smith (1989a): 392-423]

Safran, J.D., Muran, J.C. (2000) *Negotiating the Therapeutic Alliance: a Relational Treatment Guide.* New York: Guilford Press

Sanville, J. (1991) *The Playground of Psychoanalytic Therapy.* Hillside, NJ: Analytic Press

Sarno, L. (2001) Winnicott and Bion: on some Uncanny Affinities [in Bertolini, M. et al (2001) vol. 2: 204-220]

Scarfone, D. (2005) Laplanche and Winnicott Meet [in Caldwell, L. (2005): 33-53]

Schaedel, M. (2005) Working with Women in an NHS Outpatient Clinic for Sexual Dysfunction [in Caldwell, L. (2005): 126-143]

Schacht, L. (2001) Between the Capacity and the Necessity of Being Alone [in Bertolini, M. et al (2001) vol. 1: 112-125] (see also Grieve, P. (2001) for further notes)

Scharff, J.S. (2003) The British Object Relation Theorists: Fairbairn, Winnicott, Balint, Guntrip, Sutherland and Bowlby. (Paper read at a symposium "Understanding Dissidence and Controversy in the History of Psychoanalysis" – published 2004 New York: Other Press: 175-200)

Schermer, V. (2003) *Spirit and Psyche: a New Paradigm for Psychology, Psychoanalysis and Psychotherapy.* London: Jessica Kingsley

Schoenberg, P. (2001) Winnicott and the Psyche-Soma [in Bertolini, M. et al (2001) vol. 2: 147-154]

Schoenwolf, G. (1990) *Turning Points in Analytic Therapy: from Winnicott to Kernberg.* New York: Aronson

Schwartz, M.M. (1978) Critic, Define Thyself [in *Psychoanalysis and the Question of the Text* Ed. Hartmann, G. (Baltimore and London: Johns Hopkins University Press) pp. 1-17]

Schwartz, M.M. (1993)   Where is Literature? [in Rudnytsky (1993): 50-62]

Searles, H.F. (1979)   *Countertransference and Related Subjects: Selected Papers.* New York: International Universities Press

Shabad, P., Selinger, S. (1995)   Bracing for Disappointment and the Counterphobic Leap into the Future [in Corrigan, E.G., Gordon, P-E. (1995a): 209-228]

Sher, J. (1990)   *Work, Love, Play: Self Repair in the Psychoanalytic Dialogue*: Los Angeles: Doubleday

Sheridan, M.D. (1999)   *Play in Early Childhood: From Birth to Six Years.* London: Routledge

Siegelman, E.Y. (1990)   *Meaning and Metaphor in Psychotherapy.* New York: Guilford Press

Silva, E.B. (1996)   *Good Enough Mothering? Feminist Perspectives on Lone Motherhood.* London: Routledge

Sinason, V. (2001)   Children who Kill their Teddy Bears [in Kahr, B. (2001a): 43-50]

Slochower, J.A. (1996a)   *Holding and Psychoanalysis: A Relational Perspective.* Hillside, NJ: Analytic Press

Slochower, J. (2005)   Holding: Something Old and Something New [in Aron, L., Harris, E. (Eds). *Relational Psychoanalysis: Innovations and Expansion* vol. 2: 24-49. Mahwah, NJ: Analytic Press (2005)]

Slochower, J. (2006)   *Psychoanalytic Collisions.* Mahwah, NJ: Analytic Press

Smirnoff, V. (1971)   *The Scope of Child Analysis.* London: Routledge

Smith, B.L. (1989a)   Winnicott and the British Schools [in Fromm, Smith (1989a): 27-51]

Smith, B.L. (1989b)   Winnicott and Self-Psychology [in Fromm, Smith (1989a): 52-87]

Smith, B.L. (1989c)   The Transitional Function of Insight [in Fromm, Smith (1989a): 159-178]

Smith, B.L. (1989d)   Of Many Minds: a Contribution on Many Minds [in Fromm, Smith (1989a): 424-458]

Smith, B.L. (1989e)   The Community as Object [in Fromm, Smith (1989a): 516-534]

Smith, R.C. (1996)   *The Wounded Jung: Effects of Jung's Relationships on his Life and Work.* Evanston, IL: Northwestern University Press

Smith, T.S. (2002)   *Strong Interaction.* Chicago: University of Chicago Press

Sobel, E. (1978)   Rhythm, Sound and Imagery in the Poetry of Gerard Manley Hopkins [in Grolnick, Barkin, Muensterberger (1978): 425-446]

Socarides, C. (2001)   D.W. Winnicott and the Understanding of Sexual Perversions [in Kahr, B. (2001a): 95-110]

Solomon, J.C. (1978)   Transitional Phenomena and Obsessive-Compulsive States [in Grolnick, Barkin, Muensterberger (1978): 245-256]

Solow, M.J. (2003)   Face and Façade: the Mother's Face as the Baby's Mirror [in Raphael-Leff, J. (2993): 5-17]

Speziale-Bagliacci, R. (2004)   *Guilt, Revenge, Remorse and Responsibility after Freud.* London: Routledge

Spice, N. (2002) Winnicott and Music [in Caldwell, L. (2002): 193-204]

Spiro, L.H., Devnis, L.E. (1978) The Use of Onself: from Transitional Object to Illusion in Art [in Grolnick, Barkin, (1978) Muensterberger (1978): 238-254]

Spitz, E.H. (1993) Picturing the Child's Inner World of Fantasy: on the Dialectice between Image and Word [in Rudnytsky (1993): 261-277]

Spotnitz, H. (1985) *Modern Psychoanalysis of the Schizophrenic Patient* 2nd ed. New York: Human Science Press

Sprengnether, H. (1993) Ghost Writing: a Meditation on Literary Criticism as Narrative [in Rudnytsky (1993): 87-98]

Spurling, L. (Ed.) (1993) *From the Words of my Mouth: Tradition in Psychotherapy.* London: Routledge

Steiner, J. (1991) *Psychic Retreats: Pathological Organizations in Psychotic, Neurotic and Borderline Patients.* London: Routledge

Stern. D.N. (1985) *The Interpersonal World of the Infant: a View from Psychoanalysis and Developmental Psychology.* New York: Basic Books (reprinted London: Karnac 1998)

Stewart, H. (1992) *Psychic Experience and Problems of Technique.* London: Routledge

Stewart, H. (1995) The Development of Mind-as-Object [in Corrigan, E.G., Gordon, P-E. (1995a): 41-54]

Stewart, H. (1996) *Michael Balint: Object Relations, Pure and Applied.* London: Routledge

227

Sugarman, A., Jaffe, L.S. (1989)	A Developmental Line in Transitional Phenomena [in Fromm, Smith (1979a): 88-129]
Suman, A. (2001)	Interrupted Stories [in Bertolini, M. et al (2001) vol. 2: 173-176]
Summers, F. (1994)	*Object Relations Theories and Psychopathology.* Hillside, NJ: Analytic Press
Summers, F. (2005)	*Self Creation: Psychoanalytic Theory and the Art of the Possible.* Hillside, NJ: Analytic Press
Sutherland, J.D. (1994)	*The Autonomous Self: the Work of John D. Sutherland* (edited Scharff, J.S.) Lanham, MD: Aronson
Symington, N. (1986)	*The Analytic Experience: Lectures from the Tavistock.* London: Free Association Books
Symington, N. (1996)	*Narcissism: a New Theory.* London: Karnac
Symington, N. (1997)	*The Making of a Psychotherapist.* London: Karnac
Taylor, C. (1989)	*Sources of the Self: The Making of Modern Identity.* Cambridge: Harvard University Press
Tonnesmann, M. (2001)	Discussion of Innes-Smith, J. (2001) [in Bertolini, M. et al (2001) vol. 1: 233-237]
Tonnesmann, M. (2002)	Early Emotional Development: Ferenczi to Winnicott [in Caldwell, L. (2002a): 45-57]
Treacher, A. (2002)	"I Like my Life, I Just Like my Life": Narratives of Children of Latency Years [in Caldwell, L. (2002): 177-191]

Trinci, M. (2001)   With Downcast Eyes: some notes on Magherini, G. (2001) [in Bertolini, M. et al (2001) vol. 2: 228-231]

Trowell, J. (2002)   The Wider Implications of Infant Observation [in Kahr, B. (2002a): 79-88]

Tuckett, D. (2001)   Reflections on Hernandez, M., Giannakoulas, A (2001) [in Bertolini, M. et al (2001) vol. 1: 160-163]

Turk, C. (1990)   An Inquiry into the Limits of the Psychoanalytic Method [in Giovacchini (1990a): 160-178]

Tustin, F. (1972)   *Autism and Child Psychosis.* London: Hogarth Press

Tustin, F. (1981)   *Autistic States in Children.* London: Routledge

Tustin, F. (1986)   *Autistic Barriers in Neurotic Patients.* London: Karnac

Tustin, F. (1990)   *The Protective Shell in Children and Adults.* London: Karnac

Tyndale, A. (1999)   How Far is Transference Interpretation Essential to Psychic Change? [in Johnson, S., Ruszczynski, S. (1999): 53-72]

Ulanov, A.B. (2001)   *Finding Space: Winnicott, God and Psychic Reality.* Louisville, KY: Westminster John Knox Press

Urdang, E. (2002)   *Human Behavior in the Social Environment: Interweaving the Inner and Outer Worlds.* Binghamton, NY: Haworth Press

Vanier, A. (2002)   Some Remarks on Adolescence with Winnicott and Lacan [in Caldwell, L. (2002): 133-152]

Volkan, D.V., Kavanaugh, J.G. (1978) The Cat People [in Grolnick, Barkin, Muensterberger (1978): 289-304]

Volkan, D.V. (2001) Foreword [Kahr, B. (2001a): xix-xxv]

Volmer, F. (1999) *Agent Casualty* Dordrecht: Kluwer Academic

Webber, A.M., Haen, C. (2005) *Clinical Applications of Drama Therapy in Child and Adolescent Treatment.* London and New York: Brunner/Routledge

Weich, M.J. (1978) Transitional Language [in Grolnick, Barkin, Muensterberger (1978): 128-141]

Weich, M.J. (1990) The Good Enough Analyst [in Giovacchini, P. (1990a): 128-141]

Welldon, E. (2001) Babies as Transitional Objects [in Kahr, B. (2001a): 19-26]

Widlöcher, D. (1993) Freedom of Thought [in Goldman, D. (Ed.) (1993): 177-184]

Willbern, D. (1993) Phantasmagoric *Macbeth* [in Rudnytsky (1993): 101-134]

Willoughby, R. (2005) *Masud Khan: the Man and the Reality.* London: Free Association Books

Winnicott, C. (1978) D.W.W.: a Reflection [in Grolnick, Barkin, Muensterberg (1978): 17-33, in Giovacchini (1990a): 3-20 and in Kanter, J. (2004): 237-253]

Winnicott, C. (1993) Interview with Dr. Michael Neve [in Goldman, D. (Ed.) (1993): 107-110]

Wold, M.W., Fromm, M.G. (1979) Delinquency and Hope: a Clinical Illustration [in Fromm, Smith (1989a): 535-557]

Wright, E. (1998)	*Psychoanalytic Criticism: a Reappraisal.* London: Polity Press and New York: Routledge
Wright, K. (1990)	*Between Mother and Baby.* London: Free Association Books
Wright, K. (1996)	Looking After the Self [in Richards with Wilce (1996): 65-84]
Wright, K. (2000a)	Face and Façade: the Mother's Face as the Baby's Mirror [in Raphael-Leff, J. (2003): 5-17]
Wright, K. (2000b)	To Make Experience Sing [in Caldwell, L. (2000): 75-96]
Wright, K. (2001)	The Interface Between Mother and Baby [in Bertolini, M. et al (2001) vol. 2: 3-12]
Wright, K. (2006)	Preverbal Experience and the Intuition of the Sacred [in Black, D.M. (2006a): 173-190]
Wyatt-Brown, A.M. (1993)	From the Clinic to the Classroom: D.W. Winnicott, James Britton and the Revolution in Writing Theory [in Rudnytsky (1993): 292-306]
Young, R.M. (2005)	Containment: the Technical and the Tacit in Successful Psychotherapy [in Ryan, J. (2004): 165-186]
Young-Bruehl (2003b)	*Where do We Fall when We Fall in Love?* New York: Other Press
Zalidis, S. (2001)	*A General Practitioner, his Patients and their Feelings.* London: Free Association Books
Zucconi, S. (2001)	Psychosis and the Transitional Area: a Clinical Case Study [in Bertolini, M. et al (2001) vol. 2:103-112]

Reviews

Abram, J. (1994)   Dockar-Drysdale, B. (1990). *Winnicott Studies, 9*: 59-62

Akhtar, S. (1995)   Lewin, R.A., Schultz, G. (1992). *Psychoanalytic Quarterly, 64*: 583-588

Anshin, R.N. (1991)   Hughes, J.M. (1989). *Journal of the American Academy of Psychoanalysis, 19*: 497-499

Applegate, J.S. (1997a)   Kahr, B. (1996c). *Child and Adolescent Social Work Journal, 14*: 462-466

Apprey, M. (1992)   Little, M. (1990). *Psychoanalytic Books, 3*: 58-62

Bacon-Greenberg, K. (1996)   Goldman, D. (1993a). *Contemporary Psychology, 41*: 383-386

Bartlett, A.B. (1999)   Slochower (1996a). *Bulletin of the Menninger Clinic, 63*: 260-262

Bass, A. (1992)   Little, M. (1990). *Psychoanalytic Dialogues, 2*: 117-131

Berman, E. (1996a)   Goldman, D. (1993a). *Contemporary Psychoanalysis, 32*: 158

Berman, E. (1996b)   Goldman, D. (1993b). *Contemporary Psychoanalysis, 32*: 158-164

Blandy, E. (2003)   Kahr, B. (2002a). *Journal of Child Psychotherapy, 29*: 439-441

Blatner, A. (2006)   Richards, V. (2005). *PsycCRITIQUES, 51*

Bonovitz, H. (1998)   Abram, J. (1996). *Psychoanalytic Books, 9*: 435-438

Boyer, L.B. (1979)   Barkin, Grolnick, Muensterberger (1978). *Psychoanalytic Quarterly, 48*: 646-652

Boyer, L.B. (1995)   Gaddini, E. (1992). *Psychoanalytic Quarterly, 64*: 603-606

Burland, J.A. (1998) Kahr, B. (1996). *Psychoanalytic Quarterly,*
                      67: 726-727

Busch, F. (1990)   Fromm, Smith (1989). *International
                      Journal of Psychoanalysis,* 71: 553-556

Casement, P.J.   Goldman, D. (1993a). *Journal of the
(1995)   American Psychoanalytic Association,*
                      43: 223-227

Cheshire, J. (2006)   Caldwell, L. (2005). *British Journal of
                      Psychotherapy,* 22: 520-524

DeMause, L. (2006)   Issroff, J. (2005). *Journal of Psychohistory,*
                      33: 402

Dent, K. (1994)   Little, M. (1990). *Journal of the American
                      Psychoanalytic Association,* 42: 352-354

Downes, C. (2006)   Kanter, J. (2004b). *British Journal of
                      Psychotherapy,* 22: 384-388

Drell, M.J. (1991)   Clancier, Kalmanovitch (1987). *Infant
                      Mental Health Journal,* 12: 81-83

Esman, A.H. (1990)   Three Books by and about Winnicott
                      [Phillips, A. *Winnicott* (1988); Rodman,
                      R. (Ed.). *Spontaneous Gesture* (1987);
                      Winnicott, C., Shepherd, R. & Davis, M.
                      (Eds.). *Psychoanalytic Explorations* (1987)]
                      International Journal of Psychoanalysis,
                      71: 695-699

Etzi, J. (2005)   Rodman, F.R. (2003). *Journal of
                      Phenomenological Psychology,*
                      36: 247-248

Flanders, S. (1992)   Dockar-Drysdale, B. (1990). *International
                      Review of Psychoanalysis,* 19: 391-394

Flournoy, O. (1992)   Little, M. (1990). *International Journal of
                      Psychoanalysis,* 73: 593-594

Flynn, D. (1998)   Jacobs, M.(1995) & Abram, J. (1996).
                      Therapeutic Communities, 19: 334-335

Fromm, M.G. (1995) Rudnytsky, P.L. (1993). *Contemporary Psychology, 40*: 953 (also in *PsyCRITIQUES* 1995)

Gaddini, R., Bovet, A.C. (1988) Clancier, Kalmanovitch (1987). *International Review of Psychoanalysis, 15*: 534-535

Gaddini, R. (1998) Kumin, I. (1997). *Journal of the American Psychoanalytic Association, 46*: 306-316

Gargiulo, G.J. (1992b) Grolnick, S. (1990). *Psychoanalytic Books, 3*: 49-50

Gargiulo. G.J. (1994) Giovacchini, P.L. (1990a). *Psychoanalytic Books, 5*: 214-218

Gargiulo, G.J. (1996) Newman, A. (1995). *Psychoanalytic Books, 7*: 403-405

Giovacchini, P.L (1990e) Hughes, J.M. (1989). *American Journal of Psychiatry, 147*: 807

Giraldo, M. (1990) Phillips, A. (1988). *Psychiatry, 53*: 202

Goldman, D. (1998b) Slochower, J.A. (1996). *Contemporary Journal of Psychoanalysis, 34*: 645-658

Goodwin, J.M. (1997) Kahr, B. (1996). *Journal of Psychohistory, 24*: pp.302-303

Graham, P. (2005) Kanter, J. (2004b). *Children and Society, 19*: 418-419

Green, A. (2005d) *Jouer Avec Winnicott* [Playing with Winnicott] (Rabain, J-F.). Paris Presses Universitaires de France 2004. *International Journal of Psychoanalysis, 86*: 1748-1754

Grolnick, S.A. (1982) Davis, Wallbridge (1981). *Psychoanalytic Quarterly, 51*: 649-652

Grolnick, S.A. (1989) Rodman, F.R. (1987). *Psychoanalytic Quarterly, 58*: 279-282

Grotstein, J.S. (1991) Hughes, J.M. (1989). *Psychoanalytic Quarterly, 60*: 136-140

Hagman, G. (2006) Kanter, J. (2004b). *Psychoanalytic Social Work, 13*: 85-90

Hartmann, L. (2003) Rodman, F.R. (2003). *American Journal of Psychiatry, 160*: 2255-2256

Hinton, W.L. (1997) Kahr, B. (1996). *Journal of Analytic Psychology, 42*: 697

Hopkins, L.B. (2006a) Kanter, J. (2004b). *Psychoanalytic Review, 93*: 136-139

Horton, P.C. (1993) Wright, K. (1990). *Psychoanalytic Psychology, 10*: 611-619

Hughes, A. (2002) Brafman, A.H. (2001). *International Journal of Psychoanalysis, 83*: 1205-1207

Ilahi, M.N. (2005) Rodman, F.R. (2003). *Journal of the American Psychoanalytic, Association, 53*: 311-316

James, M. (1982) Davis, Wallbridge (1981). *International Journal of Psychoanalysis, 63*: 493-497

Johns, J. (2002) Caldwell, L. (2000). *International Journal of Psychoanalysis, 83*: 195-120

Kahr, B. (1996b) Newman, A. (1995). *Journal of Child Psychotherapy, 22*: 456-458

Kahr, B. (2000b) Abram, J. (1996). *Psychoanalytic Studies, 2*: 91

Kaplinsky, C, (1996) Goldman, D. (1993a). *Journal of Analytic Psychology, 41*: 150

Kegerreis, D. (2005) Kanter, J. (2004). *Psychodynamic Practice, 11*: 335-337

Keith, C. (1993) Dockar-Drysdale (1990). *American Journal of Psychotherapy, 47*: 151

235

Kermode, F. (2004)   Clutching at Insanity: Rodman, F.R.
                      (2003). *London Review of Books* (Apr. 3)

Kobrick, J.B. (1998) Kahr, B. (1996). *Canadian Journal of
                      Psychotherapy, 6*: 336-337

Kramer, R. (1994)   Rudnytsky, P. (1991). *Bulletin of the
                      History of Medicine, 68*: 540

Kupersmidt, J.   Rudnytsky (1991). *Psychoanalytic Review,
(1997a)   84*: 469

Kupersmidt, J.   Rudnytsky (1993). *Psychoanalytic Review,
(1997b)   84*: 469-474

Lanyado, M. (1999)   Abram, J. (1996). *Journal of Child
                      Psychotherapy, 25*: 143-145

Larson, L.R. (1995)   Goldman, D. (1993a) and (1993b).
                      Clinical Social Work Journal, 23: 232

Layland, M. (1996)   Kahr, B. (1996). *International Journal of
                      Psychoanalysis, 77*: 1269-1271

Lester, E. (1992)   Hughes, J.M. (1989). *Journal of the
                      American Psychoanalytic Association,
                      40*: 936-941

Levine, H. (2006)   Rodman, F.R. (2003). *Psychoanalytic
                      Quarterly, 75*: 585-591

Lomas, P. (2001)   Godley, W. (2001a). *Outwrite, 3*: 42-44
                      (Journal of Cambridge Society for
                      Psychotherapy)

Lomax-Simpson, J.   Phillips, A. (1988). *Group Analysis,
(1990)   24*: 85-86

Magid, B. (2005)   Rodman, F.R. (2003). *Journal of the
                      American Academy of Psychoanalysis,
                      33*: 408-411

Mahon, P. (2004)   Kanter, J. (2004). *Child Care in Practice,
                      10*: 405-406

Marcus, E.R. (1994b) Little, M. (1990). *Journal of the American Academy of Psychoanalysis, 42*: 937-940

Modell, A.H. (1983) Davis, Wallbridge (1981). *International Journal of Psychoanalysis, 64*: 111-112

Morris, M. (1994) Little, M. (1990). *Psychoanalytic Quarterly, 63*: 562-567

Moyer, D.M. (1995) Goldman, D. (1993a & b). *Psychoanalytic Books, 6*: 456-463

Mulder, F. (1994) Sanville, J. (1991). *Winnicott Studies, 9*: 72-75

Nussbaum, M.C. (2003) Rodman, F.R. (2003). *New Republic, 4632*: 34-38

Padel, J. (1990) Hughes, J.M. (1989). *International Journal of Psychoanalysis, 71*: 715-717

Prendeville, B. (1997) Jacobs, M. (1995). *Psychodynamic Counselling, 3*: 95-97

Ransohoff, P.M. (1994) Rudnytsky (1991). *International Journal of Psychoanalysis, 75*: 427-428

Reeves, C. (2004b) Rodman, F.R. (2003). *Journal of Child Psychotherapy, 30*: 120-123

Reeves, C. (2005d) Kanter, J. (2004). *Journal of Child Psychotherapy, 31*: 137-140

Roazen, P. (1997) Kahr, B. (1996). *International Forum of Psychoanalysis, 6*: 207-208

Roazen, P. (2004) Rodman, F.R. (2003). *Psychoanalysis and History, 6*: 117-122

Robinson, H.T. (1996) Jacobs, M. (1995). *International Journal of Psychoanalysis, 77*: 837-838

Rodman, F.R. (1992) Grolnick, S.A. (1990). *International Journal of Psychoanalysis, 73*: 594-597

Rodman, F.R. (1993) Fromm, Smith (1989). *Psychoanalytic Quarterly, 62*: 131-136

Rogers, R. (1990) Hughes, J.M. (1989). *Psychoanalytic Books*, 1: 459-463

Rogers, R. (1995) Rudnytsky, P.L. (1993). *Psychoanalytic Books*, 6: 418-422

Rudnytsky, P. (2005) Willoughby, R. (2005). *Journal of the American Psychoanalytic Association*, 53: 1365-1371

Sayers, J. (2004b) Kanter, J. (2004). *British Journal of Social Work*, 334: 1203-12

Singer, M. (1989) Giovacchini, P.L. (1986). *Psychoanalytic Quarterly*, 58: 111-116

Spezzano, C. (1993) Rudnytsky, P.L. (1991). *Psychoanalytic Books*, 4: 259-264

Spurling, L. (1998) Kahr, B. (1996). *Psychodynamic Counselling*, 4: 135-136

Steele, R.S. (1988) Rodman, F.R. (1987). *Journal of the History of Behavioral Sciences*, 24: 270-274

Strozier, C.B. (1997) Kahr, B. (1996). *Psychohistory Review*, 25: 258-260

Sussal, C.M. (1991) Hughes, J.M. (1989). *Clinical Social Work Journal*, 19: 435

Tallandini, M.A. (1996) Gaddini, E. (1992). *Winnicott Studies*, 11: 82-84

Taylor, L. (2006) Kanter, J. (2004b). *Journal of American Academy of Child and Adolescent Psychiatry*, 45: 885-887

Titchener, J.L. (1990) Hughes, J.M. (1989). *American Journal of Psychotherapy*, 44: 140

Tustin, F. (1983) Davis, Wallbridge (1981). *Winnicott Studies*, 1: 77-78

Walker, J.S. (1999) Newman, G.S. (1997). *Journal of English and German Philology*, 98: 296

Werner, S.L (1994)	Giovacchini, P.L. (1990a). *Journal of the American Academy of Psychoanalysis,* 22: 562-565
Widdicombe, A. (1997)	Kahr, B. (1996). *Journal of Child Psychotherapy,* 23: 161-163
Wolman, T. (1994)	Grolnick, S.A. (1990). *Psychoanalytic Quarterly,* 63: 367-370
Wolstein, B. (1991)	Schoenewolf, G. (1990). *American Journal of Psychotherapy,* 45: 452
Yates, S. (1997)	Kahr, B. (1996). *British Journal of Psychotherapy,* 13: 564
Young-Bruehl, E. (2003)	Rodman, F.R. (2003). *International Journal of Psychoanalysis,* 84: 1661-1666
Zuger, B. (1992)	Grolnick, S.A. (1990). *Journal of the American Academy of Psychoanalysis,* 20: 157-158

Reviews of Winnicott titles

Anshin, R.N. (1996)	*Thinking About Children - The Lancet,* 348: issue 9031: 877-888
Axelman, M. (2006)	*Playing and Reality - PsycCritiques, 51*
Bratherton, W.J. (1997)	*Thinking About Children - Journal of Analytic Psychology, 42: 535-536*
Brinich, P.M. (1998)	*Thinking About Children - Psychoanalytic Quarterly, 67: 727-730*
Brodie, K. (1993)	*Talking to Parents - Library Journal, 118: issue 3: 104*
Burland, J.A. (1989)	*Home is Where You Start From - Psychoanalytic Quarterly, 58: 283-285*
Casement, P.J. (1989)	*Human Nature - International Journal of Psychoanalysis, 70: 360-362*

Cohn, H. (1986)   *Deprivation and Delinquency - Group Analysis, 19*: 95

Davis, J.A. (1993a)   *Clinical Notes on Disorders of Childhood - Winnicott Studies, 7 (Spring)*: 95-97

Davis, J.A. (1993b)   *The Child, The Family and the Outside World - Winnicott Studies, 8 (Autumn)*: 73-76

Dunstan, F. (1997)   *Thinking About Children - Therapeutic Communities, 18*: 31-37

Fordham, M. (1972)   *Therapeutic Consultations in Child Psychiatry - International Journal of Psychoanalysis, 53*: 555-556

Furman, E. (1979)   *The Piggle - Psychoanalytic Quarterly, 48*: 324-326

Gardner, R.A. (1973)   *Playing and Reality* and *Therapeutic Consultations in Child Psychiatry - Contemporary Psychoanalysis, 9*: 392-399

Geleerd, E.R. (1967)   *Family and Individual Development - International Journal of Psychoanalysis, 48*: 106-111

Haldipur, C.V.   *Psychoanalytic Explorations - American*
(1990)   *Journal of Psychotherapy, 44*: 453

Hicklin, M. (1957)   *The Child and the Family - New Era in Home and School, 38 (May)*: 104-105

James, M. (1979)   *The Piggle - International Journal of Psychoanalysis, 60*: 137-139

Kahr, B. (1999b)   *Talking to Parents - Psychotherapy Review, 1*: 76-78

Kramer, S. (1974a)   *Therapeutic Consultations in Child Psychiatry - Psychoanalytic Quarterly, 43*: 315-318

Kramer, S. (1974b)   *Playing and Reality - Psychoanalytic Quarterly, 43: 318-319*

Kumin, I.M. (1979)   *The Piggle - Journal of the American Academy of Psychoanalysis, 7: 453-455*

Lett, M.K. (1997)   *Thinking About Children - American Journal of Psychiatry, 154: 1032-1033*

Lomax-Simpson, J. (1989)   *Babies and their Mothers - Group Analysis, 22: 347-348*

Marcus, E.R. (1994a)   *Psychoanalytic Explorations - Journal of the American Psychoanalytic Association, 42: 268-271*

Mariotti, P. (1997)   *Thinking About Children - International Journal of Psychoanalysis, 78: 166-168*

Maw, M. (1957)   *The Child and the Outside World - New Era in Home and School, 38 (July/August): 147-149*

Nelson, C.R. (1996)   *Thinking About Children - Library Journal, 121: issue 13: 95*

Neubauer, P.B. (1966)   *The Family and Individual Development - Psychoanalytic Quarterly, 35: 610-611*

Pulver, S. E. (1992)   *Psychoanalytic Explorations - Psychoanalytic Books, 3: 53-57*

Rizzuto, A.-M. (1990)   *Deprivation and Delinquency - Journal of the American Psychoanalytic Association, 38: 811-815*

Segal. H. (1951)   *The Ordinary Devoted Mother and her Baby - International Journal of Psychoanalysis, 32: 327-328*

Stone, A.A. (1991)   *Psychoanalytic Explorations - American Journal of Psychiatry, 148: 259-260*

Trowell, J. (1990)   *Babies and their Mothers - International Review of Psychoanalysis,* 17: 123-124

Weich, M.J. (1991)   *Home is Where You Start From - Journal of the American Psychoanalytic Association,* 39: 259-262

Wilce, G. (1997)   *Thinking About Children - Psychodynamic Counselling,* 3: 230-231

Yates, S.L. (1932)   *Clinical Notes on the Disorders of Childhood - International Journal of Psychoanalysis,* 13: 242-243